# Unequal Childhoods

Early childhood in rich countries is a time when children are protected, and their playfulness and curiosity is encouraged. However, this perception co-exists with toleration of political and economic conditions that grossly undermine or even prematurely end the lives of millions of young children in poor countries. *Unequal Childhoods* discusses how this poverty is recognized and defined through the following case studies:

*   Kazakhstan, once part of the Soviet Union;
*   Swaziland, a tiny country in Southern Africa devastated by HIV and AIDS;
*   Himalayan India;
*   and Brazil, one of the world's most unequal countries.

These four case studies illustrate the diversity and complexity of the responses to the attempts to globalize childhood, and highlight the need to address the inequalities of childhood experience.

*Unequal Childhoods* will be invaluable to anyone on early childhood courses with an international focus or studying childhood in an international context.

**Helen Penn** is Professor of Early Childhood at the University of East London.

## Contesting Early Childhood Series
Series Editors: Gunilla Dahlberg and Peter Moss

This ground-breaking series questions the current dominant discourses in early childhood and offers alternative narratives of an area that is now made up of a multitude of perspectives and debates.

The series examines the possibilities and risks arising from the accelerated development of early childhood services and policies and illustrates how it has become increasingly steeped in regulation and control. Each of the books in this series provides insight into how early childhood services can in fact *contribute* to ethical and democratic practices. The authors explore new ideas taken from alternative working practices in both the western and developing world, other academic disciplines in addition to developmental psychology. They also locate theories and practices in relation to the major processes of political, social, economic, cultural and technological change occurring in the world today.

**Titles in the series:**

# Unequal Childhoods

## Young children's lives in poor countries

## Helen Penn

Routledge
Taylor & Francis Group

LONDON AND NEW YORK

First published 2005
by Routledge
2 Park Square, Milton Park, Abingdon, Oxon, OX14 4RN

Simultaneously published in the USA and Canada
by Routledge
270 Madison Ave, New York NY 10016

*Routledge is an imprint of the Taylor & Francis Group*

Transferred to Digital Printing 2007

2017004371

Typeset in Baskerville
by Keystroke, Jacaranda Lodge, Wolverhampton

*British Library Cataloguing in Publication Data*
A catalogue record for this book is available from the British Library

*Library of Congress Cataloging in Publication Data*
A catalog record for this book has been requested

ISBN 0–415–32101–8 (hbk)
ISBN 0–415–32102–6 (pbk)

**Publisher's Note**
The publisher has gone to great lengths to ensure the quality of this
reprint but points out that some imperfections in the original may
be apparent

This book is dedicated to my new grand-daughter
Nobantu Penn-Kekana.
I hope it is old history by the time she gets to read it.

# Contents

# Illustrations

## Figure

## Tables

# Preface

In my utopia, human solidarity would be seen not as a fact to be recognized by clearing away 'prejudice' or burrowing down to previously hidden depths but, rather, as a goal to be achieved. It is to be achieved not by inquiry but by imagination, the imaginative ability to see strange people as fellow sufferers. Solidarity is not discovered by reflection but created. It is created by increasing our sensitivity to the particular details of the pain and humiliation of other, unfamiliar sorts of people. Such increased sensitivity makes it more difficult to marginalize people different from ourselves by thinking 'they do not feel it as *we* would,' or 'There must always be suffering, so why not let *them* suffer.'

This process of coming to see other human beings as 'one of us' rather than as 'them' is a matter of detailed description of what unfamiliar people are like and of redescription of what we ourselves are like.

(Richard Rorty 1989: xvi)

The perspective of eternity is not a perspective from a certain place beyond the world, nor the point of view of a transcendent being; rather it is a certain form of thought and feeling that rational persons can adopt within the world. And having done so, they can, whatever their generation, bring together into one scheme all individual perspectives and arrive together at regulative principles that can be affirmed by everyone as he lives by them, each from his own standpoint. Purity of heart, if one could attain it, would be to see clearly and to act with grace and self-command from this point of view.

(John Rawls 2000: 514)

These two very distinct philosophers, from the most individualistic country in the world, the USA, are concerned about social justice and inequality.

Their common theme, pursued from opposite poles of argument, is how to escape from the oblivious selfishness of being rich and privileged in a world where most people are poor and have very little, and what one might instead aim for. Rorty argues that we have to be acutely aware of difference and negotiate and renegotiate such differences with other people. Rawls argues that there are basic minimum conditions for human life, and we have to try and define them and abide by them. Both arguments run through this book. Social justice and inequality is a very old theme, but one which seems to have taken on a new urgency, as globalization – global economies and global communications – intensifies to ever greater levels.

This book explores the impact of globalization in one small area, that of early childhood. The world conference on *Education for All* (EFA) organized by UNESCO in Dakar in 2000 agreed six education goals for the South.[1] The goals of this landmark conference have been agreed (although not yet enacted) both by countries of the South, and by donor agencies in the North. The first education goal is the provision of early childhood development (ECD) programmes, especially for the most vulnerable children – although the nature of the vulnerabilities are not spelt out. This goal was adopted after much lobbying by UNICEF, the World Bank and other powerful international donors. But the arguments that underpin the adoption of the goal are deeply flawed. This book sets out to explore some of the contradictions of promoting early childhood programmes in poor countries.

Who are the key players in brokering early childhood development? The book will consider the role of major international donors such as UNICEF and the World Bank and international non-governmental organizations (INGOs) in addressing childhood inequality. Their good intentions mask a paradox; a genuine concern with the welfare of poor children, but a reliance on technocratic interventions and a justification for intervention that mostly draws on questionable paradigms of poverty.

In raising these contradictions and paradoxes I try to discuss how childhood is recognized, defined, catalogued and understood across the North and the South and in transitional countries. Early childhood in the North is commonly viewed as a time of playfulness and curiosity. However this perception co-exists with toleration of political and economic conditions that grossly undermine or even prematurely terminate the lives of millions of young children in the South.

The book includes four case studies, indicating how these assumptions and interventions unravel in four very different countries. Kazakhstan is a remote and vast Central Asian republic, once a poor region of the Soviet Union, now readjusting to the discovery of oil and gas. Swaziland is a tiny state in Southern Africa, dominated by a kingship and chieftaincy system put in place by past colonial administrations, where the rate of infection of HIV/AIDS is one of the highest in the world. These two case studies are based on material I collected whilst working for the Asian Development Bank and for the European Union Development Fund respectively. The other two case studies come directly from the South, and reflect the views of their authors, who live, work (and struggle) in the South. Pawan Gupta, from the Society for Development in the Himalayas (SIDH) in India has long been challenging the marginalization of small Himalayan communities. He argues that local interpretations of education should take precedence over national ones, especially in a country as diverse as India. Fúlvia Rosemberg, writing from Brazil, where inequality is very great, argues for minimum standards for ECD. She considers that, ironically, inequality has been perpetuated rather than addressed by the very nature of local early childhood interventions in Brazil. As the four case studies illustrate, inequality is played out very differently in different countries and in communities within these countries. In each of the four case studies the local details are myriad, and the options for action involve discussions (sometimes irresolvable) about local and national values as well as decisions about funding.

It is of course possible to be poor by the standards of the North and still lead a life of hope and dignity. Conversely, you can be poor in the North, still have access to health and education services, and receive a safety-net income – none of which can be taken for granted in the South – yet experience misery and hopelessness. As I, and many others use the term, inequality refers to the systematic control, demoralization, exploitation and dehumanization of the weak by the powerful and spans both North and South. Poverty is a matter of structure – the governments, institutions and organizations that shape societies. But it is also a matter of agency – what people believe they can do and change, however small and non-confrontational those actions are.

The book concludes with a discussion of the ethical issues raised by childhood inequality. What can be done about it? Is action possible by ordinary citizens in the North, especially early childhood policymakers, practitioners and academics, who are concerned about the inequalities children face?

In writing the book I have been mindful of the balance between scholarliness and readability. They need not necessarily be in contradiction, but I am not skilled enough to practice both simultaneously. If I have erred, then it is on the side of readability. I have kept footnotes to a minimum and I have not included specific references for facts and arguments that I assume to be fairly widely known and accepted. The difficulty is because this book crosses several disciplines, some people may be familiar with some of the facts and arguments, others not at all. There is however a comprehensive list of references at the end of the book.

# Acknowledgements

I would like to thank the many people who have directly or indirectly helped me with this book over a long period of time. In particular I would like to thank my colleagues in East and Southern Africa: Edith and Angel Mbatia in Tanzania (especially their sustaining supply of mangos and spices and batik fabrics); Norma Rudolph and Linda Biersteker who soldier bravely in South Africa; Tizzie Maphalala and her articulate and witty colleagues at the UNICEF office in Swaziland; and Cyril Dalais who is everywhere! My colleagues in Kazakhstan and Mongolia Gauchar Saimasaeva, Tamara Kalashnikova, Mandal Urtnasan and the late and sadly missed Demberel (who also showed me how to ride a camel) have provided me with valuable insights into the ex-Soviet Union and its satellites in Central Asia.

I have been fortunate in being able to undertake consultancies over a period of years for Save the Children UK, which has been a useful introduction to many of the issues raised. I especially value the projects carried out with John Beauclerk in Mongolia and Eastern Europe. (John daily reinvents the meaning of the words dedication and commitment.) My most recent undertaking for Save the Children UK, a review of the links between poverty and early education and care has been particularly relevant and overlapped with the writing of this book. Save the Children UK, and the Chronic Poverty Research Centre based at Manchester University International Development Department, have developed a programme of collaboration known as the Childhood Poverty Research and Policy Centre (CHIP). My connections with CHIP have been invaluable.

John Bennett, previously at UNESCO, now at the OECD Education Division, has been a patient foil for my ideas. I badly miss the cheer-up email dialogues with Sally Lubeck from Michigan with whom I corresponded regularly across oceans, and whose recent death was a loss for so many. I have had some useful arguments with Robin Simpson at Consumers International and some helpful suggestions from Judith Evans and Alan Pence at the University of Victoria in British Columbia. I met Alma Gottleib from the University of Illinois after I had written most of the book, but I very much wish I had met her before I started; her insights and her writing are in the gold standard category.

I am grateful to the European Union for their permission to use the materials I gathered in the EDF9 project in Swaziland, and to the Asian Development Bank for their permission to use the material from the TA3939 project in Kazakhstan. The uses to which I put the material are of course my own.

My colleagues at the Social Science Research Unit at the Institute of Education, London University have offered me a home as a Visiting Fellow for some time, and are unfailingly supportive about my travels. Veronica Burton at the University of East London kept me in touch when I was away. She also laboured unremittingly to put the text in order and it would not have arrived at the publisher's desk without her help. But its faults and omissions are still my own.

I wish I had had several more years to develop the arguments and detail the examples, but it is probably an unfinishable book, and I must cut my losses.

Above all I would like to thank my daughter Loveday Penn and my son-in-law Leslie Kekana, who in their daily lives live out the predicaments expressed in this book.

# Abbreviations

| | |
|---|---|
| ADB | Asian Development Bank |
| ADEA | Association for the Development of Education in Africa |
| CAP | Common Agricultural Policy |
| CG | Consultative Group on Early Childhood Care and Development |
| CPRC | Chronic Poverty Research Centre |
| DAP | Developmentally Appropriate Practice |
| DfID | Department for International Development (UK) |
| DNCR | The National Department for Children |
| ECD | Early Childhood Development |
| ECERS | Early Childhood Environmental Rating Scale |
| EFA | Education for All |
| EU | European Union |
| FAO | Food and Agriculture Organization |
| GDP | Gross Domestic Product |
| GNP | Gross National Product |
| HDI | Human Development Index |
| IBGE | Instituto Brasileiro de Geografia e Estatistica (Brazilian Institute of Geography and Statistics) |
| IBRD | International Bank for Research and Development |
| ILO | International Labour Organization |
| IMF | International Monetary Fund |
| INGOs | International Non-Governmental Organizations |
| MIEIB | The Interforum Movement for Early Childhood Care and Education of Brazil |
| MONEE | UNICEF monitoring project on Central and Eastern Europe, the Commonwealth of Independent States and the Baltic |
| NAEYC | National Association for the Education of Young Children |

| | |
|---|---|
| NEGRI | Nucleus for Studies on Gender, Race and Age Relations |
| NERCHA | National Emergency Response Committee for HIV/AIDS |
| NGOs | Non-Governmental Organizations |
| OECD | Organization for Economic Cooperation and Development |
| OSI | Open Society Institute |
| OVCs | Orphans and Vulnerable Children |
| PNAD | Pesquisa Nacional por Amostra de Domicilio (household survey) |
| PRSPs | Poverty Reduction Strategy Papers |
| SCF | Save the Children (UK) |
| SIDH | Society for Integrated Development of Himalayas |
| UNAIDS | Joint United Nations programme on HIV/AIDS |
| UNCTAD | United Nations Conference on Trade and Development |
| UNDP | United Nations Development Programme |
| UNESCO | United Nations Education and Scientific Committee |
| UNICEF | United Nations Children's Fund |
| USAID | US Agency for International Development |
| VOTP | Voices of the Poor |
| VSO | Voluntary Service Overseas |
| WHO | World Health Organization |
| WTO | World Trade Organization |

# Chapter 1

# Global inequalities

## Summary

This book is about the lives of poor children, children whose experiences of life are bitter – if indeed they survive. Some of the reasons for their poverty lie, I suggest, not in their own countries, but in the rich world of Europe and the USA. A root cause is the economic inequality between North and South. In order to understand the cruel and chronic poverty many young children experience, we have to come to grips with these economic inequalities, even if they do not seem, on the face of it, to be directly related to children's lives. Here I explain some of these complex economic arguments. I offer a very short primer about globalization and why it might be relevant to the lives of young children. I question the assumption that economic development is the only way to better the lives of poor children who live in poor countries.

## What causes inequality?

We live in an unequal world, where, in general, the rich have become richer and the poor have become poorer within countries, and the differences between rich and poor countries have become greater. The political and economic explanations for these trends are long-standing, complex and disputed, and can only be partially addressed in a book about young children. But what is unarguable is that young children suffer disproportionately from these inequalities. Many commentators have drawn the link between neo-liberal economic policies (particularly when abruptly introduced), the growth of poverty and the suffering of children (Cornia and Sipos 1991; Woodward 1992; de Vylder 1996; Rampal 1999).

Poor children are vulnerable in every sense; their health, their access to education, their safety in dangerous environments, their exposure to war. In short their well-being is at stake. Every year UNICEF publishes a booklet entitled *State of the World's Children*. This gives statistics concerning the position in countries in the South. It makes grim reading. In 2002 there were more than *100 million* children without access to basic education, *60 million* of them girls. There were *4.3 million* children who died of HIV/AIDS, and more than *13 million* children under 15 have been orphaned. As a result of conflict *2 million* children have been slaughtered (UNICEF's vocabulary), *6 million* children injured, and *12 million* left homeless. These figures can only be 'guesstimates', because of the difficulties of obtaining statistics about shifting, dying populations in poor countries. But we have to take them seriously because they are an outrage; the world has the resources and the knowledge to avoid such catastrophic levels of disease and despair.

A frequent explanation given for these increasing inequalities – and the effect they have on children – is 'globalization'. Critics of globalization argue that it creates poverty. The poverty that affects children so badly is, put crudely, less and less within the control of poor countries themselves. There is relatively little poor countries can do to change the grim realities of their situation. Efforts by these countries to evade the economic logic of globalization are pointless – only a handful of rogue states have resisted the pressure to conform to the economic models of the North. In the view of these critics it is globalization itself that needs to be addressed.

Yet at the same time, as we shall see in subsequent chapters, much of the aid industry is predicated on the belief that change and development is possible in poor countries. Donors – multilateral organizations, bilateral organizations, international non-governmental organizations[1] – believe that it is possible to make life better for poor children. For them, especially big international donors like the World Bank, globalization may have had its hiccups, but it is necessary and inevitable; indeed, it offers the only route to a better future.

The heated discussions about globalization – is it a good thing or not – are on the face of it far removed from the usual debates on early childhood. Most of the thinking and writing about young children is at a micro-level. Child psychology, which offers a 'scientific underpinning' for understanding children, bringing up, educating and caring for them, focuses on individual circumstances and individual learning. Many studies are highly technical and do not relate directly to everyday life. Other studies detail the effect of certain kinds of parenting or education or care programmes on young children. Such studies examine 'what works', what makes a change in the outcomes for children, what enables them to do better at school and cope with their lives.

This micro-level approach is often informed by the belief that it is not the job of researchers or early childhood practitioners to change the socio-economic circumstances of children – except possibly by chronicling it and drawing it to the attention of others. Bringing about socio-economic change is the job of politicians and economists. The only change that can be brought about at the micro-level of early childhood is to influence the individual actions of children, their parents, carers and teachers, within the home or at a crèche, nursery or school. But in fact wider socio-economic factors may be far more powerful in determining children's chances of a good life than any individual or small-scale effort to bring about change.

If we are concerned about the position of the majority of children in the world then it is important to know – or to try to find out – whether anything can be done about those shocking UNICEF figures. Do young children have to suffer and die in such numbers? Is globalization responsible?

There is a continuum of views about globalization. At one extreme, the view is that child poverty is caused by globalization. Globalization has led to inequality and exploitation, it has exacerbated the gap between rich and poor and under these conditions children suffer disproportionately. Globalization breeds misery and discontent. This is a staggering indictment, and if it is true has all kinds of ethical implications.

At the other extreme is the view that the global market is an economic fact of life – and has always been so. Advocates for globalization argue that, by today's standards, poor countries are essentially backward, with outmoded traditions, led by politicians with inappropriate expectations. Such countries have to learn to cope with the globalization. They need technical help to enter the global market. They need to learn about democracy. They must strive for the education and health standards of the North. It may be a painful road, but in the future they will be economically better off. The best way to deal with illness, lack of education, child poverty and warfare is to encourage more economic development. Krugman, a well-known gung-ho economist, put it like this:

> We've seen an enormous, unexpected improvement in the human condition over the past generation.
>
> How was this improvement achieved? Whenever I give talks about my latest book, someone asks if I still believe in free trade. The answer is yes – because every one of those development success stories was based on export-led growth. And that growth is possible only if rising economies can expand into new markets . . . over the past 25

years more people have seen greater material progress than ever before in history.

(Krugman 2003: 22)

Economists who justify and promote globalization argue that they are no more than technical experts who understand how the economy works, just as electronic engineers understand how electronic circuits work. But critics of globalization argue that the knowledge being produced is not technical but deeply cultural. In reviewing the application of health models across the world, Whiteford and Manderson conclude that:

Global forces are not acultural or supracultural. They are, rather, historical artefacts that derive from Western domination; they reflect Western values of rationality, competition and progress, in which context there is an implicit assumption that with modernization, local 'traditional' institutions and structures will be replaced by Western systems and patterns.

(Whiteford and Manderson 2000: 3)

## What is globalization?

Globalization refers to a series of economic and technological changes that have changed the way the world works. These include changes in financial markets; changes in international trade; changes in investment patterns; changes in telecommunications; and changes in the way crimes are carried out. Leading the charge towards globalization is the USA, which is the world's richest country in terms of the amount of money it earns – although there are different ways of measuring wealth, just as there are of measuring poverty. Wealth does not automatically lead to greater equality or better conditions for children (Chapter 2). Furthermore, because the USA is English speaking (although a great many of its citizens now have Spanish as a first language) English has also become the dominant language of trade, commerce, law and science.

### Financial markets

First of all globalization refers to financial markets. Money transfers across countries used to be relatively tightly controlled, but most financial markets have been liberalized, that is exchange controls have been relaxed or dismantled. Extremely large sums of money – a total of over $1,000 billion in 2000 – can be shifted very quickly around the world to where the greatest profits can be made. Most often this money shifting is speculative, a kind of betting on currency and stock markets; less than 2 per cent is for trade purposes (Khor 2001). The opportunities for greed and corruption are considerable, as the example of the American financial giant Enron illustrates. Entire economies, even quite strong ones, can be destabilized overnight, as currencies and shares crash. No wonder international news bulletins devote so much airtime to the performance of stock exchanges across the world!

## International trade

Globalization also refers to international trade. Trade is partly about marketing – persuading people that they need to buy your goods, however unnecessary. The most powerful sales techniques are used to get people to buy certain products. Coca-Cola and McDonald's are two examples of products that are relentlessly promoted throughout the world. The goods and services of the North are exported throughout the world for those who can afford them. It is possible to travel from one continent to another and have more or less the same experiences; to stay in the same types of hotel, to eat the same foods, to see the same clothes in the shops, to use the same banks. As one astute commentator suggests, to tourists from the North,

> the point of globalization, in one respect, is precisely this – the 'local' is the colour that adds a slight frisson to travel, a variation on the menu, or an item in the gift shop. Otherwise, but for the plane trip, we are always at home wherever we are.
>
> (Whiteford and Manderson 2000: 1)

The rules that govern trade, and the main ideology that now underpins it, 'the free market' are continually being revised and reinforced. It used to be up to individual countries to control the rules about trading, and through taxes, tariffs and subsidies, to decide what goods to import and what domestic industries to encourage, for instance alcohol or arms or steel. Trade liberalization – the abandonment of national taxes, tariffs and subsidies – has increased (although not at the same spectacular rate as the liberalization of financial markets). In a free trade market, goods could then be bought or sold anywhere in the world without restriction.

The world trading system up until now has favoured the exporters of manufactured goods. For a long time this disadvantaged countries of the

South whose main participation in global trade consisted in the export of raw materials and the import of finished products. A classic case of this was when Britain as a colonial power systematically wrecked the Indian cotton industry by its use of selective tariffs, in order to promote its own clothes industry. Control of trade – and profits – has always been a motive for war and domination.

Most countries – or blocks like the European Union (EU) – have tried to protect their own industries. There is a long running saga for instance about the extent to which the EU protects farmers through its common agricultural policy (CAP). It offers subsidies to farmers, and therefore makes it more economical for them to raise livestock and grow crops. Each cow in the European Union is entitled to a subsidy!

As well as subsidizing their own goods, many countries impose import tariffs on goods from abroad. Those countries that have preferential trading agreements can avoid these import tariffs. The EU for example has had a preferential agreement over the importation of bananas from the Caribbean. This was recently challenged by banana growers from the USA. The spats become retaliatory; for example the USA has in recent times banned French cheese and Scottish cashmere in retaliation for a perceived slight to USA goods.

The World Trade Organization (WTO) was set up to try to resolve these historical anomalies and inconsistencies and negotiate global free trade. In theory the WTO is a useful, highly specialized, international organization that could support poor countries, and eliminate unfair trading practices. But in practice it has been hijacked by richer nations, and multinational companies, who skew the rules to their advantage.

The trading deals being negotiated by the WTO do not redress the balance by favouring the poor, nor are they even-handed. They perpetuate the manufacturing biases which enable rich countries to buy raw goods cheaply from poor countries, and then sell on the finished goods at high prices. The WTO has negotiated a series of global deals on trading regulations for textiles, agriculture and other key sectors, backed up by international jurisdictions and fines. Poor countries are still compelled to sell their raw materials at low prices, yet are not allowed to develop their own local manufacturing industries with subsidies and protective tariffs.

One well-known example of the influence of WTO agreements is the deal over intellectual property rights, introduced because of pressure from pharmaceutical companies. This means that drugs produced in the North cannot be sold in the South at less than their sale price in the North (which is said to represent the investment spent in developing them).

Neither can they be produced locally, by scientists using the same formula. So life-saving drugs cannot be used in the South because their cost is protected, and they are unaffordable. In the case of anti-retrovirals to combat HIV/AIDS, this has become a huge medical scandal. Pharmaceutical companies making millions of dollars profit will not allow their life-saving drugs to be used at affordable prices for the majority of the world's population. Already, 4.3 million children have died of HIV/AIDS and in the worst affected countries in Southern Africa, 18–20 per cent of households are child-headed. Yet negotiations over the availability of life-saving drugs are slow and bitterly fought at every step. Protests have led to some concessions over the production of some generic drugs by poorer countries, but the situation remains fraught.[2]

These WTO trading deals are reinforced by structural adjustment programmes imposed by the World Bank. The World Bank will only lend money to those countries which engage in the world market for commodities and earn export income. This means, apart from supplying raw materials for manufacturing, many poor countries are also forced to earn export income by growing cash crops, such as vegetables or coffee for export to the North. Unlike the EU, they cannot protect or subsidize these cash crops, which are sold at rock-bottom prices, sometimes not even covering the cost of producing them.

The arguments are highly technical and detailed. But at the other end of the infighting and the deals, the tariffs and the subsidies, are people's livelihoods; what they earn to feed their families, and what they can afford to buy with the money they earn. This is why there are such big demonstrations whenever the WTO meets, as in Seattle in 1999.

### Inward investment

Another aspect of globalization is what is called foreign direct investment or inward investment. This is supposed to increase the volume of global trade and draw poorer countries into the global market. Multinational companies can shift production from the expensive North by investing in countries in the South where labour and other costs are cheap, and regulations, especially those concerning child labour, are more lax. For example Nike shoes are made in Indonesia; car and film production has been relocated in Eastern Europe; telephone-call centres are being transferred to India; garment manufacture to China or Bangladesh. Chussodovsky (1997) has tracked garment production from Bangladesh to New York and shown the mark-up at each stage of production. Workers earn very little of the profit. In the example Chussodovsky cites, garment workers typically earn the equivalent of US$5 for making a blouse that retails in New York at $292. Many goods in the South are made by children working long hours.

Foreign direct investment is supposed to benefit the countries concerned, by providing more jobs. The investment is only worth making in countries that are less poor, where there is reasonable infrastructure and communications. Poor African countries, or those with a history of conflict, are not worth investing in. But even where such investment takes place, it does not necessarily benefit those concerned. The United Nations Conference on Trade and Development (UNCTAD) reported that

> the top fifth of the world's people in the richest countries enjoy 82% of the expanding export trade and 68% of foreign direct investment – the bottom fifth, barely more than 1%. These trends reinforce economic stagnation and low human development. Only 33% of countries managed to sustain 3% of annual growth during 1980– 1996. For 59 countries GNP per capita declined. Economic integration (into the global market) is thus dividing developing and transitional economies into those that are benefiting from global opportunities and those that are not. In some cases people are poorer than 30 or 40 years ago, with little hope of improvement.
>
> (UNCTAD 1999: 31)

## Telecommunications and travel

Globalization of finance, trade and crime has been accelerated by the rapid development of technologies of communication such as electronic mail, web-based information systems, phone networks and teleconferencing. Global technologies transcend all geo-political boundaries and attempts at control.

Television and radio, available on satellite channels, also leap barriers and beam information across the globe. In theory instant communication is possible wherever you are in the world. Events are announced on the internet within minutes of them having occurred. However 90 per cent of the news comes from four news agencies, all located in the North. News is a global business too (Walt 1994).

People living in rich countries may have easy internet access, but telecommunications claims are exaggerated. In many poor countries in the South access is very difficult. If there are reliable electricity and telecommunications networks it may be possible, but almost everywhere

I have worked in the South and in transitional countries it has proved difficult, and sometimes very expensive, to access the internet or telephone networks. For example an estimated 0.5 per cent of people in Kenya have access to the internet. In any case, like print material, internet access is only available to the literate and only usable in world languages.

As well as shifting information very rapidly, it has also become possible to shift people (at least those with European or North American passports) very fast across the world. A journey from London to Johannesburg used to take 6 weeks. Now it takes 10 hours. It is possible to fall asleep in one continent and wake up in another; and increasing numbers of (rich) people do just that. The increase in air travel has been phenomenal. But it is goods rather than people that have contributed to the increase in air travel; green beans picked in Zimbabwe, or broccoli grown in Peru arrive in a supermarket in London within a day or two. The cost of the travel, the consumption of air fuel, and the pollution it causes are unacknowledged consequences of this international traffic; so too are the low wages of the people who grow or make the goods that are being shipped, so low that it is worth paying the air fares for the goods to be transported.

### International crime

One unforeseen effect of globalization, but intrinsically related to it, is the growth of international crime. Because money can be shifted around – or laundered – very easily, and because telecommunications make communication so fast, and because international law is relatively weak, unscrupulous people can benefit very easily. Where there is an especially valuable commodity such as oil, diamonds or uranium the temptations to well-placed individuals are enormous. Governments too may over-look international scruples about rights or transparency. Some of the most corrupt or dictatorial regimes in the world (according to monitor-ing agencies such as Transparency International) such as Nigeria or Turkmenistan attract investment from the North. Such investments are unlikely to benefit anyone except the rich elite who line their pockets with bribes or incentives from multinational oil companies, or who buy shares in key assets. Senior people in government can become extremely rich. For example a recent report by Lindsay Hilsum[3] illustrated the extent of corruption in Equatorial Guinea, where there is a newly discovered off-shore oil-field. The president/dictator was literally creaming off the profits for himself and his family and putting the proceeds into American banks with the connivance of international oil companies. Mobutu, in the Congo, made himself a millionaire from the diamond trade whilst his country fell apart.

The opportunities for criminal activity where valuable commodities are concerned are rife; crime has also been globalized. Recent wars in Sierra Leone and Liberia have been fuelled by the diamond trade. Kaldor (1999) suggests that most, if not all, recent wars – for example in Sierra Leone, Chechnya or in the Balkans – are perpetuated by mafiosi, international criminals who take advantage of weak international controls and regulations to profit from arms dealing and money-laundering – leading indirectly to the 2 million slaughtered children reported by UNICEF.

### The USA empire

English is dominant now because of the influence of the USA. The United States is the most important power in the world, although it comprises less than 5 per cent of the world's population. It is the richest nation and it has overwhelming military force. It has a determinative influence on anything that happens in contemporary world history. It also acts alone. It has been an unwilling signatory to most international agreements, and has refused to sign – for instance – the Convention on the Rights of the Child. It has also refused to be a signatory to the International Court of Human Justice, and has pressurized other countries to agree to exemptions for USA citizens abroad. It has undermined efforts to establish an international rule of law by by-passing the United Nations – for example in the case of Iraq.

Critics of USA policy, most notably the linguist Noam Chomsky, argue that the might of the USA is used to create investment opportunities in the South at the expense of the poor. Aid is indisputably linked to trade that benefits North Americans. Chomsky uses the example of Colombia and other Latin American countries to illustrate USA support for regimes that use paramilitary force to suppress local activists and trades unionists and peasants who oppose American investment. Chomsky may be regarded as extreme, but he has amassed considerable evidence to back his claims (Chomsky 2003). For him the claims by the USA to be spreading democracy in the Middle East through the war on Iraq are particularly hypocritical, considering the USA record of support for countries that have very bad human rights records. The USA is certainly powerful. Whether its power is used for good or bad is hotly debated. There is a spate of self-flagellating books by Americans wondering why the USA is so hated (Chua 2003).

## The dominance of English

Because of the USA, English has become the language of globalization. Almost all other languages are at a disadvantage compared with English. It is now the language of trade, diplomacy, aid, technology and academia (knowledge). It has been called a 'killer' language, because all other languages are subordinate to it. This also has repercussions for those in the South whose communications must always be through a second or third language. In addition, the orthographies of minor languages have not been computerized, and speakers of hundreds of lesser-known languages are unrepresented in telecommunications. International business is of course conducted in many languages but it is difficult to do business without English.

## The economic development arguments

Is the impact of globalization as severe as its critics imply? For our purposes here, are children at risk? Anthony Giddens and Will Hutton (2001) for example argue over whether globalization is a new phenomenon, or an intensification of economic trends that were well-established in the days of the earliest empires.[4] Hutton argues the latter; and claims that if globalization is not so very different from what has always gone on, then it is within our means to do something about it.

Giddens sees globalization as a sea change, a qualitatively different and inexorable process of modernization that can only be restrained with great difficulty, and certainly cannot be reshaped. Instead we have to learn to live with it.

Underlying these views are economic arguments. Proponents of free market economics, suggest that the free-wheeling capitalism epitomized by multinational companies, and removal of financial controls, 'freeing up the market' is the only way forward, and has led to leaps in prosperity for mankind. This economic view has been especially prevalent in the USA. Taxation is light (and lessening) and the state provides very few direct services or social welfare.

The collapse of the central planning systems that characterized communist countries appears to confirm the success of market economics. The global market is in any case now too interconnected for any other option to be possible. The more the rich get richer, the argument goes, the more wealth will trickle down to the poor. This is the new economic orthodoxy that the economic system of the USA – and to a lesser extent the UK – epitomizes. Yet the gap between rich and poor in the USA is more extreme than in most other countries of the North (Bradbury and Jantii 1999).

As subsequent chapters will show, belief in market economics is an extremely powerful viewpoint. It has heavily influenced key international financial institutions like the IMF and the World Bank, whose headquarters are in Washington (not by coincidence!). Joseph Stiglitz (2002) claims that it is the application of this crude, untrammelled economic theory, and the rush to privatize, that was responsible for the terrible downturns in the Russian economy. The overnight abandonment of social welfare supports, the rise in alcohol and drug dependency, the huge numbers of street children, and the growth of a terrifying Russian Mafia, could have been largely avoided by more moderate economic policies.

Stiglitz still believes that globalization is inevitable, but argues that economists should be better informed and more sensitive to local conditions. Others are much more critical. Susan George and Fabrizio Sabelli, in their book *Faith and Credit* (1994) argue that the IMF and the World Bank are like the medieval Catholic Church. Just as it was once unthinkable not to believe in God, now it is unthinkable not to believe in the economic orthodoxy of the free market. Countries who do not accept the World Bank are excommunicated – or blacklisted like Cuba.

Samir Amin, the North African economist, has powerfully argued that the South should develop its own economic networks and try to 'delink' from the economic and political power of the North. To a limited extent this is happening – there are already economic groupings within Africa and Asia – but they are too new or too financially weak to make a difference yet.

Ravi Kunbur (2001) is another important World Bank economist who, like Stiglitz, has resigned from the World Bank. From academia he now argues a different case. His position is that the differences of approach between the economists of the World Bank and those who criticize them arise out of profound conceptual differences in three key areas: aggregation; time scales; and the structure of the market. Economic theory works with a broad brush and considers aggregate economic trends over many millions of people, and relies on particular kinds of indicators, most notably aggregate income and expenditure. But broad brush theories cannot cope with inequalities and specificity.

Kunbur gives the example of street children in Ghana. Whilst World Bank analysts, using aggregate income-based measures, were demonstrating that levels of poverty in Ghana had fallen, NGOs were reporting dramatic increases in the numbers of street children. Both claims gave a partial picture; aggregate measures badly needed supplementing with specific instances.

Second, economists tend to rely on middle-range forecasting; what will happen in the next 5 or 10 years if present trends continue, or if certain adaptations are made. Kunbur argues that short-term measures – what children are suffering now – and long-term measures – what happens if their parents die of HIV/AIDS – must also be taken into account.

Third, Kunbur argues that there are differences over the nature and functioning of the market. There is little disagreement that the market is imperfect as a model of economic growth. The question is, how imperfect, and what kinds of adjustments should be made to it? The World Bank economists on the whole favour minimalist interventions; their critics see it as requiring more vigorous intervention and control.

As we will see in Chapter 4, World Bank economists working on early childhood issues make the common assumptions that aggregate measures are the most useful for predictive purposes; that the medium term is what counts; and that the market is a useful model for the development of services.

The small states of Scandinavia – Sweden, Norway, Finland and Denmark – are frequently cited as a workable alternative to the extreme free market ideology of the USA. These countries have successful economies, yet also have very strong welfare states. Child poverty in the USA and UK could be largely eliminated through redistributive taxes and benefits, as it has been in Scandinavia and several other European countries such as Belgium. The USA and the UK are extremely rich countries yet child poverty is rife in both. The reason that child poverty is not addressed in these countries is partly, or mainly, because economic orthodoxy argues against it. The poor must help themselves; the wealth of the rich stimulates economic activity and trade. These arguments are explored further in the next chapter.

These economic arguments may seem complex and remote from the concerns of childhood. But unfortunately they are not. Children do not live their lives in isolation; they are part of a community which in turn is part of a socio-economic system that may, and often does, affect them badly. The well-being of children is unfortunately not an accepted standard economic indicator; economics might look rather different if it was.

## Globalization – another picture

I have tried to summarize these arguments about globalization because they permeate discussions about transitional countries and the South. It is impossible to explore what is happening to children without this backdrop.

The push towards globalization – whether a recent phenomenon or an ancient one – creates a wake of poor and victimized people. But those who cannot fight back are not necessarily passive victims. As Scott has convincingly shown in his highly regarded and subtle book, *Weapons of the Weak*, confrontations between the powerless and the powerful are never straightforward. By countless small unrecorded acts, the poor fight back. Behind the public discourse are 'the hidden transcripts'; what the powerless say about powerful people behind their backs; and their subversive failure to agree with the regimes imposed on them. He argues that his study of a small village in Malaysia is a prototype for most kinds of conflicts where the rich and powerful try to insist on the hegemony of their point of view.

> The kind of conflict with which we are dealing here is singularly undramatic. At one level it is a contest over definitions of justice, a struggle to control the concepts and symbols by which current experience is evaluated. At another level it is a struggle over the appropriateness of a given definition of justice of a particular case, a particular set of facts, a particular behaviour . . . Finally at a third level, of course, it is a struggle over land, work, income, and power in the middle of massive changes.
>
> (Scott 1989: 27)

Rosaldo (1993) has also commented on the ideological resistance of the subordinate groups, who use anonymity, ambiguity and mockery as weapons against the hegemony of the powerful. These are the ways in which the poor refuse to do what they are told or accept what 'fate' has given them. Scott argues that such resistance, however trivial or annoying its manifestations, should be valued for what it is, a refusal to accept the dominant point of view.

> All the more reason then to respect, if not celebrate, the weapons of the weak. All the more reason to see the tenacity of self-preservation – in ridicule, in truculence, in irony, in petty acts of non-compliance, in foot-dragging, in dissimulation, in resistant mutuality, in the

> disbelief in elite homilies, in the steady grinding efforts to hold one's own against overwhelming odds – a spirit and practice that prevents the worst and promises something better.
>
> (1989: 350)

Even though bodies may be under the yoke, hearts and minds may remain unconvinced by the arguments of those in power. Apparent compliance with the instructions of the powerful does not necessarily signify agreement.

The yoke, however, may be a very heavy one. Scott explores in an exceptionally wide-ranging later book, *Seeing Like a State: How Certain Schemes to Improve the Human Condition Have Failed*, how governments come to override the views of the populace. Often attempts at reform, far from being cynical grabs for power and wealth, are animated by a genuine desire to improve the human condition, prompted by optimistic views of progress and rational order (a theme I return to in Chapter 4).

> If I were asked to condense the reasons behind these failures into a single sentence, I would say that the progenitors of such plans regarded themselves as far smarter and far-seeing than they really were and, at the same time, regarded their subjects as more stupid and incompetent than they really were.
>
> (Scott 1998: 343)

Amongst the most destructive of schemes are those that involve displacement of populations, for instance the construction of dams. In aggregate, in the middle term, on paper, using standardized measurements and statistical returns, economic out-turns may appear promising and justify investment in dams. On the ground, for the people who live and labour on the land, reality may be experienced very differently.

For example, the Kariba dam project in the north of Zimbabwe is a well-established large-scale investment project established with foreign aid. An entire valley was flooded in order to create electricity. The lake thus created was also intended as a tourist attraction. The land surrounding the lake was designated as a wild-life park, and wild animals within it were protected. New hotels sprung up on the shores of the lake advertising wild-life holidays.

The losers in this scenario were the Tsonga people who, for many generations, had lived self-sufficient lives as small farmers in the valley before it was flooded. They were moved to land higher up the escarpment. They continued to try to farm despite the wild animals, especially the elephants, which rampaged through their crops, but which they were not allowed to harm in any way. The lives of the Tsonga people were very carefully chronicled in the 1980s by the anthropologist Pamela Reynolds in her book *Dance, Civet Cat* (1991). She described the autonomy – and the lack of it – that the Tsonga people, especially young people, experienced. Men and some women were offered jobs as servants in the new hotels, working long hours for low pay, provided they could speak some English. The women and girls tried to continue to farm, but had to devote much more time and energy to fending off and trying to scare away the animals. They camped overnight by their fields to try to protect them, but they were frightened, and there was not much they could do if the elephants trampled on their fields. Elephants are very big and frightening close up. The Tsonga were not compensated for their losses.

A small aid project tried to offer the Tsonga people some support. In 1997 I was asked to evaluate the programme. Mostly it consisted of small clearings in the bush, where a couple of nominated women cooked porridge, donated by the agency, in a large pot. The porridge provided food for a network of local women and children. There was one hut that belonged to the project, but it was empty, unswept and unused, and the cooking went on outside it. The intention had been to provide playgroup activities for children to prepare them for school, alongside the food distribution, but this had never really happened. It required too much time and effort and it was in any case an imported concept.

I also visited the local school. The school was very overcrowded, with classes held underneath trees. There was also a language problem, since the Tsonga dialect was not catered for. The school was operating in Shona and English, so the children entered grade 1 faced with learning a new language. The aid agency carefully avoided anything that might be regarded as a political intervention; their job was to provide food and whatever support for schooling they could offer, to patch the gaps created by the economic development of the area.

The Kariba dam attracted investment. The hotels, mostly owned by white entrepreneurs, attracted many tourists. Possibly aggregated figures for the success of the dam showed a net gain; the dam contributed to cheaper and more widespread electricity for many, and for some, it generated more foreign currency. In 1997 there were rumours of eco-tourism projects to which the Tsonga were invited to contribute, if not manage. But it would be difficult to claim that over time the investment had improved the lives of the local people. Instead it had marginalized and impoverished them, and eaten away their time. Very little had directly trickled their way, and they were unimpressed by its results.

This tale of marginalization and impoverishment as a result of economic policies decided elsewhere for the apparent benefit of a majority, is a common one. The Booker prizewinner, Arundhati Roy, in her book *The Greater Common Good* (1999), has written with searing rhetoric of the way in which powerless tribal groups are treated – in particular over the Narmada dam project in India.

> The same political formation that plunged the whole nation into a bloody medieval nightmare because it insisted on destroying an old mosque to dig up a non-existent temple, thinks nothing of submerging a hallowed pilgrimage route and hundreds of temples that have been worshipped in for centuries. It thinks nothing of destroying the sacred hills and groves, the places of worship, the ancient homes of the gods and demons of tribal people. It thinks nothing of submerging a valley that has yielded fossils, microliths and rock paintings, the only valley in India, according to archaeologists, that contains an uninterrupted record of human occupation from the Old Stone Age.
>
> (1999: 47)

Identity and context are all-important. Globalism, in all its many facets, does not fill a vacuum; it replaces, or imposes on, already existing local traditions and identities. The agricultural economist Robert Chambers described this stomping all over local feelings and customs in his book *Whose Reality Counts?* (1997). He described how large-scale investments in agriculture in India, designed to stimulate cash crop production of foodstuff for Northern markets, had simply ignored the views of local farmers about what could be grown under what conditions. He designed methods called 'participatory rural appraisal' for enabling the poor to explain their position and make their priorities clear, even if they were illiterate or unused to making their voice heard. These methods are now in widespread use by aid agencies, and even the World Bank. Whilst they may be an improvement on *no* consultation, they are very often used in a tokenistic way – a point returned to in the next chapter.

There are, unsurprisingly, all kinds of direct and indirect resistances to global pressures to become the same, to adopt the same values without the same resources. The reassertion of local identities, the re-emerging importance of ethnicity and religion, demands for autonomy, self-government and independence, even civil wars are all part of the picture, the other side of the coin to globalism. It is astonishing (or perhaps not) how much the USA is criticized in the South. In Johannesburg, where part of this book was written, it was hard to find anyone with a kind word to say about the USA. The two chapters in this book directly written from the South, from India and from Brazil, document these resistances to globalism in relation to young children.

This chapter began with a recital of the statistics prepared by UNICEF concerning the appalling circumstances of millions of children. One of the arguments threaded through this book is that we cannot be parochial in our concerns for young children. Lack of knowledge or lack of information is no longer an excuse for ignoring the circumstances of poor children. There are some important and detailed studies that document the lives of poor children over time. Some of them will be discussed in other chapters. But to conclude this chapter, I quote from a recent study in South Africa, which has been following up a large group of poor children in the townships from birth onwards. South Africa in many ways offers a microcosm of global inequality; a tiny, rich, mainly white population whose standard of living is very high; and a majority of black people shut away in the townships, in what are often impoverished, fragmented communities. This is what the authors have to say:

> There is much wisdom in the saying 'as long as the poor cannot afford to eat, the wealthy cannot afford to sleep.' This statement underscores the indissoluble link between those who suffer material deprivation and those who live in abundance. This interdependence can have dire repercussions when the needs of the poor are neglected by those who live in material comfort . . . The prospect for improvement in this situation lies in part in the capacity of those who were and still are privileged to recognize their self-interest in working towards a more equitable society.
>
> (Barbarin and Richter 2001: 276)

# Chapter 2

# Interpreting poverty

**Summary**

In this chapter I try to explore what is meant by child poverty. Definitions and understandings of poverty differ – not everyone shares in the pervasive consumerism of the North and poverty is not exclusively related to lack of possessions or money. I explore some of these measures of poverty in more detail, and examine the different kinds of models that are used in the North and the South to describe and analyse child poverty. I also explore why toleration of child poverty is much greater in some countries than others – especially in the USA. I describe some of the approaches countries use to try to combat child poverty. At one end of the spectrum, especially in the Nordic countries wealth is redistributed. People pay higher taxes but very few children are poor. At the other end of the spectrum, in the USA, taxes are lower, but child poverty is high. Poverty is seen as a personal failing. In this case, a strategy for poverty reduction is to target interventions towards poor children, especially towards very young children, in the hope that they will learn skills and habits that will enable them to lift themselves out of poverty when they become adults. It is this latter approach that has been frequently advocated in the South.

## Poverty and inequality

Bessie Head, the South African writer, was abandoned at birth and brought up in a series of orphanages and foster homes under the apartheid regime. In her semi-autobiographical novella, *The Cardinals*, she describes the life of a child in the townships:

> It [the squatter camp] was a large slum area of tin shacks, bounded on the one side by a mile-long graveyard and on the other by the city refuse dump and the sea . . . The shack was a small space with every

possible bit of junk crammed into it: boxes stuffed with rags and faded clothing; an old cracked mirror in a corner; a torn stained mattress competing for space with battered pots, an oil stove, blankets and a shaky wooden table . . . Early each morning the men crept out of the tin shacks to work as labourers. Those women who had no work sat around idly and gossiped. The children had to walk a mile from the slum with pails or tins to collect water for household use, then they would spend the rest of the day raking around in the refuse dump for edibles or discarded clothing or any other treasure. During week-days life was quiet. On Friday evenings when the men received their pay, the night would be a riot of violence and drunkenness.

(1993: 3)

The child runs away, only to be placed by the social worker in another township:

The only difference between this slum and the one she had fled was that there was no refuse dump and reeking stagnant water. The pattern of life was the same with the weekends of drunkenness and violence, and the crude, animal, purposeless world of poverty. She learnt the lessons every unwanted stray has to learn: 'Work hard. Do not answer back no matter what we do to you. Be satisfied with the scraps we give you . . .'

(1993: 10)

Somehow, Bessie Head made good; her insatiable desire for learning and her talent as a writer enabled her to at least partly overcome her circumstances, but she was never at ease:

I don't think you know what it is to awaken every morning to a burning hatred against injustice. It isn't an abstract thing, you are hating people and the perpetrators of this injustice. You come eventually to the conclusion that both the hater and the hated will blow up in a great conflagration.

(1993: xii)

Bessie Head sums up the grim attributes of poverty: degraded environments, shortage of food, little or no money, few possessions, insecurity, hopelessness, violence and the daily experience of contempt. As the UNICEF Innocenti Research Centre has pointed out, in their series of reports 'The Urban Child in Difficult Circumstances', poverty is compounded by a sense of powerlessness, of exclusion, of lack of a rightful place that accompanies the failure of some of their expectations and their lack of access to the resources they need or consider they have a right to.

(Munyakho 1992: 1)

The picture of poverty was more extreme in apartheid South Africa than elsewhere, where blacks and coloureds were regarded as less than human. But in many countries the poor are despised, rather than pitied, for their poverty, especially if they also appear to be racially different.

The contempt of others is especially damaging for survival. Nancy Scheper-Hughes, the American anthropologist, has for many years been working in the favelas of Northeast Brazil.[1] In her book *Death Without Weeping* (1993) she describes the neglect shown by mothers to their infants, and the very high child mortality rates. She concludes, not that these are poor parenting practices (as many aid agencies have described the childrearing practices of the poor) but that being seen as worthless themselves, the mothers could not believe their ailing babies were worth saving. Even if they had tried to do more, they lacked the essential resources – access to clean water, sanitation, food and medicine. Resignation was a more realistic tactic than struggling endlessly against their fate. Philippe Bourgois (1998), working in the barrios in New York with Puerto Rican families, makes similar observations. The chaotic violence of daily life on the margins, in a rich country like the USA, led women to devalue themselves and to lower their expectations to the point that their own survival, and that of their children, was a matter of relative indifference.

Yet the picture of poverty is not always grim. Majid Rahnema (1997), the Iranian critic, argues that the frugality of small poor rural communities is not a meaningless existence, but one which is more meaningful and grounded than the restless, consumer bound lives of those who live in the North. He criticizes the norms of ease and plenty that characterize the North. In a vivid metaphor, he describes 'development' as a kind of socio-cultural HIV/AIDS that attacks the natural immune systems of society, destroying collaboration, co-operation and environmental respect. He asks where does one draw the line between having enough to live on, and being indulgent and greedy and dependent on the labour of others – in a sense the question asked by Rorty and Rawls, and quoted in the preface to this book. For Rahnema, refraining from excessive consumption – or most consumption – is not merely a question of self-restraint in order to avoid the exploitation of others, but a question of how the activities of daily life are valued. Money and possessions are only a means to an end. The end is the enjoyment of daily life, savouring its beauties and idiosyncrasies.

Helena Norberg-Hodge makes a similar point in her book about life in Ladakh in the Himalayas. She claims that the Ladakh people regarded laughter and enjoyment as their natural birthright. They lived in a subsistence economy, but their life was characterized by sharing, conviviality and festive activities.

> I never met people who seemed so healthy emotionally, so secure as the Ladakhis. The reasons are, of course, complex and spring from a whole way of life and world view. But I'm sure that the most important factor is the sense that you are part of something much larger than yourself, that you are inextricably connected to others and to your surroundings.
>
> (1992: 85)

She described what happened when 'development' came to Ladakh, as the Indian government tried to open up Kashmir to tourists. A remote people who had no notion of poverty, were introduced to a market economy, where they sold their labour in return for manufactured goods. New economic paradigms, stressing individuality, competition and gain led to the breakdown of old community ties and values.[2]

Both Rahnema and Norberg-Hodge have been accused of giving a romantic and unreal view of small remote communities. But definitions of poverty are complex. A key issue is solidarity, the extent to which those who experience poverty see themselves as living an unexceptional life; or perceive their suffering as widely shared; or are determined to work together to change it.

Conversely, poverty may be debilitating, and there is bitter competition over the few resources that exist; or the poor are all too conscious of the wealth from which they are excluded. William Hinton (1970) in his classic book *Fanshen* describes a poor rural community in China and the hatred that existed between landlords and peasants. The Indian anthropologist and author Amitrav Ghosh describes communal life in a rural village in Egypt. The fellaheen (peasants) question him about his life in India, and refuse to believe that there are people who are still poorer than themselves. Ghosh realises that the fellaheen are only too aware of their poverty, and see themselves shamefacedly as dirt poor.

> I realized that the fellaheen saw the material circumstances of their lives in exactly the same way that a university economist would: as a

situation that was shamefully anachronistic, a warp upon time; I understood that their relationships with the objects of their everyday lives was never innocent of the knowledge that there were other places, other countries which did not have mud-walled houses and cattle-drawn ploughs, so that those objects, those houses and ploughs were insubstantial things, ghosts displaced in time, waiting to be exorcized and laid to rest.

(1998: 200)

As Ghosh, and others, suggest, very poor people, especially in peasant communities, may live arduous lives and lack food and medicine, and know perfectly well that others possess these things, but nevertheless they belong in a community with a rich and detailed daily life. Gottlieb points to the contradictions experienced both by those 'looking in' from the outside, as anthropologists or as people involved in 'development' as well as to the contradictions experienced by the poor themselves.

The gulf between social and spiritual wealth and material poverty is difficult to reconcile. It threatens to leave an outsider alternating between envy and pity. Yet envy fosters a problematic essentialism hearkening back to a Rousseau-ian romanticizing model that is as unrealistic as any, while pity negates subjectivity and reduces humans to passive victims.

(2004: xviii)

Poverty is highly contextual. It does not always result in demoralization or passivity or anger. Understanding the nuances of poverty and its ramifications for individual lives requires, as Rorty commented, not only inquiry but imagination.

But from a distance, understanding and empathizing with poverty depends in part on the methods used to portray it. The World Bank, for example, has carried out analyses of poverty all over the world using standard economic criteria and definitions. These abstract figures have led to accusations that the World Bank has no real understanding of what it means to be poor. Stung by such criticism of its macroeconomic approach, the World Bank has made a major attempt to use qualitative participative methodologies to try to understand what poverty means to the people who experience it. It undertook a huge research exercise and attempted to document the experiences of poverty in 272 sites in 23 countries. Its 'Voices of the Poor' (VOTP) project (Narayan *et al.* 1999, 2000) provides a rich picture of the diversities and commonalities of being poor. It explores material and psychological well-being, vulnerability and coping strategies, relationships with state and civil society institutions. It confirms the multi-dimensional nature of poverty.

As Chambers (2002) points out, the ultimate justification for VOTP has to be good net effects. In the end, was VOTP 'camouflage or cosmetic'? Has it served to legitimize the activities of the World Bank, an organization which in the last resort is devoted to usury? Ravi Kunbur, who was quoted in the last chapter, was the economist in the World Bank in charge of VOTP but resigned over differences about the analysis of the data. Chambers was himself – after some self-questioning – involved in the writing-up of VOTP. He concludes from the experience of being involved in the project that,

> power forms and frames knowledge and that interpersonal power distorts what is learned and expressed. There is no complete escape from this. Each one of us has to take responsibility for our part in the methodological, epistemological and ethical struggle to achieve representations of realities which optimize a multitude of trade-offs.
>
> (2002: 159)

## Measuring poverty and inequality in the North

Poverty is relative and contextual. To understand it and explain it as it is experienced is – as the previous section has illustrated – not straight-forward. Nevertheless can it be compared and given a quantitative value? Are there benchmarks? What does standard economic analysis tell us about poverty?

Recent work by Vleminckx and Smeeding (2001) has offered a summary of the situation of children in the North. The standard measure of poverty commonly used is a relative one; households who earn less than half of the median income of their country are counted as poor. Using median income as the benchmark, unequal societies like the UK and the USA have high child poverty rates. An alternative way of rating poverty is to try to define absolute poverty, a calculation based on a 'basket of goods'. The government calculates a minimum of what is needed to live, in terms of food and utilities, and people who cannot afford these minimum requirements are classified as poor, irrespective of average income per head. The USA and Canada favour such an approach (although using different baskets). The USA again has consistently the worse child poverty ratings. However, some countries are ranked very differently, according to whether relative or absolute poverty is used as a measure. Some Eastern European countries have high rates of poverty using absolute measures, but lower rates of poverty using relative measures. In other words, in Eastern Europe income has traditionally been shared out more than in English-speaking countries.

Diderichsen has drawn on the Swedish welfare system to produce a model of a universalistic welfare state that illustrates the kind of income redistribution that takes place in countries where there is low poverty. There is graduated income tax, the poor paying relatively little, and the rich paying a great deal. The income tax is spent by the state on services (such as childcare) and cash benefits (pensions and other benefits). The two high income bands subsidize the two lower income bands. The net result is that the highest income earners are only two and a half times better off than the poorest (see Table 2.1). The comparable ratios in the USA or the UK (two of the most unequal countries in the North) are in the region of 10:1; the rich do not subsidize the poor very much.

Shelley Phipps, a Canadian economist, has tried to link values, policies and child outcomes in measuring poverty. She has extracted and combined the results of three different types of survey (one on values and beliefs; another on redistributive policies; and a third on child outcomes) in order to produce a comparative study of the USA, Canada and Norway. The three value themes were: reasons for poverty; tolerance of income inequality; and social expectations of children. Phipps shows that in the USA, and to a lesser extent in Canada there is a public view that poverty is associated with laziness, and that income inequality is not a major concern. Poor people do not try hard enough; high earners deserve their income. In Norway, only a minority held such views. As a result of these views and values, she argues, the USA and Canada are

Table 2.1 The redistributive effect of a universalistic welfare state

| Quintile | Average income | 40% income tax | Services | Cash benefits | Net income |
|---|---|---|---|---|---|
| A | 1000 | 400 | 80 | 180 | 860 |
| B | 800 | 320 | 100 | 160 | 740 |
| C | 600 | 240 | 120 | 120 | 600 |
| D | 400 | 160 | 140 | 80 | 460 |
| E | 200 | 80 | 160 | 60 | 340 |
| Ratio A:E | 5:1 | 5:1 | 1:2 | 3:1 | 2.5:1 |

Source: Diderichsen 1995: 188.

reluctant to introduce redistributive income transfers, that is tax and benefits that are pro-poor.

> Policy discussion [in the USA and Canada] is extremely concerned that 'too generous' transfers will lead people, naturally lazy, to take advantage of programmes by working less for pay and 'enjoying' more time jobless. Such thinking goes back many years (e.g. the British Poor Laws of the 17th century) but still characterizes policy discussion today.
>
> (2001: 82)

She also points out that more lone parents are in work in Norway than in either the USA or Canada even although cash and in-kind benefits are much higher for lone parents in Norway than in the other two countries.

The main difference in social expectations of children was that independence and responsibility were more highly valued in Norway, whereas hard work and religious faith were valued more highly in the USA. She included child outcomes on three measures in her comparison, asthma, child injury and feelings of fear and anxiety. Norwegian children are significantly less likely to experience asthma or injury. Only 11 per cent of Norwegian children experienced feelings of fear or anxiety against over 30 per cent in the USA and Canada. Overall she concludes that the evidence is 'consistent with the idea that both higher levels of spending and programmes with a more universal flavour are associated with better outcomes for children' (2001: 88).

The evidence from the North on poverty shows that it is possible to achieve very low child poverty rates – below 5 per cent – using either relative or absolute measures (although the kind of measurement makes some difference to ranking in some countries) by redistributive taxation. Although richer countries tend to have less poverty, it is not the case for English-speaking countries, and especially not the case for the USA and the UK. It therefore raises questions about the neutrality of economic models and forecasting which draw heavily on assumptions and evidence from the USA.

Moore (2001) has summarized the debate about perceptions of the cause of poverty in Table 2.2.

Rather than exploring redistributive taxes and benefits as a solution to poverty, a frequent paradigm in the North, especially in the USA and UK, is that poverty is primarily an individual failing, and has to be addressed by bolstering the capacity of individuals to cope, preferably whilst the individual is young and malleable enough to be influenced.

*Table 2.2* The debate about perceptions of the cause of poverty

| Perception of the cause of poverty | Policy implications |
| --- | --- |
| *Culture causes poverty:* Some poor people (the 'underclass') are and remain poor because of innate/ genetic characteristics (e.g. laziness, ineptitude, dishonesty, criminality, lack of intelligence). | Focus efforts on the 'deserving' poor (i.e. those who are poor because of external factors, e.g. widows, orphans, disabled people and some unemployed). Poverty among 'the underclass' can never be overcome. |
| *Poverty causes a culture which limits escape from poverty:* People are and remain poor because of their beliefs, attitudes and behaviours (e.g. short-termism, poor work ethic, risk aversion, unstable families, welfare dependence, substance abuse, fatalism, low expectations). A 'culture of poverty' emerged in response to poverty in earlier generations. | Focus efforts on changing the beliefs, attitudes and the behaviours of the poor. Poverty will go when behaviours change. |
| Poor people are and remain poor because of socio-economic structures. | Focus efforts on changing socio-economic structures, and providing social safety nets in the meantime. Behaviours will change when poverty is removed. |

There is an 'underclass' of poor people who perpetuate their own poverty; therefore an effective strategy is to focus efforts on their young children to counteract the failings of their parents.

Much of the evidence used to discuss poverty and children's life-chances comes from within this paradigm. If policy was directed at improving children's cognitive capacities through educational and childcare programmes, and also (or instead) addressed mothers' parenting styles, it would be possible to break through the 'culture of poverty'. Low aspirations could be challenged in a society where, theoretically, success is open to all.

## Targeted early childhood interventions to address child poverty in the USA and the UK

A very strongly held assumption in the USA is that state intervention for early childhood programmes is unnecessary and unaffordable, and too costly for the public purse (OECD 2000). The preferred approach is to target specialized services to poor young children.

Most of the evidence that targeted early intervention 'works' comes from targeted programmes for low-income families. 'Low-income' is even used synonymously with 'multi-problem', 'high-risk' and 'low IQ'! 'Multi-problem', in turn, usually refers to families who have been referred to social welfare agencies because of concerns about children – for instance chaotic lifestyles, early pregnancy, drug or alcohol abuse and so on.

There are two studies in particular that are cited over and over again, the Perry High Scope and the Abecedarian. These studies, which began in the 1960s and 1970s were conducted as longitudinal randomized, controlled trials. This methodology is borrowed from medicine and is regarded as scientifically robust, although the samples are small. It is worth paying some attention to these studies, since so very many claims are based on them.

The Abecedarian project which took place in North Carolina was a trial for 111 infants. Admission criteria to the project were based on a High Risk Index that assessed new mothers referred from hospital waiting lists and/or referred by welfare agencies. Eligible mothers had IQs of about 85, and 55 per cent were on welfare benefits. The overwhelming majority of the participants, 98 per cent, were black. Half of the sample was randomly assigned to the intervention group and the other half to the control group. The intervention group had three years of intensive high quality full-time care and education before starting school; and of this group half received after-school care from kindergarten through to the age of 8 (i.e. an after-school programme). High quality in this case means good staff–child ratios, a specifically developed curriculum, and constant university scrutiny of the project (Campbell *et al.* 2001).

At the age of 21, 105 of the participants were followed up. The major domains measured at the age of 21 included academic skills and educational attainment, employment and social adjustment which included instances of substance abuse and law breaking. Generally the group who had received intervention had better scores than the control group, with girls performing slightly better than boys. However, there was no reduction in law breaking – 44.9 per cent of individuals in the treatment group had records of one or more charges compared with 42 per cent of the controls. The mothers of the children who had the intervention had also benefited slightly from the availability of childcare, and were more likely to be employed. As the authors point out, there were layers of confounding effects – the community where the research was carried out, the standards of local schools and the levels of racism in the community may have all influenced the outcomes (Campbell *et al.* 2002).

The authors concluded that good quality full-time care in the early years did make a long-term difference, although the results should be carefully interpreted. Other observers have noted that the 'the Abecedarian program results in healthy returns for the investment of public resources targeted at a disadvantaged group' (Masse and Barnett 2003: 34).

The team from the Abecedarian have issued many papers in peer refereed journals, detailing the different aspects of the study, and their follow up of the participants over time. Generally these findings have proved durable. There has been little or no criticism of their scientific status or their claims.

The Perry High Scope project is much more problematic. The claims for the long-term effects of the project border on the fantastic: those who have been through one or two years of the (very) part-time High Scope nursery project at the age of 3 or 4 years at one time or another are less likely to have committed crimes, more likely to be house owners, or more likely to own two cars.

High Scope was an early learning programme designed originally within the school system in Ypsilanti. The programme seemed to be very successful, and those involved with it, most notably David Weikart, set up their own charitable foundation to promote the programme, to package and sell it. All the key publications describing the project have been issued by the Foundation itself, as part of its promotional activities. However, there have also been other publications in reputable journals.

There are three separate projects described in the publications of High Scope. The first, the Perry High Scope project, randomly allocated 128 children, selected on the basis of low IQ (85) to two different groups, an intervention group and a control group. Most of these children were from poor black families. The intervention group received part-time, school term, nursery education following the High Scope method, plus some home visiting. The children entered the study at the age of 3 or 4, with a new group each year from 1962 to 1965. The first group had two years of High Scope, subsequent groups only one year. Over time, 125 subjects were followed up (Schweinhart *et al.* 1993).

The second project was the Ypsilanti Preschool Curriculum Demonstration project, again in small numbers or waves through 1967, 1968 and 1969. The children were allocated to one of three groups, a High Scope group, a directed curriculum group, or a control group. It is unclear whether all the children have been randomly assigned to their groups. The numbers given for children participating in this project appear to vary; and there seems to be some overlap of groups with the previous study, i.e. some of the children in this study were carried over from the previous study. The most commonly cited number of partici- pants for this study is 68. These children were also followed up long term (Schweinhart *et al.* 1993).

The third project was the Ypsilanti–Carnegie Infant Education project (Epstein and Weikart 1979). These children were followed up for seven years but no further details of this study have become available.

Attempts have been made to quantify the impact of the first two projects in terms of cost–benefits. The cost–benefits refer mainly to the first project, but frequently reviewers have confused or conflated them. Schweinhart (2003) claims that for the children who enrolled in the Perry preschool programme, there was a benefit of $105,126 per participant. This is calculated on the following basis:

- $68,584 saved by the potential victims of crimes never committed based on typical in-court and out-of-court settlements for such crimes;
- $15,240 in reduced justice system costs;
- $10,357 brought in by increased taxes paid by participants because they had better paid jobs than expected;
- $7,488 saved in schooling, due primarily to reduced need for special education services;
- $3,457 in reduced welfare costs.

These figures amount to a cost–savings ratio of seven dollars saved to every dollar spent on the programme.

The thorough Abecedarian project showed no benefits from reduced crime figures. No other project has indicated such positive results as the Perry High Scope project. Even the Perry High Scope has had more limited impact than its supporters appear to be claiming, which has led to charges of over-selling the results.

Reviews of the evidence suggest that impact is linked with the type and quality of the provision. The low-income children who attended these programmes may do better than other children from their poor neighbourhoods, but most still lag behind middle-class children. For example, even in the Perry High Scope Preschool Project, which is known for its remarkably positive outcomes, nearly one third of the program children were later arrested, and one third dropped out of high school . . . realistic expectations are in order.

(The Future of Children 1995: 14)

As we shall see in the following chapters, the evidence, especially from the Perry High Scope study, is recycled over and over again. The conflation of low-income with low IQ and welfare referrals, and the targeting of ethnic minority groups, raises questions about the generalizability and relevance of the results. Yet despite their limited application and their limited success, these studies crop up in most of the justificatory early childhood literature that is used in the South.

Assumptions about the role of targeted early childhood interventions in the USA in combating child poverty are so widespread that they have an almost biblical status in the early childhood community. But there is some limited criticism of targeting even within the USA. Critics suggest that the aims of targeted early childhood interventions – to break the back of poverty – are in general hugely optimistic. The gains, if any, are marginal, refer only to high-quality programmes, and overlook, or divert attention from, the wider socio-economic contexts of inequality and lack of social mobility (Bickel and Spatig 1999).

The UK has followed in the USA footsteps. Drawing on the same recycled evidence from the USA, the Sure Start programme in England is another much trumpeted targeted approach to addressing child poverty. Launched in 1999, it aimed to provide a range of community-based services for children aged 0–3. It is targeted at 20 per cent of the poorest districts in England. Sure Start is currently being evaluated in three ways: for its implementation (the kind of programmes it has been developing); for its outcomes (the effect on young children of having attended the programmes); and for its cost-effectiveness (its cost compared with alternative forms of provision and child support). On each of these evaluations, the results so far are not encouraging. The programmes are low key and have been slow to get off the ground; there are no significant outcomes for children; and the programme has been very expensive to set up compared with other forms of provision (National Evaluation of Sure Start 2003/4). These and other recent evidence about the relationship between childcare and poverty also suggest that redistribution may be a more effective strategy in addressing poverty (Toroyan *et al.* 2003).

Jerome Kagan (1998) asserts that early intervention makes little difference in combating poverty; but people need to believe that it does, because
the consequences of not believing it – the poor are more or less doomed
to stay poor unless the economic system changes – are too much for well-
meaning liberals to swallow. Efforts to intervene in the lives of young
children from multi-problem families in the USA is a smoke screen to
disguise unpalatable realities:

> [S]o many people believe in infant determinism [because] it ignores
> the power of social class membership. Though a child's social class is
> the best predictor of future vocation, academic accomplishments and
> psychiatric health, Americans wish to believe that their society is
> open, egalitarian, without rigid class boundaries. To acknowledge the
> power of class is to question this ethical canon.
>
> (Kagan 1998: 147)

This discussion should certainly not be read as an argument against
providing early years education and care per se. It is worth stressing that
the OECD, sometimes called the club of developed nations, does not share
these views about early intervention as a way to combat poverty. In its
ongoing review of early education and care *Starting Strong* the OECD states,
very broadly, that early childhood services are a necessary public good
– like education or health services. They enable women's equitable
participation in the workforce and they enable children to learn and
socialize. The debate is not about such justifications for provision, which
are taken as read for a developed society, but about implementation.
The OECD review argues that children are likely to benefit most from
high quality services with trained and remunerated staff that emphasize
play and learning; that all children, especially vulnerable children, should
be able to access such services: 'Limited public investment leads to a
shortage of good quality programmes, unequal access and segregation
of children according to income' (OECD 2001: 130).

Quality services that meet conditions of equitable access and ensure
an entitlement for vulnerable children are invariably publicly funded
(although parents may make some contribution). Overall, within OECD
countries, 82 per cent of provision is publicly funded. In the absence
of any kind of state intervention or funding, it is left up to individual
providers to provide education and care on an *ad hoc* basis, and under
these conditions, the quality of provision is highly variable and access is
inequitable. This is the case, for example, in the USA (OECD 2000) which
rates poorly by comparison with other OECD countries.

My aim here has been to highlight the difficulties of using *targeted* early years provision as a strategy for poverty reduction. Targeting takes for granted that the state only has a minimalist role to play in the provision of early years services. As a strategy for poverty reduction it misleads in that it is too accepting of inequality and assumes the inevitability of poverty. It confirms the segregation and stigmatization of those that receive it. Such a strategy has led to the cavalier use of evidence to justify its claims; the claims for effectiveness have been wildly overstated. The evidence is highly specific to certain groups and cannot easily be transposed from one society to another.

The real difficulties come when this model of targeted provision is used as a poverty reduction strategy in the South without even the safeguard of 'quality'. As I attempt to show below, this happens all too often.

## Measuring poverty and inequality in the South

Poverty in the South is more life-threatening. Without any security cushion – no benefits or pensions, no services, and often no reliable, regular source of income – households are inter-dependent and vulnerable.

There are a number of standard indicators that are used to calculate a nation's poverty ranking. These include the number of people living on an income of less than a dollar a day; infant mortality; child mortality; maternal mortality; life expectancy; and access to education. These statistics are collected and compared across countries, but in many countries the statistics are simply notional. Health and education data are notoriously weak in many poor countries. A person's very existence or death may be unregistered. The one dollar a day measure does not take account of local economies; in some cities it may buy little or nothing; in other places it will buy a good meal or second-hand clothes. The bulk of economic activity of most poor countries occurs mainly in the informal sector. Petty trading, marketing, crafts, subsistence farming, itinerant or casual labour, pastoralists moving with their animals; all this means that the standard measures of economic activity used in the North are unworkable. It is impossible to calculate incomes, or predict tax revenues with accuracy. And overlaying all these difficulties, especially in Southern Africa, is the very grim fact of HIV/AIDS, making a mockery of whatever progress a country may painfully have gained.

Nevertheless, both the World Bank and the United Nations Development Programme (UNDP) attempt to rank nations into poor/low-income and middle-income nations. As the case studies in subsequent chapters show, these rankings cover very different circumstances and patterns of survival. Countries are ranked by the UNDP on their human development index (HDI) calculated on the basis of life expectancy, education, and average gross domestic product (GDP) per capita. Norway consistently has the highest HDI of any country. The USA is ranked seventh, the UK thirteenth. In terms of total income, the USA is the richest country in the world, followed by Japan, Germany and then the UK.

The amount of wealth produced by a country does not, however, translate into a better life for all of its citizens. Another index commonly used is the Gini index, that is a measure of the difference between the richest 10 per cent and the poorest 10 per cent of the population. It is a measure of the inequality in a society. Denmark has the lowest rating of 24.7. Most European and East European countries, Korea and Japan rank between 25 and 33. The UK has a rating of 36, the USA of 40. The world's most unequal countries have rankings of 60 or so. South Africa for example has a ranking of 59.8. The distribution of aid, however, is not directly related to poverty or inequality. It is geopolitical, a point discussed further in the next chapter.

The UNDP report draws on the work of Amartya Sen (1999) to describe poverty as lack of entitlement or lack of *capabilities*. Sen argues that development is about the pursuit of five freedoms – political freedom, economic facilities, social opportunities, transparency guarantees and protective security. He stresses the relationship between the means and the ends of poverty reduction. Certain policies – for instance democratic accountability, access to basic education and health services – are preconditions for enabling the poor to change their situation. Poor children who gain an education are likely to be more economically active than if they had no education; therefore investing in education may in the long term bring as many returns to a country as investing in industry. This is called 'the human capital' argument. I refer to it again at the end of this chapter.

This book includes four case studies: Brazil, India, Kazakhstan and Swaziland. They are all classified as 'middle-income' countries. They are not amongst the poorest countries, but they all have populations which include 'the poorest of the poor'. They are ranked in Table 2.3.

The UNDP has now gained widespread support for its 'Millennium Development Goals' to reduce poverty in the South. These are published and discussed in its 2003 Human Development Report, subtitled *A Compact Among Nations to End Human Poverty*. Eight goals or targets have been agreed. The eighth goal refers to the commitment of donor nations in the North. These goals are:

*Table 2.3* Ranking of case study countries

|  | HDI | Gini index | Overseas aid ($million) | |
|---|---|---|---|---|
| Brazil | 65 | 60.7 | 348.9 | ($2 per capita) |
| Kazakhstan | 76 | 31.2 | 148.2 | ($9.5) |
| India | 127 | 37.8 | 1,705.4 | ($1.2) |
| Swaziland | 133 | 60.9 | 29.3 | ($27.6) |

1 Eradicate extreme poverty and hunger: halve between 1990 and 2015 the proportion of people whose income is less than a dollar a day.

2 Achieve universal primary education: ensure that by 2015, children everywhere, boys and girls alike, will be able to complete a full course of primary schooling.

3 Promote gender equality and empower women: eliminate gender disparity in education.

4 Reduce child mortality: reduce by two thirds, between 1990 and 2015, the under-5 mortality rate.

5 Improve maternal health: reduce by three quarters, between 1990 and 2015, the maternal mortality rate.

6 Combat HIV/AIDS, malaria and other diseases: have halted and begun to reverse the spread of HIV/AIDS by 2015.

7 Ensure environmental sustainability: reverse the loss of environmental resources.

8 Develop a global partnership for development: develop fair trading and a commitment to good governance.

The goals were drawn up partly in response to evidence about widening poverty and inequality in the 1980s and 1990s. The report optimistically states that 'It is hard to think of a more propitious time to mobilize support for such a global partnership'. Unfortunately the publication of the report was singularly unpropitious. It coincided with the war in Iraq. The war immediately diverted development aid and attention from issues of poverty and inequality in poor countries.

The report sets out ways in which rich nations could help poorer ones by promoting economic growth. Rich countries are asked to sponsor fairer international trading arrangements, to support cheap drugs, and to increase debt relief. They are also asked to devote 0.7 per cent of their GDP to development aid. Only Norway, Sweden, the Netherlands and Denmark have met or exceeded the aid target. The UK donated 0.27 per cent. The USA donated 0.11 per cent, the lowest of any industrialized nation; and much of that donation must be spent on buying American goods and services.

In return for aid, poor countries are required to draw up plans showing how they will meet the millennium goals. These 'Poverty Reduction Strategy Papers (PRSPs)' are intended to provide a framework for donor co-ordination. They are required to describe 'macro-economic, structural and social policies and programmes to promote growth, reduce poverty and make progress in areas such as education and health' (UNDP 2003b: 20). The PRSPs are supposed 'to emerge from participatory processes involving civil society and external partners including the World Bank and International Monetary Fund'. This 'participatory process' is described in more detail in the case study on Brazil.

The UNDP admits that the millennium goals are very broad and that enacting them is complex. Many agencies and institutions – besides the World Bank – are working on definitional issues, trying to provide a deeper understanding of childhood poverty.

## Chronic poverty: the poorest of the poor

What does it mean to be very poor in the South? The UNICEF figures about the injury, death and dislocation of young children are very shocking. How might these circumstances be tackled?

A series of papers produced for the Chronic Poverty Research Centre (CPRC) tries to provide a framework for analysing chronic poverty and the responses to it by governments and donors. Hulme *et al.* (2001) stress the multi-dimensional nature of poverty. Whereas in the North income level is a reliable indicator of poverty, in the South 'money-metric' definitions of poverty are far less useful.

The chronically poor may fall into one or, more likely, several categories of disadvantage. They may be old, very young or on their own – widows or single parents. They may be discriminated against because of their social position – refugees, migrants, ethnic or religious groups. They may experience discrimination within the household – women and female offspring. They may have severe health problems, HIV/AIDS or mental illness. They may live in remote rural areas, urban ghettos or in regions where there has been prolonged conflict and political insecurity.

The key issues for the chronically poor are vulnerability, a lack of security of assets, and a terrible anxiety about the future:

> It can be argued that what poor people are concerned about is not so much that their level of income, consumption or capabilities are

low, but that they are likely to experience highly stressful declines in these levels, to the point of premature death. Poverty can be seen as the probability (actual or perceived) that a household will suddenly (but perhaps also gradually) reach a position with which it is unable to cope, leading to catastrophe (hunger, starvation, family break-down, destitution or death).

(Hulme *et al.* 2001: 9)

Hulme *et al.* (2001) provide a useful table schematizing the causes of chronic poverty (see Table 2.4).

The poorest of the poor have been poor for a long time, usually defined as five years or more. Some households dip in and out of chronic poverty, according to seasonal change or death of a wage earner, but the chronically poor are relentlessly so. Some may be more or less resigned to their situation; others, especially in transitional countries, are likely to be more embittered and to have higher expectations as the VOTP exercise

*Table 2.4* The causes of chronic poverty

| | |
|---|---|
| Economic | Low productivity |
| | Lack of skills |
| | 'Poor' economic policies |
| | Economic shocks |
| | Terms of trade |
| | Technological backwardness |
| | Globalization |
| Social | Discrimination (gender, age, ethnicity, impairment) |
| | High fertility and dependency ratios |
| | Poor health and HIV/AIDS |
| | Inequality |
| | Lack of trust/social capital |
| | Culture of poverty |
| Political | Bad governance |
| | Insecurity |
| | Violent conflict |
| | Domination by regional/global super-powers |
| | Globalization |
| Environmental | Low quality natural resources |
| | Environmental degradation |
| | Disasters (flood, drought, earthquake) |
| | Remoteness and lack of access |
| | Propensity for disease (tropics) |

indicated. 'The Eastern European and Central Asian respondents are filled with disbelief and demoralization and are much more likely to make comparative statements contrasting the better past with the intolerable present' (Narayan *et al.* 1999: 29).

The case studies of Swaziland and Kazakhstan bear out these findings. The chronically poor in Swaziland tend to be fatalistic; those in Kazakhstan are more likely to be angry, and to have much higher expectations about what might change.

The 'culture of poverty' argument, discussed above, is also used in the South. Poverty is not only about the lack of assets, material and social, that parents pass down to their children, but may also be about the kind of coping and survival strategies that families use.

> It is likely that the coping and survival strategies passed on from one generation to the next actually facilitate survival in the midst of bad or deteriorating conditions, keeping the poor from destitution or death, but at the same time helping to reproduce the conditions that obstruct escape from poverty.
>
> (Hulme *et al.* 2001: 16)

Harper *et al.* suggest that the most striking features of the body of evidence about intergenerational transmission of poverty is 'its ambiguity and highly context-dependent conclusions' (2003: 537). Even where evidence exists about social mobility or the lack of it, very little is understood about the processes involved. Their paper explores the evidence about micro-level social relations – how parents and older family or household members influence their children and pull strings for them. Family organization, kin or household structure is likely to be important, although certain types of family arrangements that may be indicators of poverty in the North may have no such effect in the South, and vice versa. Social norms and practices especially norms around the distribution of assets within the family may affect children, especially girls in South Asia. Certain customs may affect the roles men and women, boys and girls, may undertake in the household. Finally social connectedness, or social capital may be of critical importance.

> With strong social connections, people are able to get jobs, obtain resources in a time of crisis, share childcare, ensure children's safety, borrow money and have an increased chance of a voice or influence, and thus are able to prevent some of the most damaging aspects of poverty and help the next generation escape from it.
>
> (Harper *et al.* 2003: 541)

## Applying targeted models from the North to the South to reduce child poverty

In a significant shift from classical economic approaches to defining poverty, the World Bank has begun to draw on the 'human capital theory' of economists like Amartya Sen to justify investing in people. Investing in enabling people to better themselves through education, health and welfare services is likely in the long term to bring as good financial returns as direct investment in production and infrastructure. The World Bank and other agencies have been influenced by this approach, and do indeed loan/invest more money in education, social welfare and health than in the 1980s.

But consequences of the anti-redistributive stance in the USA (and UK) is that undue emphasis is also put on targeted early intervention measures to combat child poverty in the South. Despite the chronic levels of poverty in the South, and the many forms poverty takes, the blueprint of USA-targeted early childhood interventions has been adopted by many agencies. This is explored further in Chapters 3 and 4.

As with so many policies, it is assumed that what works – or appears to work – in the North, and in particular in the USA, will also work in the South. Early childhood is no exception. It is often implicitly or explicitly suggested that 'developing countries' are merely at an earlier stage of development than the USA; the difference is one of degree:

> factors commonplace in industrialized countries are inherited by developing countries as they advance. Thus the developmental outcomes of poor children in the United States may be predictive of outcomes of children in developing nations.
>
> (Scott *et al.* 1999)

According to such commentators, watered down versions of early childhood programmes and strategies developed (in the atypical conditions of) the USA will therefore also be a good strategy in the South.

Several World Bank economic reports have drawn attention to targeted early childhood programmes as a means of combating child poverty in the South. Van der Gaag and Tan have carried out a wide-ranging review of the (mainly North American) evidence that early childhood programmes carry economic benefits. They conclude, predictably, that

> ECD programs are most likely to be beneficial for children who grow up in the poorest households . . . well-targeted public programs can maximize society's benefits of ECD interventions while remaining

affordable . . . ECD programs are a sound investment in the well-being of children and in the future of societies.

(1998: 33)

In another version of this argument, a recent World Bank paper by Jaramillo and Mingat (2003) has claimed that early childhood interventions leads to better school performance. In the South, children commonly repeat a year's schooling if they do not achieve the required standard at the end of the school year. Repetition and drop out rates are very high in some countries. Early childhood programmes may counter these repetition and drop out rates by preparing children for school, although there are many reasons why children drop out (Serpell 1999a). School itself may be an unpleasant experience, with large classes and teachers who are either absentee or who use physical chastisement. The curriculum may be irrelevant. The assessment systems for grading children might be inappropriate and barely revised since colonial times. The school system may require children to speak and write in an unfamiliar language. Parents may not be able to afford school fees, or be able to clothe or shoe their children. Children may be too hungry to learn. Above all, in Africa, HIV/AIDS is wreaking havoc. Teachers are dying, children are required to look after younger siblings or dying parents, poverty is becoming more endemic as breadwinners die.

Jaramillo and Mingat claim to have reviewed the evidence on the impact of early childhood development programmes on schooling – citing yet again the Perry High Scope and Abecedarian figures: 'there is not much room for doubt that meeting basic health, nutrition and education needs of young children, is a key element in breaking the poverty cycle' (2003: 1).

The Jaramillo and Mingat paper analyses data on preschool take-up and repetition and completion rates in school in sub-Saharan Africa and compares this with other regions: The Middle East and Northern Africa; Eastern Europe and Central Asia; South and East Asia and the Pacific; and Latin America and the Caribbean. The authors conclude there is a link between preschool and repetition rates. They acknowledge the unreliability of the data (accurate statistics on early childhood are rarely available and rates of preschool attendance in different countries are extremely variable). They fail to mention the impact of HIV/AIDS on the children themselves and on the supply of teachers – an extraordinary omission for a study of education in sub-Saharan Africa. Nevertheless, these wobbly statistics, aggregated across wildly different circumstances, are considered sufficient to produce economic models on which to base a case for expansion of early childhood programmes in Africa. The paper calculates that in a 'hypothetical country' where preschooling was increased to a 40 per cent level, repetition rates would go down from 20 per cent to 15 per cent; and school completion to grade 5 would be enhanced by 13 per cent (2003: 21).

The authors then go on to argue that there are other greater claims on educational resources than to increase preschool education through a reception year or nursery class. For example more money could be put into improving primary or vocational education, which might bring greater returns, or crucially, have a higher political value. So they conclude that targeted community based early childhood interventions, relying on parents and community leaders, are likely to be most cost-effective, since they are less costly than school-based preschooling yet may provide similar or better educational results.

The entire paper seems an exercise in Alice in Wonderland logic. This is partly because of the cavalier economics – the aggregation of improbable statistics to provide hypothetical answers. (When challenged at a meeting about their use of statistics, the authors argued that it was better to use 'guesstimates' than not to attempt the calculations about what it might cost 'to break the poverty cycle'. They saw themselves as bringing rigour into the discussion about investment in early childhood.) But it is also seems nonsensical because of its failure to contextualize or in any way to acknowledge the reasons for repetition and drop-out in education. Instead it unquestioningly accepts that early intervention – especially if it can be provided on the cheap – is a panacea. This paper is, at the time of writing, being put forward as a basis for loan programmes in Africa.

The Inter-American Development Bank conference *Breaking the Poverty Cycle: Investing in Early Childhood* (1999) also reiterated the claims that targeted early childhood interventions are the way forward:

> [They] can foster a lifetime of improved health, mental and physical performance, and productivity. Moreover ECCD can help minimize or prevent many other problems including illiteracy, juvenile delinquency, teenage pregnancy, crime, drug use and domestic and social violence. And it can help break the tragic cycle of poverty . . . which is often passed on from one generation to the next . . . much can be increased with only modest increases in the share of national income devoted to certain early childhood development interventions. Moreover relatively small interventions can go a long way.
>
> (1999: 3)

Seen in perspective, these interventions are in fact miniscule. In 1999 alone, the World Bank spent approximately $3 billion on its education and social programmes. In contrast, at a generous estimate, the Bank has loaned $1,000 million over a 10-year period for ECD programmes (Myers 2000), that is 0.0000333 per cent of its annual education and social budget. If such ECD programmes did indeed succeed in combating poverty to the extent envisaged, they would be a terrific investment!

Moreover, the early intervention programmes in the USA on which much of the evidence is based unequivocally stressed the importance of high-quality, centre-based education and care programming in effecting any kind of long-term change to children's outcomes. In the scaled-down versions of early childhood programming in the South, it is commonly assumed that interventions can be low cost and home based rather than centre based, but that they are still likely to have the same or similar outcomes.

The idea that targeted early interventions are a good way to combat poverty has wide currency in the USA in particular. The major evidence for this is a few longitudinal studies conducted as randomized controlled trials drawn from a very narrow sample of the population. Yet almost every policy document that favours early intervention cites these studies. This wild extrapolation from limited evidence is possible partly because it fits in so neatly with other ideas about poverty and who is responsible for it. (It is also possible because of the way in which people think about child development – an argument developed in the next chapter.)

## Targeted early interventions as a solution to poverty: some views from the South

The usual view of donor agencies about providing early education and care in the South is that countries simply cannot afford it; it is an unrealistic goal. But there are also plenty of objections to this view. Transitional countries, which mostly had very well-established ECD services, regret bitterly having lost them. Hensher and Passingham (1996) point to the high expectations by the public and by the state of the kindergarten system in Kazakhstan, a finding explored further in the chapter on Kazakhstan. Similarly, there is criticism from middle-income countries where there are considerable inequities between rich and poor. The elite continue to have high expectations and buy early childhood services of good quality. The poor are expected to do with much less.

Gupta, for example, suggests that the much vaunted Integrated Child Development Services Program or Anganwadi Program in India (which has attracted substantial donor funds) created all kinds of unexpected ambiguities and resistances from the target population of poor women. The project promised to inexpensively increase the human capital of the nation, but also had the unintended effect of becoming an instrument for control of the poor.

> Investment in human capital and benevolent protection colluded with the third feature that was a necessary effect of such a program, and that was the vast increase in the monitoring, surveillance, and regulation of the 'target' population . . . Angwadi workers were not treated as state employees, and what they did at the Centres was defined as volunteer work for which they were recompensed not with a salary but with a stipend. Participation in the program subjected them to an intensive regime of regulation and surveillance.
>
> (2001: 135)

Using the example of Brazil, Rosemberg argues that assumptions about targeted early interventions as a means of combating poverty have been foisted on the South and have served, in effect, to perpetuate gross inequalities. (This argument is developed further in Chapter 8.)

> These proposals (for low-cost targeted early childhood interventions) put forward by multilateral organizations encourage programs for the children of developing countries with low state investment, low quality services and the inadequate remuneration of women's labour.
>
> (2003a: 252)

Two of the world's poorest countries have extensive kindergarten systems. Mongolia, which has one of the lowest per capita incomes (and one of the harshest climates) in the world, has a valued kindergarten system, high rates of literacy and relatively good healthcare. A World Bank study of another very low income country, Cuba, concluded that the Cuban education system – which has outstanding literacy and higher education rates – demonstrated that high quality education and a universal kindergarten are sustainable and affordable in a poor country. 'Most inspiringly Cuba demonstrates that a poor country can build an education system of very high quality that truly reaches all' (Gasperini 1999: unnumbered).

However relative poverty may be in the North, chronic poverty in the South is life-threatening. Children die in large numbers because they do not get enough to eat, they do not get medical care and they live in unsafe environments. It is important that any policies or practical initiatives to help them do not make things worse rather than better.

# Chapter 3

# Understanding early childhood

**Summary**

Children grow up with a radically different sense of self and relationships to others depending on time and place and where and when they were brought up. The study of child psychology or child development claims to offer especial insights into understanding early childhood, but has difficulty explaining these differences in children's self-perceptions and habits. Child psychology as a topic is mostly a sprawling, and sometimes contradictory collection of experimental data about tiny and discrete aspects of infant and child behaviour. Practitioners and policy makers, and researchers themselves, have extrapolated from this data to describe and explain children's journey or 'development' from infancy to adulthood, and to justify particular kinds of childcare and education practices. I argue that much of what is considered 'scientific fact' in understanding childhood is in fact biased towards a particular societal view. For instance, a key idea is that early intervention has a profound effect on later life. This may be partly true, but it is grossly exaggerated in much of the childcare literature. I go on to explore some common assumptions about childhood and parenting. There are pervasive views about the ideal family, the ideal child and the ideal surroundings that imbue understandings of young children. These views contrast sharply with understandings about young children in the South.

## The science of child development

In Chapter 2 I discussed how poverty is interpreted. I argued that in the USA and UK in particular there is a long tradition of regarding poverty as a personal failure, rather than as a societal one. Put at its crudest, people who are poor do not have enough ambition, nor do they work hard enough; they are too disorganized, or they cannot be bothered to learn. They cause trouble if not dealt with firmly. Anyone can succeed; if they do not, they only have themselves to blame.

If poverty is a personal shortcoming one of the ways to deal with it, so the argument runs, is to try to correct it when children are still young and malleable; to target the children of the poor and their mothers, and give them (non-financial) support. This support might be highly structured centre-based education and social programmes, or parenting advice, or home visiting or a mixture of these and other programmes.

These ideas about the correction of poor children are closely linked to ideas about child development. If we know how children develop, that is how they change as they grow older, then it might be possible to intervene in their life in such a way as to maximize their progress, to make sure that nothing is lost by the wayside, that they achieve their 'full potential'. Child development or child psychology is said to offer a scientifically based account of children's behavioural progress. It offers rationales for intervention in young children's lives. Child development is obviously an important area of study for those concerned with young children, if for no other reason than as a topic which is exclusively focused on what children do. It has provided an immense body of knowledge about young children's capacities and behaviour.

Like all knowledge, however, child psychology and explanations of children's development is not a straight accumulation of facts. What is known is partial and organized into theories and categories, sometimes contradictory ones (Penn 2004b). Prout and James (1990) argue that there are three pervading themes in child development: 'rationality', 'naturalness' and 'universality'.

*Rationality* is the universal mark of adulthood and childhood represents a period of apprenticeship for its development. Children's ages and stages, and the activities that are said to characterize each stage, are seen as markers of developmental progress towards rationality. Child development ceases at some point in late adolescence when the child has become a fully rational adult. Rational means being able to use logical reasoning and being competent in mathematical thinking. Children are essentially irrational and have to learn to think logically and rationally, whereas adults have acquired logical thinking skills. This theme of rationality, developing throughout childhood in age-related stages, features most strongly in the theories of Jean Piaget, but has been very widely influential.

This simplistic notion of rationality has been criticized strongly by child's rights advocates such Alderson (2000) who argues that even very young children are capable of making rational and considered decisions, within the limits of their knowledge. By contrast the notion of ages and stages of development implies that children are always inferior to adults in their understanding of issues. The relatively new discipline of the sociology of childhood also puts forward an alternative view, that children's behaviour and attitudes are better explained in a generational framework, in which power belongs to the adult and children are relatively powerless. Childhood is the other side of the coin to adulthood; and the nature of childhood in a given society can only be fully understood in relation to adult assumptions about, and behaviour towards, children (Mayall 2002).

*Naturalness* refers to the biological underpinnings of behaviour inherited through the genes. The sociobiologist Hrdy has pointed out in her landmark book *Mother Nature* (1999), that biological behaviour is very diverse. For instance parenting behaviours across species vary widely. Biological mothers do not always care for their offspring; offspring do not always attach themselves to their mothers. The evidence from primate studies suggests that claims for a biological basis to human behaviour are very complex. Attachment behaviour, for instance, the very close bond a very young child shows for its mother, is commonly interpreted as an example of the biological roots of infant behaviour. The most recent World Health Organization report (2004) on early childhood insists that attachment behaviour is biologically based and universal, a basic and essential human behaviour. Yet Gottlieb (2004) in a landmark study of childrearing in Côte d'Ivoire convincingly argues that the attachment of young children to their mothers (or other carer) and fear of strangers is learnt as much as it is biologically based. Infants are undoubtedly highly dependent, and their survival depends on the care they receive, but the care can be offered in a variety of ways.

*Universality* refers to behaviour that occurs independently of culture, behaviour that is common to all children wherever in the world they live. Typically, in comparing behaviour from accounts drawn from many societies, researchers assume that behaviour can be directly compared. They simplify and cherry-pick the experiences, perceptions and habits of children from one group and match them with those of another different group to make a general point, with little acknowledgement of the context or history of either. Many anthropologists and cultural psychologists would question whether universal traits and behaviours are possible independently of context, and instead argue that no behaviour can be comprehended outside of the context in which it has emerged (Rosaldo 1993; Spiro 1990).

Super and Harkness (1986) in a well-known paper put forward their theory of the developmental niche – the nature of parenting reflects the physical and social setting in which the child lives; the customs of care and childrearing; and the psychology of the child's caretakers. A significant number of psychologists now accept that child-rearing is 'culturally embedded' (Jahoda and Lewis 1987; Shweder and LeVine 1984; Rabain 1979; Reynolds 1989; Stigler *et al.* 1990; Ochs and Schieffelin 1984; Cole 1990; Serpell 1993; LeVine *et al.* 1994; LeVine 2003; Harkness and Super 1996; Goodnow and Collins 1990; Lamb and Sternberg 1992). The French anthropologist Jaqueline Rabain puts it still more strongly:

> The observation of the attitudes, the behaviour and the events taken by themselves teaches us nothing of their psychosocial significance, precisely because the absence of the location of words and deeds in a discourse, in a code which positions conduct in collective meaning.[1]

> (1979: 21)

What is taken as 'scientific evidence' about child development is mostly drawn from the results of observations and experiments with mainly white middle-class children in North America and Europe, and directed at a similar audience of middle-class white readers (Serpell 1999b). Approximately 18 per cent of the world's children live in North America and Europe, and the evidence is mainly drawn from the better off amongst that 18 per cent. Yet this evidence is assumed to be applicable to all children in all circumstances. If indeed child development is making claims that various kinds of behaviour and learning are universal, then at the very least the evidence base needs to be considerably widened. Norms of child behaviour differ considerably across the world. Where detailed evidence has been obtained from the South, some of the conventional understandings of child development have been profoundly challenged. As Gottlieb writes about her work:

> My major aim has been to challenge the assumption of an Everybaby that somehow exists outside of culture. Such an assumption implicitly underlies for example the two thousand or so parenting manuals now sold in bookstores and the myriad parenting advice columns dotting newspapers and magazines so popular in many Western countries. In challenging the basic operating model behind the fact of such widely consumed folk models passing as neutral expertise, I hope to present an alternative model of a baby that is deeply constructed by culture.

> (2004: xvi)

# Early experience: is it long-lasting?

An important strategy in poverty reduction in the USA and to an extent in the UK has been an emphasis on early experiences: are they profound and long-lasting or not? Can early interventions reshape the future prospects of children? I have discussed this at length elsewhere and suggested that there are serious ideological and methodological problems about trying to link past, present and future in human development (Penn 2004b). LeVine, looking at the issue from an anthropological perspective concludes that:

> Theories advancing the idea that childhood experience has a lasting impact gain plausibility in our society from the prescientific folk beliefs and philosophical traditions of our culture . . . persistent belief in early experience as formative or injurious is due to a prevalent orthodoxy of thought reflecting the influence of persuasive clinicians such as Freud and Bowlby and our ideological heritage of child-rearing determinism and egalitarianism.
>
> (2003: 71)

As LeVine and others have pointed out, a powerful mythology has grown up around the idea of early intervention. This has been fuelled by the Perry High Scope project, which has made extreme claims for very limited data, but nevertheless is a primary source for many of the secondary reviews that argue for early intervention – especially the World Bank literature.

The mythology of early intervention is also propped up by (mis)readings of neuroscientific research. Over the last ten years, many advocates of early intervention consider that their argument has been strengthened by 'brain research'. Certain nutrients are essential to foetal and neonatal growth, and malnutrition carries the risk of deformity and retarded growth. From this kind of evidence it has been a short, but careless, leap to discussion about brain growth. The argument put forward is that the brain is at its most malleable in the first years of life, and the synaptic connections formed at this stage in response to stimulation are critical in determining later cognitive abilities. 'Stimulation' of babies by concerned caretakers is the psychological equivalent of nutritional supplementation. If mothers were taught how to 'stimulate' their babies this would be a cost-effective intervention.

Bruer (1999) robustly asserts that these arguments are absurd. On the one hand ideas about 'stimulation' are very imprecise and highly culture-bound. On the other hand the evidence about brain functioning is scanty. He has shown how the results of a few obscure and not very relevant studies such as that by Chugani[2] have been blown out of all proportion. He argues that the popular claims for more stimulation of babies based on brain studies feed into the preoccupations and prejudices of those who wish to see early intervention as a panacea for change.

The claim that early stimulation is critically related to brain development has very little, if any, foundation in neuroscientific evidence. Rose and his colleagues (1998) have comprehensively reviewed the evidence on brain functioning, and concluded that neuroscientific knowledge is too fragmented, and technology is still too primitive to justify the claims to predict how the brain works – indeed Rose questions the possibility of the endeavour. Patterns of synaptic connectivity in the brain are relatively little understood, and their relationship to consciousness is unknown and probably unknowable. But in any case synaptic connectivity simply cannot be measured in babies – or in any human subject – without massively intrusive technology.

Yet these claims about the stimulation of babies leading to brain development are used to give extra, ultra-scientific, support to early intervention strategies. They are used over and over again.

Mary Eming Young, who is Senior Public Health specialist at the World Bank, and who has been responsible for much of the justificatory literature on the Bank's early childhood development (ECD) policies, has reviewed ECD programmes, almost all from the USA (and not at all from Nordic countries) and concludes that:

> Evidence suggests that (ECD) programs are effective in addressing such vital human development issues as malnutrition among children under five, stunted cognitive development and unpreparedness for primary education . . . early childhood interventions can increase the efficiency of primary and secondary education, contribute to further productivity and income, and reduce the cost of health care and public services . . . Deficits in individuals caused by early malnutrition and inadequate care can affect labour productivity and economic development throughout society. Properly designed and implemented interventions in the early childhood years can have multi-dimensional benefits.
>
> (Young 1998: 209–10)[3]

Young makes heavy use of the analogy between micro-nutrient deficiencies and their effect on body growth, and 'cognitive deficiencies' and their affect on synaptic growth of the brain. Her influential perch at the World Bank has influenced many of the international agencies concerned with young children. For instance the UNICEF programming guide recently issued for Central Asia, *Early Childhood Development in the Central Asian Republics and Kazakhstan*, devotes a whole chapter to explaining brain research. Here is an extract:

> Sometimes a complicated concept can best be illustrated by a simple example.
>
> A child starts playing peek-a-boo. In a matter of seconds thousands of cells in the child's growing brain respond. Some brain cells are turned on whilst some existing connections amongst brain cells are strengthened. At the same time, new connections are formed, adding a little more definition to how the brain is structured. Science did not always know this was happening. A child's game of peek-a-boo is far from being simple and ordinary . . . When a connection is used repeatedly in the early years it becomes permanent. When synapses are used or fired as when a child plays peek-a-boo they get stronger. When connections are repeatedly fired together, they are wired together. In contrast a connection that is not used at all is unlikely to survive . . . For example a child who is rarely spoken to, read to or encouraged in self expression in the early years, may have difficulty in mastering language skills later on. At the same time, a child who is rarely played with may have difficulty with social adjustment as he/she grows up.
>
> (2002b: 29)

In the USA, the Perry High Scope and Abecedarian interventions at least defined themselves as 'high quality'. They had generous child–adult staffing ratios, carefully worked out curricular programmes and they were centre-based. They claimed that the long-term benefits they observed would not have happened without this quality input. But the brain research findings have enabled a second generation of researchers and policy makers to cut corners and claim that all that is needed is 'stimulation', and teaching mothers to stimulate their children is an effective intervention to combat poverty.

The evidence from intervention studies and from brain research is used in a cavalier way to support particular policy stances. But other evidence, especially anthropological evidence, does not support these claims for early intervention. It suggests, for instance, that stimulating young children to be verbally precocious through babytalk and intense caregiver attention is above all a white middle-class Euro-American practice. Ochs and Schieffelin, who have compared language development in young children in different societies, point out that:

> To most middle-class Western readers the description of verbal and non-verbal behaviour of middle-class caregivers and their children seem familiar, desirable and even natural . . . the characteristics of caregiver speech (babytalk) and comportment that have been specified are highly valued by members of white middle-class society, including researchers, readers and subjects of study. (But) the general patterns of white middle-class caregiving that have been described in the literature are characteristic neither of all societies nor of all social groups.
>
> (1984: 283)

LeVine and the group of anthropologists working with him have systematically compared early childhood experiences (in context) across North and South. LeVine contrasts the intensely collective upbringing of the East African children he studied where there is little or no explicit caregiver focus on the development of word games or language (although there may well be bilingualism or multilingualism), with that of a typical North American child. He concludes that:

> The constant presence of young children in family life whilst rarely being the focus of attention, and their participation in the productive and other activities of the household from an early age appear to offer emotional security without the verbal expressiveness by the mother and others . . . making sense of this will require changes in our notions of emotional and communicative development.
>
> (LeVine *et al.* 1994: 272)

LeVine points to the extremes of upbringing that are taken as normal in the North. A warm, caring stimulating responsive relationship – the basis of so many tests of quality – can also be construed as a lesson in self-centredness. A young child is taught to expect that it is natural for her to be the exclusive focus of attention.

> Compared with Africans, American infants experience a particularly sharp distinction between situations in which they are alone and those in which they are with others – for African infants are never alone and are often present as non-participants in situations dominated by

adult interaction, while the American infant is often kept in solitary confinement when he is not the centre of adult attention. This creates (for the American) a bifurcation between the extremes of isolation and interpersonal excitement that is unknown in Africa and may underlie some of the striking differences in interactive style between peoples of the two continents.

(2003: 94)

'Stimulation' of young children is a cultural phenomenon. To talk it up as a counterweight to poverty is, as Kagan (1998) has pointed out, a way of avoiding the painful truth that many children are suffering. Promoting early childhood intervention is easier than addressing fundamental social inequalities, and may appear to be a way around them.

I do not want to throw the baby out with the bathwater or suggest for one moment that responsive caregivers are not essential for young children. Nor do I want to deny that there are valuable and useful insights that have accumulated as the result of careful analysis of practice in working with young children over many years in Europe and North America. But misapplied and exaggerated claims are in no-one's interest; they perpetuate injustice and lead to inappropriate practices.

What are inappropriate practices? It is more or less impossible to act outside one's own cultural norms (although this is what is often expected of parents in the South). But if one accepts the position – as I do – that the way we bring up children is essentially culturally embedded, then humility is necessary when confronting the practices of others. Some of the everyday practices with young children which seem like common sense, say, to a person living in a village in West Africa, may seem bizarre or wrong to a visitor from the UK or USA. An obvious example is leaving babies to be carried and cared for by barely older siblings; or allowing young children to engage in adult tasks such as using a sharp knife or machete for chopping twigs.

Conversely, common practices in the North – leaving babies in carry cots; finding excuses for young children who are not helpful and obliging; tolerating children who are not self-effacing in a group; permitting rudeness or failure to greet and respect others, especially elders, in public places; restricting children's physical explorations in the interests of safety – all these aspects of caregiving may seem neglectful to those not versed in Euro-American ways. The difficulty is that relatively little is known, except at a fairly superficial level, about the ideas and beliefs that shape and inform childrearing in many societies and groups. The detailed, pioneering work of anthropologists and psychologists such as LeVine

(1994, 2003) (who describes himself sadly as a gadfly to psychology) Gottlieb (DeLoache and Gottlieb 2001, 2004) and Serpell (1993) is rarely cited in the literature.

In the North we are largely ignorant of the practices of childrearing in the South. The converse is not true. Those who hold 'traditional values' in the South are continually being made aware of the practices of modernity. They are engaged in continuous renegotiation of those values through migration or through engagement with visitors and foreigners. Gottlieb (2004) captures the ironic contradiction between her position as an anthropologist respectful of local tradition and the villagers' embrace of modernity. She describes an incident at the baby clinic she ran, when she recommended a mother to consult the local diviner about a child's fractiousness – much to the amazement of the mother who had come to the clinic for a Western remedy!

## Ideas about parenting

Early intervention strategies, particularly as portrayed in the South by donor agencies, assume that education in child development for parents or caregivers will lead to long-term improvements and enable children to better cope with poverty. Promoting intense verbal stimulation between the caregiver and young child is one strategy. There are also some other very basic assumptions that underpin child development as it is currently practised in the North: what I call the ideal family; the ideal person; and the ideal surroundings.

My account of these idealisms is deliberately partial, and I have short-cut some important issues. I have also left out some underrated topics: for example it is clear that multilingualism and the position of high-status languages warrant much more investigation. Indeed there is some evidence about the adverse impact of high-status languages. Put popularly, English is known as 'a killer language' and obliterates other languages; little-known oral languages do not stand much chance of survival (Abley 2003). Multilingualism is the norm in the South, but discussion about it barely reaches the surface in English-speaking countries.

I can best illustrate my argument with a personal example; a ready-made ethnography! I live for part of the year in South Africa. My daughter has married an African, a man from the Northern Southu group whose family comes from a small township in Limpopo Province in South Africa. His first language is an oral language, Pedi, although he also speaks seven other languages fluently, only one of which he was formally taught. Multilingualism means that ambiguity and awareness of difference pervades everyday existence in the very words you speak, especially if one of those languages is unwritten (Goody 1990).

My son-in-law is the eldest in a family of five, and is the only one who has a substantial income, although his job takes him away abroad for months at a time. He now has a large house in Johannesburg. In the African tradition his house, and indeed his income generally, is considered as a family resource. Willingly or not, as the eldest of the family, and as someone who is well-to-do, the demands on him, and on my daughter, are endless. His brothers and sisters and other relatives visit, stay and borrow and cook; they explain to me firmly that this is also their house and they have an entitlement to be in it. His 16-year-old niece lives with them semi-permanently and attends a local school although she regularly goes back to the township to stay with her grandmother. Her own mother, my son-in-law's sister, used to live nearby and often dropped in, but has just moved back to the township. Also living in the house, in separate quarters, is the domestic servant, who has a 9-year-old son, who sometimes lives with his mother, and sometimes in another township with his grandmother. As well as this, my daughter had a friend living in the house for several months. The friend has three children. The eldest sons aged 12 and 7 years live with her; and a third child, who is under 2 years, lives in a township with her grandmother. Many teenage women have children and it is a common practice to send babies away to older relatives to be brought up. In fact many women of all ages do this, a reflection of the hardness of servitude and city life under the apartheid regime; but also a distant reflection of older traditions about upbringing.

In the house no-one sleeps alone. This is not just due to lack of space but it is an understanding of conduct that regards privacy as peculiar and physicality as an important part of life. My grandson, aged 5, will happily sleep with any available adult or child rather than sleep alone; as will other people in the household. Companionship is valued at night as well as during the day although of course there are also strict rules about gendering once children grow beyond puberty.

These permutations of adults and children seem to shift constantly. People disappear for long holidays, or for other reasons, and reappear. Other people appear who seem to be strangers, at least to me. Daily life is conducted in at least two languages, sometimes more.

The adults in the house have a generally benign view of children but would regard it as their duty to admonish *any* child who appears to be doing something naughty – although expectations and standards of child behaviour vary greatly. Children are expected to get on with things themselves. They do not need nursing and nourishing. Adult attention and direction is unnecessary and even inappropriate, unless it is a direct instruction to avoid danger (and even ideas about what constitutes danger and risk are very different). My daughter, in middle-class English fashion, tries to reason and discuss. Other adults give children shorter shrift, give fewer explanations and expect obedience with alacrity.

My son-in-law and my daughter are the heads of the household. Their word is law, at least to everyone except my grandson who is already aware of his status, privileges and obligations as eldest son of the head of the household, and the negotiating power this gives him. (When I have finished speaking to him on the phone he usually says to me politely 'Would you like to speak to your daughter now'.) My son-in-law and daughter dispense money and justice, arbitrate and adjudicate; and if there is a breakdown the miscreant will be banished from the house, at least temporarily.

Their household is more like a small feudal court, in the midst of a society where one echelon has embraced modernism very fast but where the majority of people are still vulnerable and dependent. The tensions in the household – and there are many – come less from the way of life per se, but from the gradual consciousness that in the new South Africa this way of doing things may, in the future, no longer be acceptable or desirable. Ideas about allocation of time; dependence, independence and deference; about possessions and purchasing; about personal space and privacy, about the status of languages: in many if not most ways, ideas are shifting rapidly.

Conventionally, the Euro-American literature on parenting makes many assumptions about the obligations and responsibilities that parents bear towards their young children. Many of them are not met in this household.

## The ideal family

Central to the idea of child development is the family. In the North the discourse of the family has become increasingly narrowly focused on the nuclear family, the biological mother (and sometimes the father) and one or two children; sometimes grandparents.

As Lamb has pointed out, the pervading – but unjustified – assumptions about the family in the psychological literature are:

1   Children need two parents, one of each sex;
2   Family responsibilities should be divided between the parents, with

fathers as the economic providers, and mothers as home-makers and caretakers;

3    Mothers are better suited for child-rearing and care-taking than fathers are;

4    Young children should be cared for primarily by family members; and

5    White middle-class parents have superior parenting skills and have children who are more likely to excel.

(1999: 4)

Lamb's own work, and that of his colleagues, explores, and refutes, these assumptions in the USA, not least because of the confounding effects of poverty and wealth. In the South, in many countries, the family may be a still more misleading concept. It is more appropriate to talk about multigenerational households and peoples' ranking within them – as with my South African family. This rank may be partly gender and age related, but only partly. It may depend on order of birth, on marital status, or on wealth. It may reflect consanguinity or matrilinearity or patrilinearity; it may be affected by polygamy or polyandry. Maturity may be a sign of status rather than of age. (This common lesson about the eldest son being head of the household in his father's absence is one my grandson has already learnt.)

Even if the 'conventional' family was a standard and desirable norm, for many poor men and women, 'normal' family life is an impossibility. UNDP estimate 1 in 37 people in the world is a migrant in search of work and livelihood, either from countryside to city, or from one country to another. Studies of township (slum, favela) dwellers suggest that a majority are recent migrants to the city, and the households they create are characterized by considerable mobility (Munyakho 1992; Bourgois 1998; Barbarin and Richter 2001).

Alternatively, entire villages may be sustained by remittances of absent men and women. Hochschild (2001) writes of the care chain in the USA, whereby middle-class American mothers employ (im)migrant women from the South to care for their children, whilst the (im)migrant's own children are left behind with others; her earnings supporting the household that remains behind. (History suggests that the well-to-do have always relied on the poor to supplement the care of children in their families, irrespective of the psychological and economic costs to the childcarer's own family.)

In situations of extreme need, multiple unstable partnering is likely to be the norm, with disastrous consequences in those countries where

HIV/AIDs is prevalent (Barnett and Whiteside 2002; Campbell 2003). In the worst affected countries around 40 per cent of pregnant women are sero-positive, that is without medical intervention they and probably their new-born children will die within five years.

The extreme economic pressures on millions of men and women in the South trying to bring up children under unbearably adverse circumstances, and the complexities of household ordering in so many situations, makes a mockery of simplistic championing of the importance of family life. Yet we know relatively little about what happens to young children under these circumstances, and how they cope with pressures that are so very far from ideal.

## The ideal child

The ideal child in the North is above all an 'individual'. Child development is dominated by 'the individual and self-contained child' to use Kessen's famous phrase (1981: 29). Parents, caregivers and teachers emphasize those characteristics that will enable a child to articulate her wants and preferences, to choose, to establish her selfhood; her separateness, self-sufficiency and self-confidence – in the novelist Malcolm Bradbury's words, to become 'a push-push-pushing individual'. 'Every child is an individual' is almost a mantra of practice in early childhood.

To give an example of the opposite extreme to North American individualism, many pastoralist or nomadic communities put great emphasis on achieving group harmony. Fitting in with others is a prime goal (Briggs 1970). I describe this phenomenon in my study of childhood in Mongolia (Penn 2001). From the earliest age, children are quietly and affectionately schooled into taking notice of others around them, of avoiding any discord or disturbance. Children are loved and not repressed; but nevertheless no child would dream of calling attention to herself in a public place; it would be considered rude and shameful.[4] This is not merely a matter of being obedient and respectful to adults, as was the case in the African groups described by LeVine. It is that under certain circumstances people actively cultivate mutual tolerance and self-restraint.

As DeLoache and Gottlieb point out in their witty and imaginative book *The World of Babies: Imagined Childcare in Seven Societies* (2001) expectations vary considerably about how children should fit in with those around them, what attributes are most valued and most encouraged, and how pain, anger and emotion are accommodated. In each society that they consider, they show how what is 'normal' is considered as 'common sense'. It is only when the commonsensical is transposed elsewhere that it becomes a folk theory, and an idiosyncracy. The Euro-American beliefs in individuality, competition, personal striving and success may be regarded as sheer bad manners elsewhere.

## The ideal surroundings

Individuality is achieved above all through the articulation and exercise of choice over possessions. LeVine, who has spent an anthropological lifetime exploring childrearing, argues that becoming an individual in the North is learning to discriminate and exercise preference over the material world.

> The American infant, unlike his African counterpart, has numerous possessions earmarked as belonging to him alone; their number and variety increase as he grows older, permitting him to experience the boundaries of his self represented in his physical environment . . . From infancy onwards, the child is encouraged to characterize himself in terms of his favourite toys and foods and those he dislikes; his tastes, aversions and consumer preferences are viewed not only as legitimate but essential aspects of his growing individuality – and a prized quality of an independent person.
>
> (2003: 95)

Sutton-Smith (1986) also critiques how children's development (and parents' love) is given expression through the provision of toys. Nurseries compensate still further for the absence of love, and emphasize a view of development that relies on the use of 'appropriate' toys and stimulation. For instance, Tobin describes how nurseries in the USA epitomize consumerism: 'Consumer desire is reproduced by the material reality of our preschools. We create cluttered overstimulating environments modelled on the shopping mall and amusement park' (1995: 232). By contrast, Viruru who has written an interesting study of early childhood in a nursery in Southern India describes how frugality underwrites the pedagogic approach:

> although the nursery could have undoubtedly have bought more things for the children, they seemed to purposely refrain from doing so. This is very much in keeping with the general Hindu philosophy of regarding materialistic things as having secondary importance.

A good Hindu is encouraged not to be enmeshed with worldly objects.

(2001: 127)

## Developmentally appropriate practice

At one level the arguments about childcare in the North are political rather than psychological. They concern the broad childcare systems that are put in place within a country, and the role of the state in subsidizing and regulating those systems. The OECD, for example, is carrying out a review across its members of such provision. At one extreme is the USA which regards childcare arrangements as essentially a private contract between parent and carer, and responsibility rests with the parent to identify, find and pay for good childcare. At the other extreme, in the North, in Nordic countries and Eastern Europe, the state assumes responsibility for the funding and standards of the childcare (OECD 2001).

The OECD reports suggest that where the state assumes responsibility for funding and regulation, the childcare *tends* to be of a uniform good standard. If access is not related to ability to pay, if the childcarers meet minimum (and not so minimal) initial and in-service training requirements, and if there are generous accommodation requirements, then there is some guarantee that the provision will be satisfactory. But over and above these structural guarantees, what distinguishes good systems is that there is also an active debate about what constitutes quality. In Finland, for example, there is constant discussion (and a virtual network), led by the Ministry of Social Welfare, about the quality of children's collective life outside home; about the values that might inform such care, and how they might be put into practice.[5] Regulatory control is paradoxically unprescriptive. It is assumed that the childcarers are competent and knowledgeable, as are parents, and within very broad parameters set by a statement of values, parents and staff together will discuss and arrive at appropriate local solutions.

Where the state does not assume responsibility for funding and regulation, childcare proceeds on a much more ad hoc basis. The quality of childcare in nurseries or with childminding (family daycare) is very variable. The childcarers are not reliably trained or vetted, and they come and go with alarming frequency – childcare staff turnover in the USA and UK is very high. Pay is poor and conditions of work often unattractive.

In the absence of state funding or regulation, as in the USA, it is left up to voluntary and private organizations to advocate for some kind of (unenforceable) self-regulation and standards, to try to weed out the worst childcare. One widely cited attempt to offer guidance on quality of childcare in the USA is outlined in *Developmentally Appropriate Practice in Early Childhood Programs* produced by the National Association for the Education of Young Children (Bredekamp and Copple 1997). This guide is implicitly based on the ideas of rationality, naturalness and universality outlined at the beginning of this chapter. It spells out the needs of each age group, how these needs are manifested in behaviour. It demonstrates how childcarers, whether institutionally based or at home, can recognize the behavioural cues and provide the kind of care and the range of activities that best meets the needs of the child at each stage of its development (a stage can be as little as three months). Developmentally Appropriate Practice (DAP) claims to draw on 'neutral' research evidence (almost exclusively from the USA) as a basis for its guidance and presents the guide as 'state-of-the-art knowledge' about young children.

DAP does not attempt to discuss values or cultural perceptions as a basis for practice. Instead it assumes a relative lack of knowledge and competence in parents and childcarers. It compensates for this by giving detailed and prescriptive advice about what to do at each 'age and stage' of a child's life. The first edition in 1987 was criticized on the grounds that it assumes that knowledge and practice are, or can be, more or less context-free, and that it ignored controversies and debates in the field. The main challenge has come from the 'reconceptualizers' group of early childhood educators, mostly post-modernists. Tobin (1996), for example, argued that such a fixed construction of good practice rules out alternative approaches and solutions.

The second edition of the guide to DAP in 1997 highlights the complexities of many of the issues involved. It acknowledges some of the criticisms that were made, but is still strongly wedded to an ages and stages approach. It implicitly perpetuates the notions described above, of the ideal family, the ideal child and the ideal surroundings. It does not acknowledge the havoc that can be wreaked by poverty. It stresses individualism and does not, for example, regard helpfulness and co-operation as a mark of maturity and intelligence, as would be the case in many societies in the South (Serpell 1993). It takes for granted the material basis and assumptions of choice and consumption that underlie so much of ECD programming.

Viruru quoted above, also argues that 'so much of early childhood education and care is written in the language of affluence and privilege and is far removed from the realities of so many children' (2001: 19). Play-based pedagogies, in her view, are predicated on a level of material resourcing which is simply not available for many children. She also argues that the very notion of play as a separate fantasy world for children, requiring its own special play equipment, is a denial of the experiences of children 'who grow up with the world rather than protected from it' (ibid.: 19).

DAP is mirrored by the widespread use of the Early Childhood Environmental Rating Scale (ECERS) commonly used to measure the quality of settings where young children are being cared for. This uses a range of sub-scales to measure different aspects of the provisioning and staffing in the nursery. Like DAP, ECERS is used as a tool to root out the worst care practices in poor systems, although the question remains what anyone can do about it in the absence of state funding or intervention. Desperate mothers, compelled to work, have little flexibility or choice in finding childcare; and there are few sanctions against poor practices.

DAP and ECERS would merely be a reflection of a particular system of childcare if their applications were confined to North America, where they originated in a market dominated early education and care system. But DAP forms the basis of the work in early childhood that major donor agencies sponsor in the South. The World Bank Institute, the arm of the Bank which was established in 1955 'to train officials concerned with development planning, policy making, investment analysis and project implementation in member developing countries' has published a 'definitive' handbook for early childhood programming (Evans *et al.* 2000). The book contains many practical suggestions, but the over-riding assumption at the heart of the handbook (and the accompanying CD-Rom) is that of 'developmentally appropriate practice'. It is generally assumed that precepts of understanding and practice – such as the National Association for the Education of Young Children (NAEYC) manual on *Developmentally Appropriate Practice* – forged for children in the USA are seen as perfectly legitimate for the South.

The manual takes individuality for granted, and stresses what makes children different from one another, rather than what they might have in common. 'Each child is a unique person with an individual temperament, learning styles, family background and pattern and timing of growth' (Bredekamp and Copple 1997: 11). It repeats the ages and stages approach. It carves out intervals, 0–3 months, 4–6 months, 7–12 months, etc. and for each of these stages explains what children need and what children can do. Similarly, in describing projects, it explains what project goals and objectives are suitable for each age stage, and what kinds of strategies might best support these goals. It evidences the same familiar findings – the Perry High Scope and the Abecedarian. It brings in the brain studies, collapsing (mis)information into one overarching claim:

> The influence of the early environment on brain development is long-lasting. Children's early exposure to good nutrition, toys and stimulating interaction with others has a positive impact on children's brain findings at age 15 compared to the brain findings of peers who lack this early input.
>
> (1997: 80)

Yet the authors are also very experienced and committed to working in the South, and are aware of contradictions in repeating the familiar adages. They stress that 'context is (almost) everything' (1997: 2). They point out that 'the alert reader will recognize that there are some obvious (turns) and potential trade-offs among the different principles and guidelines' (1997: 27). Their mission is to bring the hard-won knowledge of child development to others who may not know about it but who will surely benefit from it. The difficulty is, as they partly realize, that this knowledge may not be so hard-headed, so value free and so useful as they would wish.

This guide has the imprimature of twelve major international donor agencies concerned with early childhood, including UNESCO, UNICEF, USAID, the Christian Children's Association, Plan International and the Inter-American Development Bank. It is issued by a multi-donor organization called the 'Consultative Group on Early Childhood'. The handbook took several years to produce, and drew on earlier, similar guides produced by UNICEF and other agencies. It is a standard reference for those wishing to work with young children in the South.

## Another vision of childhood

There is a Yoruba saying 'My child is my crown' (Zeitlin 1990). Children are intrinsic to being alive; if you are alive you want to create more life. It is unthinkable not to want children or not to welcome their presence. They link past and future and ensure continuity of the lineage. Gottlieb (2004) calls her book about child-rearing in West Africa *The Afterlife is Where We Come From* in recognition of these ancestral feelings and beliefs. But children are still more than that. They are not separate autonomous beings, but part of a web of mutuality. They are insurance against old age in societies where there is no other security. They share in household tasks, in the immense labour of daily tasks in societies with no mod cons.

Their play requires no special toys or equipment, but there are always playfellows at hand.

Children are systematically trained by adults (and not only by their parents) from the earliest age to undertake responsibilities – for running errands, for looking after younger siblings. Often this training is gendered; girls and boys are required to undertake different tasks and may be rewarded for doing them in different ways. But this training takes place in an intensely collective environment, where meaning is shared, adults can easily assume each other's roles, and peer groups are a powerful source of reinforcement.

The difficulties arise where these intricate understandings about child-rearing break down. There is of course no such thing as a halcyon past except for a favoured few. Human history is full of accounts of wholesale movements of peoples, of warfare, slavery and displacement, and such massive disruption is, sadly, not new. The Greek and Roman empires ran on the slave labour of conquered peoples. Whitfield (1999) writes about the effects on ordinary people of the clashes of Chinese, Tibetan, Turkic and Islamic empires in Central Asia, and the death and enslavement of hundreds of thousands of people from the sixth to the tenth centuries. Every continent and every age has been witness to man's inhumanity to man. So much so, that it is a leap of faith to assume benignity as a basic condition for bringing up children; and adaptiveness and flexibility are probably the most necessary of human attributes.

Some people[6] argue that globalization is yet another round of conquest and colonization. Economic pressures have grossly distorted the 'traditional' lives of millions of families in the South. But whilst a majority of those in the North have secured for themselves some recent immunity from catastrophes,[7] in the South life remains more precarious. Epidemics such as HIV/AIDS are causing further havoc.

Then the donor agencies arrive with their new prescriptions about childcare imported from the North, and in particular from the USA. Somehow, reciting nursery rhymes and providing toys has become a recipe for challenging poverty. Child development, like so many other things, has become globalized. But for a body of knowledge concerned with young children it has very little to say about how most young children live (or lived). It does not recognize the catastrophes that undermine so many millions of young children's lives.

Child development is a discipline that argues we should focus on young children; we should not neglect them because they are such an important part of life. To ignore the specifics of children's lives would be like ignoring the specifics of women's lives in giving an account of society.

As a discipline it is unique and important, and without it our understanding of others would be very limited. But child development is also a discipline that has been forged in a Euro-American context, making use implicitly of common societal assumptions, and drawing on a very narrow evidence base. Despite its subject matter, it can distort and distract, as much as enhance, our understanding of the unequal lives that so many children live.

# Chapter 4

# Lending a helping hand

## Summary

This chapter describes some of the difficulties in bringing aid to poor countries. Most poor countries in the South are struggling to overcome a colonial inheritance: the language, the structure of government, and even the boundaries of the country, are the result of foreign interference and domination in the past. Aid also comes in cycles; what is fashionable in one decade is replaced in another. I describe some of the main international non-governmental organizations (INGOs) that give aid and illustrate their way of working: the World Bank and its satellites; the United Nations and its many offshoots; international consultancies; corporate donors; international NGOs like Oxfam and Christian Aid; and those few organizations concerned mainly or exclusively with early childhood. I point to the difficulties that most of these organizations face, as bureaucratic agencies located in the North, relying on a particular kind of technocratic knowledge and expertise. I also briefly discuss how governments in the North provide aid programmes. Whatever the source of the aid, it is sometimes counterproductive and not always welcomed.

## What the critics say

Most people are concerned about poverty, particularly the poverty experienced by young children. It would be very wrong to imply that people or organizations or businesses or governments are callous (although some certainly are) and that childhood poverty and inequality is ignored. There are many international responses to poverty. The last chapter explored how knowledge about child poverty in the South has been constructed. This chapter explores how help is delivered.

There is a widespread popular view that aid has been a failure. The novelist Paul Theroux, revisiting Africa, where he was once a Peace Corps teacher, is condemnatory about United Nations and other aid agency staff, driven around in expensive cars and living in air-conditioned premises in the midst of tropical squalor. Graham Hancock's book *Lords of Poverty* claims that official aid agencies such as the World Bank and USAID have 'high-jacked our kindness'. He describes the bureaucrats who work for them as 'freeloaders' and 'masters of disaster'. He concluded that so much money is spent on organizational issues and on staff, and so little directly on the recipients of aid, that 'development assistance should be stopped in its present form – something that might prove to be in the best interests both of taxpayers of the rich countries and the poor of the South' (1991: 193).

More recently, Bob Geldof, the pop musician who set up Band Aid for famine relief in Africa, has written an open letter about his appointment to a commission to investigate poverty in Africa, chaired by the UK Prime Minister Tony Blair.

> I am asking for your help in a constant demand for a fundamental and radical rethink of our deadly tango with Africa. If this (the commission) turns out to be another meaningless development tract, I'm out of there. And I will weep.
>
> (2004: 27)

Aid is supposedly a benevolent intervention. It superseded colonialism, the rule of one country – in their supposed best interests – by another.[1] But colonialism has left all kinds of legacies. The imprint of the colonizers can be found everywhere. Many of the borders of ex-colonial countries are arbitrary, cutting across tribal or ethnic or religious borders – like Kashmir or Southern Sudan or some of the islands of Indonesia – leaving a legacy of unresolved and probably irresolvable disputes. On achieving independence the language of colonization was usually adopted as the language of government, whatever the local languages. English, French, Portuguese and Spanish are used in this hegemonic way, even although these European languages could not be more dissimilar from some of their local counterparts in grammar, orthography and script.

Above all, colonial powers created what Mamdani calls 'decentralized despotism'. The British and the French typically reinforced, rewarded or even invented, amenable native chiefs, kings and princes whom they allowed to rule locally, providing they did what they were told when it mattered.[2] 'The natives' were allowed to continue with their traditional laws and customs under the jurisdiction of these chosen chiefs. As Mamdani points out, the diversity of forms of self-government in Africa, such as the egalitarianism of pastoralist communities in East Africa or the autonomous female organizations in West Africa, were at best ignored, at worst wiped out:

> That [colonial] model was monarchical, patriarchal and authoritarian. It presumed a king at the centre of every polity, a chief on every piece of administrative ground, and a patriarch in every homestead or kraal. Whether in the homestead, the village or the kingdom, authority was considered an attribute of personal despotism.
>
> (1996: 39)

This colonial model was imposed throughout the British and French empires.[3] It led to the corruption and self-enrichment of many chiefs or princes, and to the build-up of tribal or ethnic power bases where none had previously existed. It is the legacy inherited by post-colonial governments. After independence, the division between the new governments and the native rule continued, causing all kinds of frictions. In many countries – as in Swaziland – the rule of native elites continues today despite token parliamentary democracy. Ironically, such elites now claim that they are defending local culture and tradition in the face of an alien modernity.

Colonial administrators set up structures of government which had devastating and unforeseen consequences, yet are still in operation. For example, there are many problems about land registration, not least in Zimbabwe where the disputes over land annexed in the 1930s by white settlers are still bitterly contested. Land in rural Kenya, once communally held, was reregistered in the name of male householders, leading to an exodus of women from land they had once farmed.

> The official registration of land that begun under the colonial era meant that farms were almost always registered in the name of individuals, invariably men. This put an end to the group ownership systems that used to pertain, where a village might own land communally and plots were then allocated to families according to their need . . . For women whose husbands had migrated to cities this was a double blow. Forbidden [in colonial times] to accompany their husbands to the towns, they then found their access to land was forfeit because their husbands were not there to register the land in their names . . . [In the slums] of Nairobi an in-depth study [in 1990] revealed that only 20 per cent of the parents had been born in the area. The rest had all come in from the surrounding countryside . . .

the reasons they gave for migrating illustrate the problems women in
rural areas have in maintaining their access to land.

(Munyakho 1992: 10)

Once in the city, in temporary shacks in squatter camps, without water
or sanitation, women had to maintain themselves and their families by
working long hours as domestic servants or as market traders, or by illegal
activities such as brewing beer or prostitution. They were simply unable
to spend the time, and often did not have the money, to look after their
children, many of whom took to the streets.

Education systems still bear the marks of their colonial administrators:
from methods of financing and collections of statistics to inspectorial
systems and curricula. For instance in Swaziland the guidelines still in
place for the registration of nurseries, might have come out of – and
probably did – an English local authority handbook from the 1950s![4] Even
eating habits have a colonial heritage. It is possible to get baguettes and
croissants in most ex-French colonies, whilst in ex-English colonies, hotels
may still serve English breakfasts, down to the kippers, smoked haddock
and marmalade!

Transitional countries are struggling with their one-time Soviet over-
lordship, and how to transform their services when the very concepts
which they use to understand government and administration are derived
from their former regime.

Aid agencies have to come to terms with these colonial inheritances, in
a very practical sense if not in a moral sense. It is questionable how many
aid staff are aware of the colonial histories of the countries in which they
work, or consider that it is of any relevance in dealing with present
problems.

Any aid agency worth its salt, however, also has to explore present
inequalities, the extraordinary difference in living standards that charac-
terize North and South. Many aid agencies in the UK, such as Oxfam,
Save the Children and Action Aid attempt to do this. The Church of
England booklet *New Start Worship*, written with the charity Christian
Aid, advises that:

If, when we ourselves are not on the poverty line, we always go for
the cheapest price without considering that this price is achieved
through ethically unacceptable working conditions somewhere in the
world, we are making a statement about our understanding of
the word neighbour.

(2000: 23)

Who should carry responsibility for the present situation in the South, and does it make any difference to assign responsibility? In their book *A Moral Critique of Development* Quarles van Ufford and Giri argue that we should all, whether living in the North or the South, think of ourselves as global selves. We share a global responsibility for the past, as well as the continuance of the planet and for the well-being of the people on it. The problem is not for the North to articulate an ethics of care, how 'we' might make 'their' lives better. Instead the challenge is how to articulate a joint enterprise of change and sustainability.

> In mainstream development institutions such concerns [for the poor of the South] have been separated from the conditions and problems of ourselves, the rich. We propose . . . a shift from a focus on poverty and under-development – which explicitly or implicitly takes 'Western' industrial living as normative . . . towards a perspective that places the developers and the developed, self and other, within a common framework. One way to do this is to focus on consumptions and lifestyles instead of 'poverty'. How are valued lifestyles produced? What and how do people consume? What are the social and environmental effects? A focus on 'lifestyles' enables the driving forces of high consumption in 'the West' to be considered in the same frame as 'poverty'.
>
> (2003: 24)[5]

## Cycles of aid

Quarles van Ufford and Kumar acknowledge the widespread disillusionment with aid. In a penetrating analysis they trace the history of attempts by the North to offer help to the South. They argue that since the Second World War, when the United Nations was set up, there have been three identifiable stages or periods of intervention:

- first, a period of hope and optimism, offering simplistic technocratic solutions through investment in industry – roads, peanut farms and similar agricultural enterprises, hydroelectric power stations, new universities – largely controlled by the newly independent countries themselves;
- second, an emphasis on financial solutions, on marketization and privatization and reform of banking;
- third, most recently there has been an emphasis on managerial solutions, on improving governance and administration, and the development of 'human capital'.

All these interventions hold out great hope of improvement; the rhetoric of aid intervention is always one of optimism. The new solution is just around the corner:

> in the 1960s, newly independent governments in a hurry displace the private sector (Nationalization plans, government led projects . . .). In the 1970s donors in a hurry displace government (donor-driven projects with their own management structures . . .); in the 1980s governments return ownership to the private sector (structural adjustment, privatization . . .); in the 1990s donors begin to return ownership to governments (sector-wide programmes, direct budget support . . .) and in the 2000s agencies emphasize accountability to domestic institutions (governance, participation, poverty reduction papers . . .).
>
> (2003: 15)

In so many countries aid projects reflect this chequered history of past interventions, often ignored or forgotten by the incoming donors. When I was based at the Education Ministry in Swaziland, the room used by our team had been used over the years by previous consultants. Some of their material was still there, under layers of dust on the bookshelves, buried amongst out-of-date computer packages, proposing policies that had never been enacted and might always have been irrelevant. Similarly, in Kazakhstan the first task of our consultancy team was to identify relevant previous consultancy documents, and work out what had been recommended and compare it with what had actually been carried out. The ideologies, rationales of – and funds offered by – donors have changed considerably over the years. But whilst the cynical and weary staff in the Education or Health or Finance ministries or those working in projects on the ground might remember some of the comings and goings, amongst donors themselves there is usually very little institutional history.

Judith Justice traces the history of UNICEF funding for child immunization. She shows how at first in the 1960s and 1970s there was international pressure to reach globally agreed immunization targets under the slogan 'Saving Infant Lives' irrespective of the capability of health services within countries to explain or maintain such programmes. As UNICEF priorities changed from child survival to other areas, international funding for the immunization programme waned, leaving countries without the resources and incapable of continuing the programmes. Immunization programmes in some countries are now at a lower level than in the 1960s when UNICEF began the programme. The immunization programme was promoted as part of a global agenda, and as so often happens, when the agenda changed the project could not be sustained.

> In Uganda, for example, many mothers did not even understand that immunization was related to the health care of their children ... Global health initiatives are frequently promoted without enough regard to the particular local setting in which they are being introduced; for instance the availability of trained personnel, ability to deliver supplies, ability to finance currrent costs to operate internally provided capital investments and follow-up.
>
> (Justice 2000: 32)

It is common for any kind of project, whether for early childhood education and care or anything else, to have many funders over time. Most funding is for a short term – three years or less – since donors are unwilling to commit themselves to long-term funding. They conceive of their funding as 'seed money' to establish the validity of a particular intervention (and their own credibility as an aid organization). They hope that the government, or some other agency, will take over the project if it proves worthwhile. Adroit project staff seek other funders as money runs out.

One consequence of this is that if a project proves 'successful', any donor that at any point has had a hand in the funding may list it as their success. Many early childhood projects crop up again and again in the development literature of different agencies. The World Bank in particular, as an umbrella funder, draws on the work of those with whom it may have had no direct contact, as evidence of the success of its policies. For example, it describes the work on early childhood in Kenya carried out by a variety of other agencies long before the World Bank itself was on the scene as 'pre-project strengths' and assesses them as if they were a scheduled aspect of their own programming (Balachander 1999).

The balance between international donors coming in with their own priorities and slogans and local priorities in a resource-poor country is invariably fraught. The question of agency – who is really in control – has never really been resolved, and the pendulum has swung backwards and forwards about what kind of change or development is necessary, what strategies are most appropriate to bring about change and who should carry them out. Who should set the priorities? How should money be distributed? To whom and under what conditions? And for how long?

And what is the appropriate way to behave for those bringing the money from North to South?

## The big-time aid agencies

### The World Bank

The major institution set up to address poverty across the world is the World Bank. Its most recent mission statement reads:

> Our dream is a world free of poverty. Our mission is to fight poverty with passion and professionalism for lasting results.
>
> [We value] personal honesty, integrity, commitment; working together in teams – with openness and trust; empowering others and respecting differences; encouraging risk-taking and responsibility; enjoying work and our families.

Not everyone agrees with the World Bank's assessment of itself. Kumar (2003), for example, describes World Bank literature as a kind of gothic fantasy literature, a bizarre genre of escapist reading for economists and politicians. The World Bank evokes very hostile reactions from some of its clients; and from some notable ex-employees like its former chief economist, Joseph Stiglitz. Ravi Kunbur, who was in charge of the Poverty programme at the World Bank until he resigned after disagreement with its policies, pointed out dryly that: 'In the year 2000, the Governors of the World Bank, whose mission is to eradicate poverty, could only meet under police protection, besieged by those who believe instead that the Institution and the policies it espouses cause poverty' (2001: 2).

The original, laudable, intention of the World Bank and its predecessors and partners[6] was to assist in the redevelopment and reconstruction of debilitated economies after the Second World War. It has interpreted its brief liberally, and now has a monetary interest in almost all 'developing' and transitional countries. It regards itself – and is mostly regarded as – the bank for the world, to where almost any country can turn for help with redevelopment. Its power as an institution is unrivalled.

The World Bank is 'owned' by 181 member countries, whose views and interests are represented by a Board of Governors and a Washington based Board of Directors. The World Bank is a generic title for a number of international financial institutions such as the International Bank for Research and Development (IBRD), the International Finance Corporation and the International Development Association. In order to belong to the IBRD a country must first join the International Monetary Fund (IMF).

The largest shareholder in the World Bank is the USA, which has 16.49 per cent of shareholder votes. The USA and four other major shareholders (France, Germany, Japan and the UK, who together hold a further 16 per cent of votes) each appoint an executive director. A further 19 executive directors are elected by a group of countries or in the case of China, the Russian Federation and Saudi Arabia, form single constituencies. Wade (2001) argues that the USA has a disproportionate influence on the World Bank, not only as the largest shareholder. (In fact the shareholders rarely meet to vote, although the USA uniquely exercises a veto on various key constitutional issues.) The Bank is very closely intertwined with the US Treasury, which heavily influences, if not directly controls, its key appointments. Its location in Washington reinforces these connections. The World Bank, Wade claims, lends US policy a cloak of multilateralism, whilst enabling it to push hard for free market policies which serve its own financial interests. 'The World Bank has been an especially useful instrument for projecting American influence in developing countries and one over which the US maintains discreet but firm institutional control' (Wade 2001: 127).

The World Bank nevertheless attempts to project itself as an independent, caring institution. It sees itself as a kind of broker between the rich nations of the North and the poor nations of the South. It employs some of the best regarded analysts in their respective fields. It has recruited highly respected economists, education, health and social development specialists from many countries besides the USA.

The World Bank operates on two major conditions. First, it only works in tandem with the International Monetary Fund (IMF), which assesses the economic stability and viability of any country to which development loans are offered. If the IMF does not give a country a clean bill of economic health, the World Bank will not provide loans to its government. The IMF espouses free market economics, and believes that the state has a very small role to play in the economy or in the provision of services. Its structural adjustment policies have forced many poor countries into downsizing their health and social sectors and privatizing most of their assets in order to qualify for loans. Tanzania, for example, is one of the world's poorest countries, yet had nevertheless attempted to provide universal free primary education. The IMF forced Tanzania to cut its education budget to the point where it was widely acknowledged that it was no longer realistic to expect that all – or even a majority of – children would go to school.

Joseph Stiglitz, the economics Nobel prizewinner, has critized the IMF for the rigidity and extreme nature of their views. As mentioned in Chapter 1, he argues that IMF policies have badly damaged transitional countries like Russia, with the result that great suffering occurred. As one Namibian colleague joked with me, 'structural adjustment means that now everyone has more choices about when to eat. We can choose between breakfast and lunch, or lunch and supper, or breakfast and supper. Sometimes we can choose just one'.

The second condition of World Bank investment is that it is a loan, on which interest must be paid. Long-term loans are made to one political regime, but, in the course of events, are paid off by another. As the campaigning group Jubilee 2000 have frequently pointed out, long-term loans totalling around $450 billion were made to dictators and other corrupt regimes such as Soharto, Mobutu and the military junta in Brazil.[7] Their more democratic successors were still forced to repay the debts. These loans were mostly prompted by the geo-political interests of the USA, including the sale of armaments, rather than for reconstruction purposes.[8] Raffer claims that indebtedness and rescheduling of international debts 'violates all the most basic principles of the rule of law' (1992: 3). No country has been able to refuse to pay their debt, since the economic consequences would be too dire. But the debt repayment burden has proved crippling to many poor countries. The Inter-Church Coalition on Africa has commented: 'Every child born in Africa is born with a financial burden which a lifetime's work cannot repay. The debt is a new form of slavery as vicious as the slave trade.'[9]

The international campaign by the organization Jubilee 2000 to highlight poor nation indebtedness was successful in that certain very poor countries earned debt relief – including Tanzania where education and health statistics immediately improved! However, the fact remains that the World Bank is precisely that, a bank representing the interests of its shareholders, rather than any redistributive mechanism between North and South. Overall, like any other bank, the World Bank has *earnt* money from its customers, the poor countries of the world.

The World Bank's attempts to measure the extent of poverty and most recently to solicit the views of the poor on the poverty they experience, rely on extremely sophisticated economic modelling. But as Kunbur has pointed out, at root are arguments about the concept of 'development' and whether a neo-liberal economic approach can be extended unproblematically to all nations. The World Bank acknowledges that the world fiscal system has serious weaknesses and institutional and governance reforms are badly overdue. But it sees these weaknesses as flaws that can be eliminated, given suitable expertise. The World Bank argues that its interventions are more, not less, necessary as a vehicle for achieving economic stability and progress; and that more technological expertise can solve global problems.

The World Bank acknowledges that world-wide, education rates are falling and child mortality is increasing (although these figures are also now a reflection of the HIV/AIDS epidemic). The Bank invests in education and health to try to combat these trends. In a significant shift from purely economic definitions of income and expenditure, and import and export trends, it draws on the 'human capital theory' of economists like Amartya Sen to justify investing in people. The World Bank now considers that suitably constructed health, education and other welfare investment policies might also in the long term enhance economic productivity.

The Bank is now focusing many more loans on education and social development projects. A recent promotional booklet claims that 'the World Bank is fully committed to pro-actively and comprehensively improving the quality of life for children' (World Bank 2000: 1).This gradual refocusing of endeavour has led to their adoption of early childhood programmes. The World Bank has so far loaned over $1000 million dollars over a ten-year period to support a range of early childhood development and care programmes (ECD) throughout the world including countries such as Bolivia, Colombia, Brazil, El Salvador, India, Indonesia, Nigeria, Uganda and Morocco. It maintains a lively website, with pages of material on early childhood. It commissions papers and promotes the topic through publications and regional and global conferences. It regards itself as an important contributor to the debate about early childhood; and conversely it is lobbied by many organizations who regard it as a major player in the field. It states that: 'The World Bank is the largest single source of external funding for health and education in developing countries. Increasingly much of that investment has been directed towards helping young children – the human capital of the future' (World Bank 2000: 1).

However, as indicated in the last chapter, its adoption of early childhood relies on paradigms forged in the USA, which are in themselves highly questionable. It then applies them with token acknowledgements of context and setting. These precepts of understanding and practice forged for children in the USA are seen as perfectly legitimate for the South, and likely to deliver untold benefits. To the women living in the townships described by Munyakho, or the favelas described by Scheper-Hughes,[10] whose lives are unutterably hard, such visions as this must seem not only insulting, but downright cruel.

Not only is the physiological basis for good health laid during these early years but the essential values that have such high pay-offs in competitive labor markets are transmitted from parents to children. These transfers include such critical assets as self-esteem, a work ethic and a sense of discipline, an awareness of family traditions and of the community to which one belongs, a vision of opportunity and a thirst for knowledge.

(Evans *et al.* 2000: foreword)

### The United Nations family

The setting up of the United Nations was an idealistic attempt to define the global future, to move away from the cataclysmic experience of war, to redefine human rights. It was 'a practice of hope' setting out visionary goals, but without any clear ideas about the means of achieving them or any clear acknowledgement of the changes – and damages – wrought by colonialism. It was almost immediately hijacked by the Cold War (Bergesen and Lunde 1999).

It was originally a loose organization for international co-operation, but gradually widened its membership and its powers. A majority of members now come from the South. The General Assembly, the overall decision-making body; and the Security Council (dominated by its five permanent members, the USA, the UK, France, Russia and China) are based in New York. The United Nations now consists of sixteen specialized agencies, all semi or mostly autonomous within the UN and based mostly in capital cities in the North; for instance UNESCO (United Nations Education and Scientific Committee), which specializes in education, is based in Paris. Besides UNESCO, the three biggest agencies in terms of staff and financing are the FAO (Food and Agriculture Organization) based in Rome, the WHO (World Health Organization) based in Geneva, and the ILO (International Labour Organization) also based in Geneva. Others include the UNDP (United Nations Development Programme), which specializes in analysis of development issues and is based in New York. (The UNDP issues the annual *Human Development Report* which compares members on various kinds of development indicators and has recently set the *Millennium Goals* to reduce poverty.)

Membership of these agencies is mostly by subscription from member states (the UK government under Thatcher, for example, withdrew its UNESCO subscription, as it suspected UNESCO of being too left-wing; the USA still does not subscribe to it). The big UN agencies have regional offices (Latin America, Central Asia, etc.) and in addition often maintain an office in each poor country in the region.

As well as the specialized agencies, there are eleven UN commissions. These commissions are governed by elected member states, and serviced by the UN Secretariat. There are also five regional commissions with regional secretariats. There are two High Commissioners (for refugees and for human rights, appointed by the Secretary General).

There are eleven funds and programmes with funds raised from outside as well as from within the UN. UNICEF (United Nations Children's Fund) based in New York, operates on a fundraising basis, hence its programme of using well-known filmstars as 'ambassadors' for its fundraising strategies.[11] Hence also its sloganizing campaigns like the one described above on immunization. When, for fundraising purposes a particular slogan like 'Saving Infant Lives' is exhausted, the organization needs to find another. UNAIDS, based in Geneva, is the latest of these special programmes, tasked with raising money for global programmes to combat HIV/AIDS.

There are also five research institutions and an infinite number of expert and ad hoc committees. The research institute that is concerned with childhood is the UNICEF Innocenti Research Centre in Florence. It has, for example, produced well-regarded reports on child poverty and a series of monitoring reports on the position of children in transitional countries.

As Bergesen and Lunde (1999) comment, this is a chaotic profile. Despite having overlapping briefs, these agencies see themselves as distinct agencies each with their own mission and priorities. Attempts at reform have been unsuccessful. There has been some reshuffling but the sprawling agenda is not really in question. UNESCO, UNICEF and the WHO, for example, are all concerned with the health and well-being of young children and have all issued their own statements on early childhood. They may work closely together (for example UNESCO tends to take the lead on French-speaking Africa rather than UNICEF) but they are also liable to compete with one another, and may not even be housed together or plan together within a particular country. The protocols surrounding their relationships to each other and to other aid agencies are considerable, presenting a kind of diplomatic end-game to the outsider. UN staff in these agencies are paid at international rates (less for local staff but still above local rates) and are relatively well looked after and protected – in secure air-conditioned offices, travelling in four-wheeled drive vehicles with distinctive logos emblazoned on the side. It is these accoutrements, this image of a well-to-do, well-cushioned elite that give rise to the scorn evinced by Paul Theroux, Graham Hancock and others, cited above.

UNICEF has a benign image as the international organization most closely concerned with the well-being of children. Like the World Bank, with whom it collaborates, it has been very influential in shaping ideas about childhood in the South. At the New York headquarters it formulates global priorities and programmes; and this framework is then used at regional and country level to determine the work undertaken. It has most recently adopted a 'Child Rights' approach to programming, although the ramifications of this are loosely worked out, and the universalism implicit in such an approach is unexplored. At a country level it may enter into all kinds of arrangements and deals with other agencies to fund particular local projects, but has relatively little 'free' money to spend on such projects. In some countries, like Swaziland, its work is outstanding and makes a real difference to children on the ground; in others like Kazakhstan, it appears to be out of tune with local needs and priorities.

### The international consultants

International aid is as subject to the pressures of globalism as any other industry. Many aid projects, especially large ones, are put out to tender. The EU, for example, runs its aids projects (which are at least grants rather than loans, and worth many millions of euros) on a techno-cratic tender basis. Tight tender specifications are issued, specifying the technical details of the project in advance and the time scales in which it must be carried out. In response to these tenders, a huge consultancy business has grown up. Companies whose prime business may or may not be concerned with the aid industry compete for tenders. Italian oil companies, German pharmecutical firms, Finnish forestry specialists may all – and do – bid for education or health contracts. The British Council in the UK is also a major bidder for contracts.

These firms may have a core of permanent staff to put bids together, but their bids are based in turn on subcontracting teams of free-lance consultants who are brought together (often very hurriedly) to do the work on a short-term contract. A successful bid may bring together a team of people from, say, Canada, the UK and Australia, who have never worked together before, and are unlikely to do so again, and may have no particular knowledge of or commitment to the country in which they will be working, and no obligation to it once their contract has finished. At the point of bidding, they are known only on the basis of their CVs. The consultants are mostly men in their 50s and 60s who may have worked in a senior capacity in administration or a university but now specialize in free-lance work – and have the freedom from domestic obligations to work in this way. The perk of the job is not only the salary but the per diem expenses – living expenses that are modelled on cost of living in the North. A per diem for one day may be in excess of a local salary for one month in the country where the consultancy is being carried out.

Successful consultants who build up a profile of contracts zig-zag from one side of the world to another for a one- or two-month stay (or even less), applying their expertise in the country in which they happen to find themselves. The EU even contracts out the overseeing of such work to other consultants. In countries where they have several projects, they tender for another consultancy firm to oversee the implementation of the projects, to make sure the tender specifications and time scales of other tenderers are being met. Although there are rules about fairness and competition, some collusion between firms, and between individuals, inevitably takes place, although certainly nowhere near the scale of the corruption that operates on many international business deals for oil or gas or infrastructure projects like dams. Transparency International is an organization set up precisely in order to monitor international corruption, and some of its reports make dire reading.[12]

These tendering practices, which are widespread, arise from a vision of aid as a technocratic exercise, modelled on the business world, rather than as a kind of global responsibility. Advising on health financing, or social care, or even on early childhood education, is conceived as a highly specific task requiring free-floating expertise rather than commitment or local knowledge. The collegiality and team effort that usually characterizes successful professional work has to be established (and often is not) within the foot-loose group of consultants, rather than with local people. When the consultants leave, their expertise often – or usually – goes with them; only their recommendations remain.

The tendering approach and the work of the consultancy firms raise important questions about the ethics of aid. Just who are the free-floating, technocratic elite? What obligations and loyalties do they have? Is there a moral dimension over and above the business transaction? These are rhetorical questions only. There is no evidence of a wider ethical debate in the competitive world of tendering and contracting.[13]

### Corporate charity

Noreena Hertz, in her analysis of global corporatism, points to the work of what she calls 'evangelical entrepreneurs' – the super-rich who are lightly taxed and who are encouraged to show their generosity through corporate giving. (Indeed the Harvard Business School offers a workshop in 'strategic philanthropy'!)

> With personal fortunes rivalling those of states and a global presence that mocks states' limited reach, they are bypassing mainstream electoral politics to achieve political ends. Rather than seek election to office, many of them clearly believe that they can achieve much more as business people than as politicians, using the leverage of their business empires to gain access to world leaders . . . These real life Citizen Kanes are effectively becoming a class of unelected politicians, ambassadors and advocates, raising popular support, acting in defiance of government policy, donating money to supranational organizations, playing the role of unofficial diplomats and using their power, wealth and influence to effect political and social change to an unprecedented degree.
>
> (2001: 208)

One of the most well-known corporate donors is Bill Gates of Microsoft. He has set up the Bill and Melissa Gates Foundation to support health care in the South, giving money to HIV/AIDS organizations. Ted Turner, the media giant, has written off some of the UN debts. George Soros made a billion dollar fortune on the stock exchange (his speculation at one point caused the UK to devalue the pound). He set up the Soros Foundation and has used his considerable fortune to set up the 'Open Society Institute' (OSI) in more than fifty countries. This institute fosters capitalist entrepreneurship, risk taking and creativity in order to loosen what Soros sees as the mindset of dependency in ex-communist countries.[14] The OSI supports a wide portfolio of activities, including social and economic analysis, public sector reform, independent media and human rights.

The Soros Foundation also supports an early education programme in all the countries in which the Foundation operates, based on Head Start in the USA. Unapologetically American in approach, Soros offers kindergartens equipment grants and other resources if they agree to try out its preschool approach, 'proven' to work in the USA.[15]

These entrepreneurs are merely the most well known. Many voluntary or non-governmental organizations in many countries look to corporate donors for funding. Most early childhood organizations in South Africa, for example, rely on such corporate sponsorship. Such donors do some good, but on their own terms; and often their interventions are intended to promote the good image of their own company or their own name.

Their social responsibility is dependent on their profits. As Hertz points out, 'downgrading the role of the state in favour of corporate activism threatens to make societal improvements irreversibly dependent on the creation of profit' (2001: 250).

## The early childhood organizations

Apart from the World Bank, UNICEF and UNESCO there are a number of agencies that include early childhood projects in their work. There are also a few international organizations that specialize in projects aimed at children and childhood in the South. Some of these are also foundations set up by rich individuals. The Bernard Van Leer Foundation, which derives its money from packaging, specializes exclusively in early childhood; and the Aga Khan Foundation, funded through the personal wealth of the Aga Khan, works with young Muslim children mainly in East Africa, India and Pakistan. Unsurprisingly, neither of these agencies engage with 'political' issues but see their role in more limited terms of delivering aid. Soros is more political, but with the very specific political intention of developing capitalist entrepreneurship.

Save the Children (SCF), is a loose federation of organizations from a number of different countries concerned with children and childhood. It raises its money through fundraising. Save-US is much more business orientated (as it has to be in order to bid for USAID contracts) but other members of the federation, especially the Swedish SCF, Raada Barnen and SCF-UK, maintain a highly critical stance on globalism and the activities of the World Bank.

Some governments support early childhood projects through their bilateral aid programmes. The Dutch government, for example, supports the early years section of the Association for the Development of Education in Africa (ADEA) which brings together African Ministers of Education and Senior Civil Servants to exchange information about education planning and projects. But bilateral aid tends to be strategic and supports policies and approaches rather than offering direct funding to individual projects.

There are a number of umbrella groups which attempt to share and co-ordinate the work being done. The Consultative Group on Early Childhood Care and Development (CG) describes itself as 'an international inter-agency group dedicated to improving the condition of young children at risk'. The CG grounds its work in a cross-disciplinary view of child care and development. It is based in Toronto, Canada, but is very closely linked to UNICEF and the other children's agencies listed above, as well as to the World Bank and USAID. It is also 'apolitical' and does not engage in any of the wider debates about poverty or inequality but by and large showcases the work of its constituent agencies. It does not include SCF or Soros, and so far it has not made links with the EU (which has a far more ambitious aid programme than USAID).

A new organization, the World Forum on Early Education and Care, also based in Washington, is an offshoot of a North American advocacy organization, the Childcare Exchange. In their own words:

> The objective of the World Forum is to promote an on-going global exchange of ideas on the delivery of quality services in diverse settings. We have two goals for delegates: first, that they acquire a wealth of new ideas and new perspectives to enrich their work; and second, that they develop meaningful relationships that continue into the future with their peers from other nations.
>
> (www.ccie.com)

Whilst this is an open forum and has brought together many new actors, it relies on, and blurs the influence of, corporate sponsors. Its leading funders are Johnson and Johnson and Vivendi. It has established a hierarchy of benefactors, donors, friends and champions for its corporate donors, mainly firms that seek to sell children's products. Its website lists a 'Market Square' where it is possible to find a product by company or category. This commercialism is regarded as so normal that it is seen as a source of strength rather than weakness to the organization. Given this kind of corporate sponsorship, the idea that children's development is intrinsically linked to the accumulation of possessions (LeVine 2003: chapter 2) is unlikely to be questioned.

The organizations described here have their roots in the North and operate within the kinds of knowledge frameworks described in the previous chapter. Many radical organizations exist in the South, in South-East Asia, in Latin America and in Africa but they have a grass roots focus and draw on sources of inspiration which are relatively unfamiliar in the North – an emphasis on non-violent protest, or on spiritual traditions, or on the work of the famous Brazilian educationalist and activist Paulo Freire, and on particular understandings of solidarity, communality and obligation. By contrast, most ideas about childhood espoused by aid agencies in the North draw, implicitly or explicitly, on traditions of individuality and personal success and advancement; they are locked into globalizing discourses. Chapters 5 to 8, which cover the four case studies from the South, illustrate these differences of approach between North and South.

## Do INGOs work?

The aim of most of the organizations mentioned is to draw attention to the plight of children in the South and to suggest ways in which their position might be improved. Almost all aid projects are problematic, in that they involve ideas from the North being applied like sticking plaster to the sores of the South. In the case of the World Bank, because the Bank lends rather than grants money, the justification for aid has to be in economic terms: a promise, however contrived, of a future prosperous enough to pay back the loan. In the case of early childhood, the assumptions are that poor children will be better educated, healthier citizens, earn more, and be in a position to help their country perform better in world markets – as Kumar (2003) suggests, a fantasy of gothic proportions, given the obstacles that chronic poverty, HIV/AIDS and globalism pose.

Boli and Thomas (1999) in their book *Constructing World Culture* examine the work and reach of all these different agencies – the big time agencies like the World Bank, the United Nations group, the charities, the corporate bodies – collectively called International Non-Governmental Agencies (INGOs). They argue that there has been a massive growth of all kinds of INGOs (from the World Bank and UNICEF to the smallest charity). These INGOs, although outside the international political systems of governance, nevertheless exert great influence. Like corporations, they act independently of nation states, and are unaccountable to them, although they seek to influence policy and practice within those countries. Because they exist independently of government and to an extent are free-floating and unaccountable, they have to justify their power and influence by claiming they act more fairly, more independently and more flexibly than do individual governments, and they take a wider perspective. They do that by making certain kinds of arguments.

- Universalism – they argue that there are supra-national standards of conduct, welfare and well-being to which everyone aspires; the Convention on the Rights of the Child, for example, or anti-discrimination policies on gender or race. As neutral international agencies, they can push for these universal standards, without getting embroiled in trade or diplomatic bargaining. They are 'above' politics.

- Individualism – they argue that they care about people or children wherever they are. They are humanitarian agencies who care about the welfare of individuals whatever their situation or the tensions in the community to which they belong. They can help in times of crisis and draw attention to pain or suffering, no matter what causes it.
- Rational voluntaristic authority – since INGOs have no legal or bureaucratic authority, they can only appeal to reason; they argue that they are doing the best possible job at all times. Scientific or pseudo-scientific claims – like those of child development – are stressed over and over again as a justification for action. INGOs cannot easily accommodate the irrational or what does not fit into standard approaches.

Boli and Thomas examine the work of a number of organizations or movements in these terms: the women's movement, the Red Cross, and population control bodies. They conclude that whilst all of the organizations they examine have brought about change, they have done so at a price. They have been constrained 'by a vision of progress that reifies both science and individual welfare' (1999: 248).

## How governments give aid

The United Nations has agreed a target for the aid that rich countries should donate towards poor countries: 0.7 per cent of GDP. The UNDP annually lists the amount of government aid and which countries are the main beneficiaries. As pointed out in Chapter 2, only four countries – Norway, Sweden, the Netherlands and Denmark have met or exceeded the aid target. The UK donated 0.27 per cent of GDP in 2001.[16] The USA donated 0.11 per cent of GDP, the lowest of any industrialized nation.

The aid that ex-colonial powers (for instance Spain, France, UK, the Netherlands and Portugal) give is mainly directed towards their one-time colonies. They maintain regional offices in those colonies. In the case of the UK Department for International Development (DfID) much aid giving is now decentralized to regional offices. DfID specifies the broad categories of funding (currently governance and helping the poorest of the poor), but decisions are made regionally.[17] Aid from governments is distributed mainly in three ways: directly to governments in the South to undertake particular programmes, for example, reform of governance; as grants to INGOs working in the South; and as tenders for particular tasks, for which consultancy firms apply.

The EU subcontracts almost all of its aid budget to consultancy firms that have successfully bid for tenders. USAID offers tenders, as does DfID especially for technical projects. Governments may also fund research projects.

Aid budgets, especially in the USA and UK are also used to boost sales of US and UK goods and services – for example, weaponry or engineering projects. The UK formally delinked aid and trade in 1997 (although inevitably there are informal links) but many USAID projects specify that a substantial proportion of aid must be spent on such goods and technical services from the USA.

Government aid budgets also reflect geo-political concerns. The USA offers a considerable proportion of its aid to Egypt to buy support for its Middle Eastern policies; and similarly it has over the last decade provided money for ex Soviet and Central Asian republics – especially Georgia and Uzbekistan, which have strategic importance because of oil and gas pipelines, despite the difficulties posed by their undemocratic regimes. Much US and UK aid money is now being diverted to Iraq. For example, the amount of money DfID allocated to Africa has been reduced, in order to fund reconstruction in Iraq.

The USAID budget, despite being only 0.11 per cent of GDP, is still the largest single aid budget because of the size of the US economy. Its influence is a powerful one. Over and above the restrictions on goods and services and geopolitical considerations, new evangelistic condition-alities have been imposed on grant giving under the present US regime of George Bush. For example, in South Africa USAID has set aside money for projects dealing with HIV/AIDS. However, in order to be eligible for money, most projects have to be faith-based and to put forward abstinence (from sexual intercourse) as its main preventative strategy. As a result, much of the money is unspent; few projects wish to adhere to such terms.

The Nordic countries and the Netherlands, who do meet their 0.7 per cent target (although this is a small amount compared with the USAID budget), are generally more open in their funding, and more radical. One Swedish Foreign Minister has even advocated that instead of aid, rich nations should pay an aid tax and the tax revenues should be paid directly to governments in the South.[18]

Many countries, including the USA, the Nordic countries, the Netherlands, France, Spain, Italy, Canada and Japan, have supported early childhood projects either directly or indirectly through INGOs. The UK is an exception. It argues against the funding of early childhood, which it sees as a low priority.

## A helping hand?

At the beginning of the chapter, I mentioned some of the antagonism that is felt towards the aid industry. Aid workers are sometimes seen as yet another set of colonialists, living a life of relative ease in very poor countries and ignorant of the history and cultural traditions of those countries. In a controversial book about famine relief, for example, Alex de Waal argues that only political action within countries can in the long term improve circumstances. Interventions, especially those of INGOs, have served to undermine the ability of people to argue for and negotiate their own solutions. Emergency appeals for famine relief also serve to bolster the image of aid agencies rushing to the rescue.

> The minimum duty of the humanitarian is therefore to tell the truth. The problem of famine will be solved by political action, and humanitarians must never hint otherwise, nor allow their existence or actions to imply otherwise. They must not inflate the marginal contribution they make to saving lives and livelihoods.
>
> (De Waal 2002: 221)

As Quarles van Ufford comments, the aid industry is characterized by an inane optimism that predicts all kinds of wonderful solutions from tiny drops of aid. It may do more harm than good in distorting expectations of what is possible or desirable. Those in the North who promote early childhood programmes are particularly guilty of promising the world and delivering peanuts.

Giving, then, is not that simple. The inequalities between North and South are shocking. But the way in which aid is distributed can distort both the giver and the recipient.

# Chapter 5

# Kazakhstan

## Summary

This chapter explores the details of early childhood services in a transitional country and discusses how inequality amongst children has arisen and is being addressed. Across the ex-Soviet Union and its satellites, the fall of communism and the rapid privatization of state assets has generally resulted in a fall in income, an increase in unemployment, especially for women, an erosion of welfare services and a growth in inequality. The changeover from a command economy to a capitalist one also resulted in an influx of consultants advising – sometimes unwisely and in ignorance – on almost every aspect of policy and provision.

In Kazakhstan, kindergartens were once highly regarded as the best in Central Asia. Since transition, the percentage of children aged 2–6 attending kindergarten has fallen from 50 per cent to 11 per cent, the biggest fall being in rural areas. Many of the kindergartens that remain are in poor condition; as with schools, there has been little or no capital investment since 1990. The government has attempted to compensate by providing nursery education for 5–6-year-olds attached to schools.

Much of the material I use here was originally obtained as part of field trips and two case studies that I undertook in 2003 as part of a consultancy commissioned by the Asian Development Bank. I was part of a team reviewing the Kazakh education sector (although I am responsible for the interpretation of the data presented here).

## Background

Kazakhstan is the ninth largest country in the world, part of a land mass that freezes in winter and bakes in summer. The land is mainly central Asian steppes, vast areas of plains once home to nomadic peoples. To the east and south are China and Mongolia. Almaaty, on the edge of the Tien Shan mountain range, a spur of the Himalayas, was until recently the capital of Kazakhstan. The capital has now been relocated hundreds of miles north to a town (previously called Zelinograd) in the steppes, transformed and reborn as Astana. There the oil and gas wealth is fuelling a building boom. Glittering skyscrapers command views over the marshes and endless flat grasslands of the steppes. The wide Ishim river flowing through Astana is hemmed in by concrete banks and the paved tow paths are extravagantly punctuated by little pavilions, and by flashing fairy lighting spun along the lamp-posts. The new capital is proud of its image, although in the suburbs, not so far out of sight, there are still derelict factory complexes, disused rail-yards and all the rusting debris of the Soviet regime.

In the west is the inland Aral Sea, one of the most polluted areas in the world. It was once the site of extensive Russian bio-chemical weaponry testing. Extensive drainage for cotton farming has dried out the sea and lethal winds blow across the contaminated earth. In the west, also, Kazakhstan borders on the Caspian Sea, where there are extensive reserves of oil and gas. To the north is Siberia; this is the borderland country of Semiplatansk, the Russian nuclear testing site, where more than 500 nuclear tests were carried out. The north-east complex of Baykonur is still an important base for space exploration.

Just as Kazakhstan's geography shapes the lives of its people, so too does its history. Successive waves of invaders passed through the land until, in the fifteenth century, the Khanate of Kazakh emerged. The Kazakh people were mainly nomads, grouped into three main hordes or clans (*zhouzes*) herding flocks on the plains and moving with the seasons. As Central Asia came under Russian rule in the eighteenth and nineteenth centuries, Ukranians, Belorussians, Germans, Bulgarians and Polish, Jewish and Tatar people moved into the region and settled in the towns and cities and on the more productive lands. Russia also used Kazakhstan as a place of exile for political revolutionaries.

In 1936 Kazakhstan officially became one of the Soviet republics. Under the Soviet Union, more land was brought into cultivation and the considerable mineral assets of Kazakhstan were exploited (New Internationalist 2003). Many more Germans and Russians, even Koreans, were forcibly resettled in Kazakhstan, so that Kazakhs were no longer a majority people in the country. An estimated one million Kazakhs died during Stalin's enforced collectivization. Almost all nomads were sedentarized and the Kazakh language and lifestyle were held in contempt and seen as 'backward'.

Despite these gross assaults on identity and livelihood, there were also gains, especially for children. 'Traditional' Kazakh society is nominally

Muslim but religious observances blurred with older shamanistic rituals. Women were relatively independent and unveiled. Children enjoyed considerable freedom and mobility within the limits set by other social norms, such as respect for elders. Nomadic families were traditionally extended households; children always had a place in them, and upbringing was shared within the household.

The Soviets also considered children to be valuable. Children were thought of as 'true revolutionaries' who could reshape the future (Kirschenbaum 2001). Soviet ideology chimed in to an extent with nomadic tradition (UNESCO/MoE 2000). The manner in which children are held in high esteem by the family, society and government is rooted both in the nomadic culture of Central Asia and the socialist values of the former Soviet Union. Children had a special role in Soviet society; they were the citizens of the future in whom it was important to invest. The state provided wide-ranging institutional support for children. There was a comprehensive social safety net that included family support payments, maternity and health care. There was a successful education system that turned a mainly illiterate society fully literate within a generation, an extraordinary feat (Demberel and Penn 2005). These standard services were complemented by a wide range of public or state enterprise services for children, including kindergartens, milk kitchens, holiday camps and after-school care centres.

In 1990 the Soviet Union disintegrated, and Kazakhstan became an independent nation, initially reluctantly. A few entrepreneurs, often well-placed communist officials in a former life, made fortunes buying state businesses and concessions at knock-down prices, and then capitalizing the profits. The great majority of the population had the ground kicked from under them as welfare safety nets abruptly disappeared, jobs were lost and salaries remained unpaid. The state enterprises, the factories, mines and collective farms, were broken up and if possible sold. With them went the welfare services that they had provided.

In 2003 I visited a rural district in the Pavlodar region of the steppes, where there had once been a collective farm. It had offered employment to the local village population, two kindergartens, health services, water and sanitation systems, and ensured local food distribution and transport services. It provided local entertainment facilities, youth clubs and organized holidays. All this disappeared within the space of a year or so in the early 1990s. There is now high unemployment. The kindergartens have closed, most of the health services can only be obtained by visiting the city, at considerable time and expense; the water system has broken down through lack of maintenance and the poorest families must buy water. Others, who can afford it, have dug wells. Few goods are available in the local store. Some fields were bought by local entrepreneurs and are being farmed, but much of the land is fallow, and equipment lies rusting. Only the local school remains, valiantly attempting to keep the local community together. Some of the mothers we met, although grateful to the school, were overwhelmed and helpless. One woman told us that she could not afford to travel to the city to obtain a simple eye test for her child. How would her son manage at school if he could not see?

This disintegration was not unique to Kazakhstan. The break-up of the Soviet Union and its satellites, and the extent to which the process of transition was accelerated and exacerbated by poor economic advice from international organizations such as the International Monetary Fund, has been well-documented (Stiglitz 2002). So has the rapid impoverishment of women and children (Falkingham 2000; Bernard et al. 2000). In the worst years of transition, average income fell by 50 per cent, with women more likely to be out of work than men. Many mothers, even with good qualifications, feared that they would never get another job. 'It's impossible for women over 40 to find a job . . . that's my fate, children', one mother, a trained accountant, told us sadly. At the same time as incomes plummeted, education, health and welfare expenditure also fell dramatically. In Kazakhstan in the first five years after transition the proportion of GDP spent on social security decreased by about 90 per cent, and education and health spending by more than 50 per cent. Falkingham comments that:

> Given that in the Central Asian region children take pride of place within the family and, culturally, are prioritized within the family's hierarchy of needs, the observed levels of malnutrition amongst young children and growing absences from school are indicators of a society in severe distress. Families alone have been unable to protect children from the negative outcomes associated with transition. Governments in Central Asia need to intervene, both to protect the future human capital of their countries, and to minimize the multiple risks of material and capability poverty children face during transition.
>
> (2000: 21)

In Kazakhstan, as in other Central Asian republics, the story of Soviet breakdown intertwines with a reasserted nationalism. The Kazakh president, Nursultun Nazarbayev, a former top communist official and a member of the senior of the three Kazakh clans (now one of the world's richest men through his ownership and development of what were previously state assets), considered it important to try to reassert Kazakh nationality. Kazakhs were appointed to important political and official positions. The Kazakh language was reintroduced as an official language, alongside Russian; and Kazakh traditions and heritage have become part of the school curriculum. There has been a widespread emigration/ repatriation of non Kazakhs to Russia and Germany. The majority of the population are now Kazakh, although Kazakhstan is still a diverse country and there has been a great deal of inter-marriage between groups. There are still 130 nationalities represented and they are tolerantly treated, although many Russians say they experience discrimination.

Kazakhstan is relatively fortunate. There has not been civil war as in Tajikistan or Kyrgyzstan, and there is not political repression, as in Uzbekistan and Turkmenistan. Kazakhstan has valuable natural resources, in particular oil and gas, and it is governed moderately well. Despite some extremes of wealth and poverty, it is still a more equal country than the UK, as measured on the Gini index (31.2 as against 36 for the UK and 40.8 for the USA). On most human development indicators it ranks about 76th in the world, ahead of the other Central Asian republics, although it is ranked lower on environmental issues and on transparency. A recent report commissioned by the UNDP on perceptions of corruption in Kazakhstan suggests that people believe corruption is widespread. Their view is that the most effective way to combat it would be to improve standards of living and address inequality – in the authors words, the 'pre-conditions for corruption'. Ordinary citizens are often fatalistic about corruption. One is quoted as saying 'Corruption will always be there, and although we can mitigate it, we will never be able to eradicate it . . . the entire system is based on bribes' (UNDP 2003a: 35).

Kazakhstan is in the throes of transition. Its turbulent recent history affects what services are available for children and who gains access to them. Hopes and expectations are shifting rapidly. Services strongly reflect their Soviet heritage, yet at the same time, there are conflictual pressures for change and development. The government is secular, but is keen to stress the values of a Kazakh upbringing. It is not altogether clear what this national identity is, over and above reviving the language, respect for physiognomy and dress, and honouring the remnants of forgotten or dying traditions such as living in a yurt (round felt tent). The government at the same time also wishes to become and be seen as part of the modern international community,[1] to provide services that match those of the developed world – although it is also not clear to those making the changes what the developed world might offer.

As a middle-income country Kazakhstan attracts less INGO interest than poor countries. The Soros Foundation which has an office in every transitional country is well represented and pursues its Stepping Stones project (see Chapter 4). The Asian Development Bank, World Bank, UNICEF, UNESCO, UNDP and other international and national NGOs analyse, aid and abet change, through research reports, advocacy and funding, and in the case of big donors, usually with conditionality agreements. There are also missionary groups, mainly Baptists and fundamentalist Christian sects.

## Early childhood services

The kindergartens in Kazakhstan, as elsewhere in the Soviet Union, were a demonstration of the importance the state ascribed to the upbringing of young children. The origins of this system in revolutionary Russia have been well described by Kirschenbaum (2001). By the 1960s and 1970s it was firmly embedded. Bronfenbrenner (1974) describes the Soviet kindergarten system in his book *Two Worlds of Childhood*. He praised their emphasis on mutuality and citizenship, and commented on the all-encompassing services they provided for children. His picture in retrospect seems a little rosy. Nevertheless it does justice to the extraordinary amount of care, intelligence and resources that went into developing the kindergarten system. The ossification and disintegration of this system, and current attempts to revive it, are discussed here.

At independence in 1990 Kazakhstan had the best preschool provision of any Central Asian republic, covering approximately 50 per cent of children under 7. There were 8,743 kindergartens, over half of which were in rural areas. Much of this provision was workplace based. In rural areas the local factory or collective farm employed most people in the district, and provided them with a range of health and welfare services including kindergartens. In towns and cities factories and industries also provided kindergartens for the children of their workers, often to a very high standard which included on-site swimming pools (heated throughout the sub-zero winters). Local authorities (oblast – region, or raion – district) provided kindergartens for those not already provided for in the workplace.

There was little, if any, difference between workplace and other kinder-gartens. Staff were trained in state teacher education institutes, and were offered state-run in-service training. Staff were paid the same wherever they worked. All kindergartens followed the same curriculum, and offered similar facilities. All the kindergartens were free. As the state owned the workplaces, and the government was highly centralized, this made educational and economic sense. However, once privatization was introduced, and the state's economic activities were drastically curtailed in favour of a private market, then the services offered by industrial and economic enterprises were calculated on an entirely different basis. Most large workplaces closed; those that remained could not easily accommodate facilities for workers in their profit and losses balance sheets. We visited one kindergarten that had previously been provided for airport workers. The airport had been privatized and expanded, but the new owners did not see why they should support the kindergarten. The kindergarten was one of several we saw that had been taken over by a local school, in order to try to keep it going.

As factories and collective farms closed, so did the services they provided. Seven out of eight kindergartens closed, the majority in rural areas. The number of children covered fell to 11 per cent in 1998. Education generally experienced problems, but the percentage of the education budget spent on kindergartens fell, and continues to fall (see Table 5.1). There are now 937 kindergartens left, although since 1999 the government has introduced part-time (minimum four hours) preschool classes for 5–6-year-olds in most schools.

Kindergartens have been neglected by default. I carried out an analysis of kindergarten budgets which showed the gap between government subsidy and the costs incurred by the kindergarten. All food costs – an expensive item – are now paid for directly by parents. Basic salaries and basic services – such as electricity and telephone – are met. But there is no budget for maintenance or other capital costs, and very little budget

*Table 5.1* Kindergarten share of the education budget (in tenge)

| Year | 1997 | 1998 | 1999 | 2000 | 2001 | 2002 | 2003 |
|---|---|---|---|---|---|---|---|
| Preschool budget (000s) | 5,253 | 3,999 | 2,481 | 2,976 | 3,322 | 3,880 | 4,307 |
| General education budget | 73,375 | 69,462 | 78,692 | 85,416 | 107,884 | 123,980 | 150,772 |
| Share of budget (%) | 7 | 5.75 | 3.1 | 3.48 | 3 | 3.1 | 2.85 |

Source: Ministry of Education.

for equipment. Staff benefits such as national insurance or holiday pay are being eroded.

A few kindergartens in the big cities which can tap into a more wealthy clientele are doing well, and operate as in their heyday, with teams of specialists and lavish premises.[2] But in general, in order to cover costs, kindergartens have to charge more fees and increase the numbers of children attending. Many kindergartens now house many more children than originally intended.

The result has been that although there is still considerable government subsidy for the kindergarten sector, only those families that are dual earner households or who earn considerably in excess of the basic wage can afford places. The average wage of a teacher or doctor, for example, in the local currency of tenge, is between T6,000–T12,000 per month. The average income of a parent using a kindergarten is T24,000 per month.[3]

## Government responses to the provision of preschool education

The government has been under constant, if low-level pressure, from international agencies to do something about its falling kindergarten enrolment. In particular the series of monitoring reviews of transitional countries (MONEE reports) from the UNICEF Innocenti Centre have provided many revealing studies about the situation (UNICEF 2000, 2002a). The UNESCO Education for All (EFA) agreement, ratified in Dakar, Senegal, in 2000, to which Kazakhstan is a signatory, also sets out the case for inclusive preschool provision. The first of six EFA goals put forward is to 'expand and improve comprehensive early childhood care and education especially for the most vulnerable and disadvantaged children'.

An analysis of options for the government in developing preschool provision was put forward in a 1995 World Bank Social Protection project analysis in Kazakhstan. Hensher and Passingham, who contributed to the analysis, wrote about it in more detail in a subsequent study. This study focused on the possibility of transfer of workplace (enterprise) kindergartens to the public sector. The study also emphasized the wider care and health benefits of the kindergarten system, but concluded that,

> given the reality of decreasing public finances, the government and the people of Kazakhstan face a choice between achieving more comprehensive provision of immediate preschool education for older

infants or a more explicit acceptance that the kindergarten system aims to provide childcare and early education for only a proportion of children '. . . [T]he alternative of shifting resources to schools may be of limited feasibility given the high utilization of capacity, and the non availability of resources to undertake significant modification or expansion of the school system's capital stock.' The study concluded that 'the attachment to subsidized childcare is deep-rooted in Kazakhstan and has long been regarded as an important entitlement'.

(Hensher and Passingham 1996: 312)

Nevertheless, faced with financial constraints, the government chose to introduce a system of part-time preschool classes within schools as an alternative to taking over the kindergartens. Enabling legislation was laid down in November 1999 in the Decree on Compulsory Preschool Education for Children and the implementation of the policy was detailed in the main regulations for preschool education and training (Republic of Kazakhstan 2001). By 2002 an estimated 70 per cent of children aged 5–6 attended four hours of preschool classes, from 8 a.m. to 12 a.m., in school terms.

There was therefore a major shift in preschool provision away from free-standing kindergartens to nursery classes attached to compulsory schools. The Kazakh government had the resources and the authority to implement the new system very quickly, within a period of three years. There have been a number of government papers outlining the role of the preschool sector.

The government's most recent 'Development Concept' issued as a Ministerial Discussion paper (February 2004) states that the goal of preschool is 'to ensure equal starting opportunities for children by gradually increasing coverage of children with preschool educational, recreational and correction programmes'. The main objectives of preschooling education and upbringing are:

• Improving the quality of preschooling for children;
• Life protection and strengthening children's health and the promotion of a healthy life-style;
• Harmonious personality development, satisfaction of the child's interests and development of abilities, formation of social and spiritual qualities.

The Kazakh preschool system aims to prepare children for school by giving them a sound grounding in the skills seen as necessary to cope with school. They should be able to enter school being able to form letters (Cyrillic) neatly; memorize, recite and count; and have a positive attitude towards the tasks they are expected to undertake. The system also takes responsibility for their health. In kindergartens, at least, children are well fed and closely monitored for any illness or disability.

All nursery classes and kindergartens must provide an option of Kazakh (as opposed to Russian-medium) classes. As with schools this has produced some difficulties over staffing, since all teachers were trained in Russian until relatively recently. In most schools and nurseries there is now a corner or a small room devoted to traditional Kazakh artefacts – a round felt tent with traditional hangings and implements; romanticized portraits of chieftains from the three clans; and drawings of famous Kazakh writers and poets. The way of life being celebrated is now remote for most people. Unlike in neighbouring Mongolia, the Soviet regime stamped out pastoralism in Kazakhstan. But the revival of Kazakh tradition and cultural values within all schools and kindergartens harks back to this pastoral tradition; the social and spiritual qualities draw on a partly mythical and vanished past.

Whilst kindergartens are still directly funded by the Ministry of Education, and their funding can be tracked, nursery education funding is not demarcated. A notional amount for nursery education is attached to the general allocation of the government budgets disbursed to the oblasts (regions). The Ministry of Education has also issued guidelines for setting up nursery classes. But it was left up to the local district and the school to allocate the money.[4] Often the amount allocated was insufficient to meet the guidelines. The problems noted by Hensher and Passingham about the school system's capital stock were unresolved. In our visits to school sites we found that the standard of provision in schools was, in almost all cases, less than that provided for kindergarten places.

The situation was further complicated by the fact that all kindergartens were allowed to introduce a free preschool nursery class for their eldest group. Since kindergartens already provided for the 5–6 age group, this had the effect of offering a subsidy to all children aged 5–6 *already* attending kindergartens – a perk to the better-off parents who tended to use the kindergartens.

There are various hybrid arrangements now starting to emerge by default (i.e. local arrangements for the use of buildings as described above) rather than by design. These include kindergartens based in schools, and private–public partnerships where private owners have bought the buildings but teaching staff are still provided by the oblast or raion. One of our case studies was a kindergarten taken over by a school.

The kindergarten had been a workplace nursery attached to a factory. The original building had been well-equipped and offered a range of services including a swimming pool. In order to save the kindergarten when the factory closed, it had been rehoused in the school in much more cramped accommodation. The kindergarten lost its director and was managed by the headteacher of the school. Many places were lost and staff dismissed. Age grouped classes were combined into multi-age groups. Access to specialist provision was curtailed. The training opportunities offered to staff were reduced. Staff felt that their concerns had a low priority within the school. They expressed a wish to move. Neither did parents express much confidence in the running of the kindergarten by the school. The school itself was a poor school, in a poor district, and it may be that poverty and poor resourcing was the overriding factor, rather than disregard of the claims of kindergarten teachers within the school.

The second case study was a public–private partnership. The kindergarten had originally been intended as a sanatorium for children with, or at risk of, tuberculosis. Referred children automatically received free places. Alongside the sanatorium was a normal kindergarten. A private operator had been persuaded to take out a long lease on the building but staff were still paid directly by the raion. The staff attended local in-service training, and there was little difference in operation between this private kindergarten and other public kindergartens. The sanatorium places were renegotiated, and a few places continued to be funded directly by the raion, but far fewer than before. Although the kindergarten was not very different from other kindergartens, and operated on very similar principles, the new autonomy of the Director was welcomed. Staff and parents expressed a much higher degree of satisfaction than did those in the school kindergarten. However, this kindergarten was also historically better resourced and offered a wider range of services than did the school-based kindergarten.

Perhaps the weakest aspect of the system – as elsewhere in the ex-Soviet Union and its satellites, is the exclusion of children with disabilities. The Soviets called the study of children with disabilities 'defectology' – a word coined by Vygotsky, who at one point was employed as a defectologist. Defectology meant identifying weaknesses and disabilities in children, and addressing them by carefully worked-out programmes of treatment in dedicated institutions. In some cases the remedies were good and worked[5] but arguably, for the most part, children were simply labelled, institutionalized and largely ignored. In Kazakhstan children with disabilities are sent to specialized kindergartens, where they are available, and subsequently to special schools. This policy, already problematic, has become completely untenable in the polluted region around the Aral Sea, where the level of congenital defects is so high, and a majority of children may have some kind of disability. This is rarely publicly discussed. This omission is particularly sad and ironic in view of the great emphasis on health and well-being of children in ordinary provision. Our remit in Kazakhstan did not permit us to investigate this issue further.

Nursery classes are replacing kindergartens, and the kindergartens themselves are changing. There are increasingly hybrid arrangements like the ones I have described. Yet despite the catastrophic cutbacks and the changes, there is still a national conception of early childhood as a universal service. At a political level, early childhood services feature in discussions about the education system; there is political concern and statements about the importance of the role of the state in the 'upbringing' of children, and making sure that their education includes moral and spiritual values, as well as instruction in reading and writing. There is an infrastructure for early childhood services at national, regional and local level. There are many competent and experienced people working in the sector, working against the odds perhaps, but with clear memories – and secret hopes – of what still might be achieved. There is support for training and curricula development, for inspection and advice through a system of 'methodologists' and regional training institutions.

## Parents' and preschool teachers' views of preschool services

Despite the closures and the cuts in subsidy, 12 years after transition, the high expectations, forged in the communist heyday, have proved remarkably resilient. The following comments are drawn from two case studies of kindergartens discussed above, the school-based kindergarten and the semi-private kindergarten.

> I am a housewife and don't have to send my children to the kindergarten. But I don't have enough knowledge in development and upbringing. They know how to do it in the kindergarten.

> I think that huge support to the family is rendered by the kindergarten director. She arranged a health complex in the kindergarten. There our children are either given aftercare, or health protection procedures (swimming pool, sauna, physiotherapy, herbal remedies). And all this is included in the kindergarten charge.

At this kindergarten our children get enough of high vitamin food, as there are a lot of vegetables, berries and fruit in the nutritional ration.

The kindergarten should have a family consulting room where parents with the help of a professional psychologist could share their experience and obtain information in regard to child development and upbringing.

This kindergarten is convenient for us because they have a round-the-clock group there. We work in the market and sometimes we have no opportunity to take the child home in the evening.

The preschool institution lacks some of the specialists and facilities necessary for the provision of quality preschool education and children's health monitoring – methodologist, speech therapist, swimming pool, gymnasium, etc.

These views of kindergartens as places that offer far more than a family can or should provide is uniquely Soviet. Kindergartens offer education *and* comprehensive childcare and health care, all nutritional requirements, specialist teaching services and a methodologist to oversee and help teachers. The teachers are regarded, both by themselves and parents, as highly professional and a fount of knowledge about children's upbringing. Western services, especially those in the English-speaking world, rarely aim to be so comprehensive. They do not usually offer such long hours, provide specialist teaching and supervision of teaching. It would be *extremely* unusual to have specialist rooms such as music rooms, gymnasiums or swimming pools. Nurseries would not see it as part of their remit to oversee children's nutrition, rest or exercise, nor to provide detailed health monitoring, nor to employ specialists or supernumerary staff to deliver these services. Nor do services in the West usually inspire such confidence from those who use them.

The unique status of the kindergarten system is reflected in the fact that both the wealthiest and poorest families wish to use it for their children, although the latter are now unable to do so. In this context, preschool classes are seen by almost all parents as crumbs compared with what their children might otherwise receive in kindergarten. As Hensher and Passingham commented there is 'a danger that those children with the greatest needs, and those parents with the least political power, have the least access to the benefits that kindergartens offer' (1996: 550).

Reconciling access and uptake to these different forms of provision – kindergartens and preschool classes – would seem a priority for the government.[6]

Parents greatly value the comprehensive approach of kindergartens above the provision offered by nursery classes. The (mostly poor) parents who took part in the focus groups we organized during our visits to a range of kindergartens across the country were grateful for nursery class places, but still continued to express a preference for kindergarten places, where they felt that social benefits to their children were greater. They also consider that those children who start kindergarten at the age of 3 or 4 have an advantage over their own children who cannot start until the age of 5.

Several consultancy reports, undertaken between 1990 and 2000 suggested that the demand for kindegarten places had dropped. We found no evidence for a drop in demand, only evidence of lack of affordability. Instead of being used as a redistributive social policy, kindergartens are in effect supporting a relatively well-to-do minority of families, and further exacerbating social divisions. Those unable to afford kindergarten fees regard themselves as socially excluded, as second-class citizens.

Those staff who have managed to retain their jobs in kindergartens also experience sharp losses as resources dry up and they are no longer able to provide what they once had and consider to be appropriate. Staff feel that they can no longer maintain the high professional standards of education and guidance they once offered to children and parents. Many staff are also aware that the material resourcing – toys, equipment and books, and building maintenance – in the West is far in excess of anything that they can afford, but they are unable to see the other side of the coin, which is that in terms of the range of services they offer, and the level of teaching they provide, they are still fortunate.

## The role of NGOs and INGOs in Kazakhstan

Kazakhstan has just emerged from a period when over half of its population, especially in rural areas, experienced stark and chronic poverty (Sange Agency 2001) but it is regarded internationally as a potentially wealthy and viable nation state. For this reason, apart from evangelical Christians, it has not attracted many international non-governmental organizations.[7] The role of voluntary organizations, or indeed any kind of civic society outside of official communist circles, is an unfamiliar one. Voluntary organizations are regarded with some suspicion, and have to register with the region or district bureaucracy.

The main exception is that the Soros Foundation, whose widespread role in transitional countries was discussed in Chapter 4, supports a number of kindergartens in Kazakhstan. These were selected on the basis of competition. Kindergartens were invited to bid to become eligible for Soros grants, to become demonstration kindergartens. The successful bidders we saw tended to have the most affluent users, and to charge the highest fees.

Soros gives grants for resources to the kindergartens in order to assist them in providing a child-centred, individualistic pedagogic approach – although not in any way curtailing their range of services. The Soros rhetoric, explicitly taken from Head Start in the USA, is that individualism is a good thing, and developing individual autonomy is best achieved by giving children a choice between many toys and games, set out in 'corners' or 'work stations'. Soros kindergartens were as generously equipped as any Western nursery. The children using the Soros kindergartens also seemed – to my eye – more spoilt and sulky than elsewhere, as if, having been indulged, they saw no reason to co-operate. Children undertook tasks on their own without reference to other children; or ignored the teacher, or misbehaved; all behaviour unheard of in an ordinary Kazakh kindergarten!

The Soros rejection of the collective ethos of the Soviet era in favour of USA-style individualism and consumerism has produced a mixed reception amongst parents and staff. The resources Soros provide are eagerly sought. In a resource-poor environment, unlimited books, stationery, equipment, furniture, and best of all refurbished buildings, are precious indeed. On the other hand the Soros interventions are some-times seen as proselytizing, a triumph of the West over communism. 'Everything Soviet is seen as bad; it is insulting', as one parent informant told us. 'I removed my child from their kindergarten.' On the other hand, any discussion about increasing children's autonomy is potentially very challenging in an authoritarian system.

UNICEF is attempting to develop community-based, self-help models in rural areas, but these are at an early stage and have not yet succeeded in becoming established. As this chapter has stressed, there is a deep and widespread belief that preschool provision should be a state-provided service. It maybe that in the absence of any other provision, community groups and parent education will be seen as better than nothing. As in other Central Asian republics, it is likely to be an uphill task to establish them.

# Conclusion

The concept of preschool services in Kazakhstan is much broader than in the West, where preschool generally has a much narrower focus on learning. It is more or less unheard of in OECD countries to provide the range of services and facilities that Kazakhstan (and other ex-Soviet republics and ex-communist countries) take for granted as an indication of quality in their kindergartens. Even although these kindergartens are now being disbanded in favour of an extra year at school in many transitional countries, their remnants evoke admiration.

The kindergarten system is undoubtedly authoritarian by Western standards.[8] But so is Kazakh society generally, if one can make a generalization about so mixed and transformed a society. Pedagogies in the West are generally more child-centred and open-ended in their approach, but rely considerably on good resourcing – a generous supply of books, toys and equipment – which is simply unavailable elsewhere.

But what is so striking about Kazakh kindergartens – and other ex-soviet systems – is the amount of care, attention and ambition that went into setting them up in the first place. The history of Soviet kindergartens is slowly being written (Kirshenbaum 2001). It seems very likely that they contributed to the extraordinary changes in literacy in the Central Asian populations, from very low levels in the 1920s to very high levels by 1990. However disregarded they may appear now, the kindergartens offer some lessons about setting up and maintaining an early education and care system in the most unpropitious of circumstances in remote and poor regions of the world.

# Chapter 6

# Swaziland

## Summary

This chapter explores early education and care in Swaziland, a small, traditional country of about one million people in Southern Africa, bordered by South Africa and Mozambique. Just as Kazakhstan bears the indelible imprint of the Soviet Union, Swaziland was shaped by the British Empire. Colonial traditions permeate the country, from the bacon, egg, porridge and scones served for breakfast in the hotels to the most minute structures of government. I discuss the history of government and the role of the monarchy in Swaziland, and how these impact on the delivery of early childhood services. The provision is mostly ad hoc and offers a very low key service to children; it does very little to relieve the poverty or improve the prospects of the 15 per cent of children who attend. Above all, children's lives are affected by HIV/AIDS. An estimated 15 per cent of households are child-headed. The exceptionally vulnerable position of young children in Swaziland is an issue which should concern anyone involved with children.

Much of the material I use here was originally obtained as part of interviews, field trips that I undertook and documentation obtained in 2003 as part of a consultancy commissioned by the EU under the EDF9 education programme. I was part of a team reviewing the Swazi education sector (although I am responsible for the interpretation of the data presented here).

## Introduction: the governance of Swaziland

Swaziland is a tiny country in Southern Africa, whose independence as a separate state was only precariously established last century. It has a population of little over a million, although this is now falling because of HIV/AIDS. There are also many Swazis in South Africa. In the north it is very hilly and beautiful, and a draw for tourists – although erosion is changing the landscape. In the south of the country it is flatter, drier and hotter, and drought has been a severe problem. Swaziland has been in receipt of food aid from the World Food Organization on and off for some years (although there are also extensively irrigated sugar plantations in the south, owned by multinational corporations). Swaziland is ranked 133rd out of 175 in the 2003 world development index (South Africa is ranked 111). It is classified as a 'middle-income' country. It has a GDP per capita of US$4,367 but it is also one of the world's most unequal countries – its gini index rating is 60.9 (UNDP 2003b).

In Chapter 4, I pointed out that an explicit tactic of the British Empire was 'divide and rule'. Mamdani (1996) has analysed how this was applied in Africa, where local chieftains were given authority over their subjects – backed up by the armed forces of the Empire when necessary – in return for compliance with colonial rule.

Swaziland is a prime example of this policy. But in the case of Swaziland, there was an exceptionally able and long-lived chieftain/king, Sobhuza II, who neatly out-manoeuvred his colonial masters.

Sobhuza became King of the Swazis after a period of regency, in 1918, in the midst of colonial squabbles between Britain and South Africa about the future of Swaziland. He might easily have become another South African chieftain, ruling over a small province, propped up by a racist regime.[1] For a long time he was treated in just those terms, and received a substantial allowance from the British to govern the natives.

But Sobhuza was clever and adroit; he was anxious to preserve Swaziland's autonomy as a nation, and to reject attempts to reduce his position to that of a minor and irrelevant chieftain. He went to Johannesburg to hear the famous anthropologist Bronislaw Malinowski speak. After hearing him, Sobhuza invited him to Swaziland to visit his kingdom, and to assign a researcher to document his people's customs and traditions.

Malinowski did both. The anthropologist who came with him was called Hilda Kuper, and she was gifted and thorough. Sobhuza had reinstated many rituals and traditions that had fallen into disrepute or disuse and gave them sacramental status. In her book *An African Aristocracy*, and in her subsequent biography of Sobhuza, Kuper detailed – and legitimated – the daily rituals and complicated and mystical rites that were used to confirm the authority of kingship.

Sobhuza convincingly justified his absolute power through these ritual practices and through a system of seeking advice and taking soundings about all decisions within the chieftaincy system. The king's function was to be his people's symbolic representative and the slave of his people's wishes or needs; a function replicated by chiefs at the local level. 'If a chief does good it is because his people are good; if he does evil it is because his people let him. A chief must feel with his people and take his stand with their wishes, not from his own self-interest' (Kuper 1978: 113). Sobhuza made decisions after consulting with a council of handpicked, mainly royal advisers. When controversial matters arose, he held councils with his chieftains or even with the public. In these councils important matters were discussed and consensus reached.

Swazi society is polygamous, and those rich or powerful enough to do so took many wives. Sobhuza, as king, saw himself as having a duty to procreate. He took a new wife almost every year and had more than 100 children, referred to as 'the eggs of the nation'.

Sobhuza was hardworking and relatively modest in his lifestyle. He had enormous dignity and a gift of rhetoric. He was widely admired as a servant of the people, and as a nation builder, who preserved the independence of Swaziland against successive South African regimes and British colonial attempts to redraw national boundaries. He avoided bloodshed and strived for peace at a time when apartheid violence ravaged Mozambique and South Africa.[2] Throughout his long reign he moderately but resolutely opposed colonial exploitation and the appropriation of tribal land by white farmers – although he accumulated it for himself and his many wives and children.

He objected to the imposition of parliamentary democracy in the run-up to independence in 1969, and argued that his council of chieftains was more democratic and better reflected Swazi custom and practice. 'If only we could be able to extricate Africa from this idea of one man, one vote . . .' (Kuper 1978: 217). A British-style parliamentary system was nevertheless imposed, with some concessions given to customary law and adjudication. In 1973, four years after independence was granted, Sobhuza suspended parliament indefinitely, and for the rest of his reign, ruled as king without parliamentary intervention. Yet such is his reputation that even today, 20 years after his death, he is spoken of by ordinary Swazis with the deference and respect accorded to Mandela in South Africa. Kuper describes his reign as an attempt to realign race, class and nationalism. 'Swaziland provides a classic example of the interaction of race, class and nationalism – three overlapping but analytically distinct factors motivating political action and receiving different weightings at different times and situations' (1980: ix).

The present king, Mswati III, was one of Sobhuza's youngest sons. He was educated in an English public school, but was plucked from his English education at the age of 18 to become king. Parliament has been reinstated, but it operates alongside the king's own appointees, the Council of Advisers. All senior officials in the ministries are appointments made by consent of the king. This dual system of governance and customary law has several times broken down, most recently when the king abducted a schoolgirl as a bride. Donors are heavily pressurizing the king to adopt a constitution that limits his powers and demarcates between state and kingship.[3]

'Culture' is always located in time. Just as Sobhuza successfully reintroduced and reinvented certain traditions, the culture is now buckling under the tensions of accelerated capitalist consumerism and a weak king. Levin (1997) has shown how the monarchy under Sobhuza and under the present king has legitimated the accumulation of land and wealth by the aristocracy.[4] Mswati has adopted all the royal privileges of his father, including polygamy. He presently has eleven wives (the abductee was the tenth), all of whom receive generous state allowances. He does not appear to have his father's sense of service or his frugality and perceives himself as having first call on the country's budget.[5]

Swazis are divided about the king and chieftaincy system. Many are deferential, and are very uncomfortable or resent any criticism from outsiders about it. Kingship and chieftaincies define and give dignity and meaning to Swazis' daily existence; it provides a context in which they can place themselves. To criticize the king and chieftains is to criticize the people. Kuper argued that 'Swazi accept economic and social inequality and approve of wealth as the privilege of men of noble birth' (1980: 154).

Others, including many exiled Swazis, are cynical and say the kingship is an anachronism that cannot continue.[6] Donor agencies are split between trying to use the chieftaincy system on the grounds that it is the best way to reach the rural poor; and those who insist that more constitutional changes must take place before more aid is forthcoming.

These tensions between Western-style governance and local tradition have been brought to a head because of Swaziland's current economic and social position. It was classified by the World Bank and others as a middle-income country in the South (although at the bottom of the group of middle-income countries). It is less eligible for donor aid than very poor countries, and many donors have withdrawn their support.

But the overall level of income, on which such judgements are made, masks gross inequality. As pointed out above, Swaziland is one of the world's most unequal countries. It is agriculturally productive. It has profitable forestry and sugar industries (part owned by members of the royal family). As a legacy from distribution of land in the colonial era, many whites, including South Africans, own farms and businesses in

Swaziland. There is a successful tourist industry centred around game parks and lodges, mainly owned by whites. The celebratory dances and rituals associated with kingship feature heavily in the tourist trade. The king is a tourist attraction, a manifestation of 'genuine' African culture. There is a large handicrafts industry, also largely organized by white entrepreneurs. Swaziland's privileged trade relationship with the EU has attracted Asian entrepreneurs, mainly in garment manufacture and in handicrafts, who are thus able to access European markets.

As elsewhere, the poor, especially the rural poor, have very little. They are wage labourers dependent on seasonal employment. Many still work in the South African mines. The land tenure system – tribal land is communal and its use is governed by the chieftains – has resulted in significant erosion. The last few years have been drought ridden (despite the major irrigation projects for the sugar industry) and large areas of the country have been dependent on food aid for survival.

Some donors, most notably DfID,[7] argue that governance is now the critical issue in Swaziland. Until the government has real powers and the judiciary is independent, all development monies are likely to benefit the king directly; or to be spent on showy projects that bolster his prestige.[8]

But all these contradictions of governance, and the modernization and development of trade have been thrown into crisis by the epidemic of HIV/AIDS.

## HIV/AIDS in Swaziland

HIV/AIDS is the most immediate and overwhelming issue facing Swaziland. Reliable data suggest that 38.6 of pregnant women are seropositive, that is, they will die, probably messily and painfully, within six to eight years. Unless they have access to neprovirene, a drug that inhibits or prevents mother-to-child transmission of HIV/AIDS, their children will also die before they are 5.[9] Approximately 25–30 per cent of all children in Swaziland are orphans, that is they have lost one or both parents (but if they have lost one parent, they will almost certainly lose the other). Around 10–15 per cent of households are child-headed, that is the main carer is a person under 18 (Whiteside *et al.* 2003).

This scale of death is unimaginable in the North. We consider children need support and counselling and all the resources of the state if they lose one parent through a traumatic event – or even if they lose an acquaintance, a friend at school, for example. In Swaziland, by contrast, the painful deterioration and death of parents, cousins, aunts, uncles, brothers and sisters are everyday events; they frame daily life. Many people explained to me the pervasiveness of the catastrophe. 'Children are already caring for sick parents before coming to school; they do not know whether their parents will still be alive when they come home' (regional guidance counsellor). 'Saturdays used to be funeral days. Now we bury on Thursdays, Fridays, Saturdays and Sundays and it is not enough' (community worker).

The impact of HIV/AIDS is similar to the Black Death in Europe in the Middle Ages when three out of ten Europeans were wiped out. The difference is that the Black Death struck rapidly; the development of symptoms was followed immediately by death. With HIV/AIDS it can take years of infection before debilitating symptoms show in an individual. By then it is too late to prevent the spread of infection to others, especially if the individual concerned has had many sexual liaisons.

Barnett and Whiteside (2002) argue that, like other epidemics, the incidence and spread of HIV/AIDS is not accidental. It is harder to diagnose, prevent, mitigate or treat under certain social conditions. The epidemic is invariably worse in unequal, unstable societies where migration is common, poverty is rife, levels of education are low, and where health services are too fragmentary to offer diagnosis or treatment. It is compounded in those countries where the state has dubious legitimacy – the colonial legacy of 'decentralized despotism' that has become the case for much of Africa, and for Swaziland in particular.

The HIV/AIDS epidemic spans many years, and its effects are cumulative, skewing populations. Children, and the elderly, rather than adult earners, predominate. As Alex de Waal comments:

> According to traditional patterns of life expectancy, a child who reaches adulthood might be expected to live for a further four or five decades. This forty or fifty years of adult life is the unexamined foundation of much of our economic and social life, and of our economics. On it is based the further expectation of handing on assets and skills to one's children and living to be a grandparent . . . it sustains the complex world of institutions which require people with prolonged personal experience to staff them. We are only just beginning to understand what happens to a society in which these assumptions no longer hold good.
>
> (2003: 13)

## Childhood in Swaziland

Procreation in the kingship system is a natural duty. Having as many children as possible is a good thing, to perpetuate the lineage and as a security for old age. Children are valued and cherished, but they are also there to serve their family. Obedience is a pre-requisite, enforced by physical punishment. Kuper comments that the scope of the individual is defined by age–class–gender boundaries ' "respect and obey your elders" . . . its meaning is, when necessary, beaten into the young, but usually less drastic teaching is sufficient' (Kuper 1980: 117).

Sobhuza frequently reflected on upbringing and childhood:

> A person will bring up his children in the spirit that they are his children, his responsibility and the future prop of his declining years. Even if he beats the child he only does so in order to teach him or give him training of some kind, and when he is grown, the child will say 'oh, how my father did beat me' but the father will be in a position to say 'I wanted you to be a man and by my discipline I have brought you to what you are now'.
>
> (Kuper 1978: 211)

Sobhuza valued education and made attempts to introduce schools for Swazis during the colonial era when the only schools available were for whites. But he held that 'true education is more than book learning, wisdom is greater than knowledge' (Kuper 1978: 105). Such wisdom comes with age, and Western education must be viewed cautiously. 'Why should our children be taught to despise our customs and disobey their elders' (Kuper 1978: 155). Young people with education should still be deferential to those older than themselves. Kuper commented that she often heard older youths being told 'Be quiet. You are still young. You know nothing' (1980: 117).

In this traditional system, girls have even less authority and status. The school system is not discriminatory in that girls and boys attend in equal numbers. There are also significant numbers of women in public life (almost all from senior clans). But, nevertheless, girls are expected to be more domestically orientated and more compliant, especially in sexual matters.

One of my most interesting informants in Swaziland was a history teacher, a distant member of the ruling royal family, and utterly opposed to it.[10] She was particularly concerned about the everyday treatment of children. She said that physical beatings in schools were commonplace, even for trivial occurrences such as being late, even if it was through no fault of the child. Children were also beaten at home. Children had no voice, and although Swaziland was a signatory to the Convention on the Rights of the Child, children's rights had little currency.

In 'traditional' culture children were subjugated, but they also had a place. They were an integral part of a close kinship system, united under a local chieftain. Their identity was shaped and directed by that wider community. The HIV/AIDS epidemic has turned that world upside down. The UNICEF 2001 Swaziland Progress Report on the position of orphans and vulnerable children comments that children have

> lost parents or have become nurses to their own ailing caretakers. They have been forced to drop out of school for want of fees, or to labour or scavenge for food. They live in collapsing homes under leaking roofs, in a world of fear and collapsing hopes, often surrounded by human predators who thrive in a social environment which is itself collapsing under the weight of AIDS.
>
> (2001: 5)

As parents die, if the children are fortunate, women, mainly elderly women, step in. Grandmothers look after their grandchildren; sympathetic women in the local community try to help out. The maid who cleaned my room was a grandmother who was looking after three young children, two of whom were her grandchildren. I asked how she managed, especially since one of the children was not even a relative.

> She is not really mine but she comes. That is why I say I have three. She comes and says 'can I get under the blanket?' What can you do? You cannot say no. She has a stepmother and she is not happy there.

The central assumption of child-rearing in the North is that children grow up in a benign environment, where adults – mothers, fathers and close family, or paid carers – will look after them. Their living spaces will be safe and their basic needs will be met. All the psychological investigation of children's behaviour and capacities is underwritten by this assumption. In many countries, especially those afflicted by HIV/AIDS, this assumption does not hold good. Children's resilience, solidarity, capacity for sharing, their stamina, their sense of time, place and the future, are rarely conceptualized or investigated. But these are the attributes that will enable them to survive in Swaziland and countries like it.

## Early education and childcare in Swaziland

I have provided this long introduction to try to show how the social and economic context sets the frame for what is provided in early education and care. Long as it is, I have left out a great deal, including any discussion of the education and health systems. These are modelled on those of the North. The capacity and efficiency of education and health systems are critical for children's survival. Like all other aspects of government, they reflect the struggle between tradition, modernity and inequality.

What follows is a description, and then an analysis, of the early education and care system. Under the British colonial regime, the preschools that existed were freestanding nursery schools. This model persists, and the weak regulatory framework that exists is cast on the assumption that preschool is freestanding, and operates on a termly basis, adopting school holidays. Hours are usually 8 a.m. to 1 p.m.

There is a large private sector, where the medium of teaching is mostly English rather than Siswati. Some of this private provision is highly sophisticated, on a par with European nurseries in the range of activities and the resources provided. Much of it is designed to prepare children for school, which does not begin until the age of 7. The children of whites and of the black elite – the royal family, the aristocracy and senior government officials – usually attend such schools.

Most preschools are community based, however; small enterprises (so poor that to speak about profit or non-profit is irrelevant) run by community groups or churches in whatever local space is available. In rural areas, the community (the church and/or the local chieftain) chooses the person to work in the preschool from within the local community. All provision, private and community is self-supporting from fees. There is no government support. Some community-based nurseries have donor support but most struggle from day to day.

A comprehensive survey of preschool provision was undertaken in 1987 by Magagula. The survey identified 210 preschools: 83 urban and 127 rural, catering for 7,855 preschool pupils aged between 2 and 10. The majority (61 per cent) were community based. Facilities in some preschools were limited. In at least 17 per cent of preschools there was no direct water supply. Only 35 per cent of preschools had outside space or gardens, and of those, only 58 per cent were fenced. In 52 per cent of preschools, there were no books and inadequate learning materials.

A second survey was funded by UNICEF and carried out by officials from the Ministry of Education in 2001. This survey was intended to update the picture of preschool provision in Swaziland. The analysis of the data was not completed, but I reworked the raw data, to provide information about the current situation. The survey collected returns for 813 centres,[11] catering for 17,281 children, or an estimated 14.6 per cent of the population of 3–6-year-olds. These centres have been opening at a steady rate since the previous survey was undertaken.

Approximately 34 per cent of centres are private, and 66 per cent are community based. A typical community-based centre caters for between 15 and 25 children, and charges between 150 and 300 emalangeni (E)[12] per term. 'Teachers' are paid on average between E100 and E500 per month. Approximately 60 per cent of centres have electricity; 75 per cent have water; and 35 per cent have fenced and equipped outside playspace. Generally the higher the income of the preschool, the better the services it offered. The poorest preschools offered least to children. Very few of the community-based preschools in rural areas that I visited had books, play materials, furniture, outside play equipment or fencing.

The data about qualifications of staff is confusing. There is no pre-requisite for working in preschool. Many of the staff have not gone beyond grade 5 of primary school (i.e. left school at the age of 12). Only one man was recorded as working in preschool, and he was wheelchair-bound and illiterate. His community designated him as a suitable person to care for children.

In Shiselweni, the poorest of the four Swazi regions, some fees are as low as E20–30 per term ($3 dollars). These fees may be paid irregularly, and may not be sufficient to cover the teacher's salary, who may then decamp until more money can be found. The fees leave nothing over for materials, equipment or maintenance. Also, in Shiselweni less than 10 per cent of centres have electricity and outside playspace.

At the other extreme, in large private urban preschool centres, fees may be as high as E2,000 per term and the most senior qualified teachers can earn as much as E3,000 per month. For those that can afford it, preschool provision is a good preparation for school. For the poorer communities, preschool centres are makeshift arrangements surviving on very few resources.

Preschool centres, like schools and other institutions, were not designed to cater for orphans and vulnerable children (OVCs). If they do, on the whole, they are too poorly resourced to be able to offer extra support over and above what is already offered. Most preschool centres for example, although they are open for at least four hours, do not provide food or drink. There are, however, a few centres, run mainly by small NGOs, that do specifically offer support to OVCs.

There is one preschool inspector based at the Ministry of Education, and one in each of the regions, who are nominally responsible for regulation of preschool and who try to offer some in-service training. As noted above, the regulatory schemes are a left-over from colonial times, and require unobtainable and unenforceable facilities (kitchen, sickbay, sanitation, outdoor equipment, etc.). The inspectorial team try to provide some in-service training but are hampered by lack of transport and lack of funds. A rural preschool might be visited, exceptionally, once every three years.

The preschool sector has grown up on an ad hoc basis without governmental support. In the poorest communities centres are barely self-sustaining, and offer relatively little input for children. A standard method for schematizing problems used by development agencies is 'a problem tree', showing how issues relate to and lead on from one another. The problem tree for early childhood in Swaziland is shown in Figure 6.1. The early childhood sector is self-supporting; there is no legal framework in place and no government strategy for dealing with early childhood. The result is that preschools benefit only a few children whose parents can pay for decent services. For everyone else, even orphan children, it is too ad hoc and too low key to offer much more than minimal care. There are no measurable outcomes, and it would be foolish to suppose that, except for the few centres that have enough money to operate, it prepares children for school or for any other social or educational development. It is a far cry from the rhetoric embedded in the first of the six goals, spelt out in Education for All. Early childhood development and care cannot change inequality and injustice; it merely reflects it.

## The role of NGOs and INGOs in Swaziland

In the absence of any strong governmental policy or commitment towards providing asocial welfare, there have been a plethora of small initiatives, one replacing the other. A project that has been funded by one donor on a short-term basis of three years may have to seek other donors, if the original donor decides to reschedule its programmes or decides that the project is now 'sustainable'. We visited one preschool project that was just about to lose its funding from a German church organization; it had previously been funded by two other, unrelated donors. It was now casting around for a replacement donor.

Some churches and small national and international organizations support preschools.[13] Whatever the rationale may have been for opening such preschools in the past, the main motivation for opening them now is to provide some kind of safe space for vulnerable children. Invariably, in rural areas, these preschools are set up with the permission of, and in

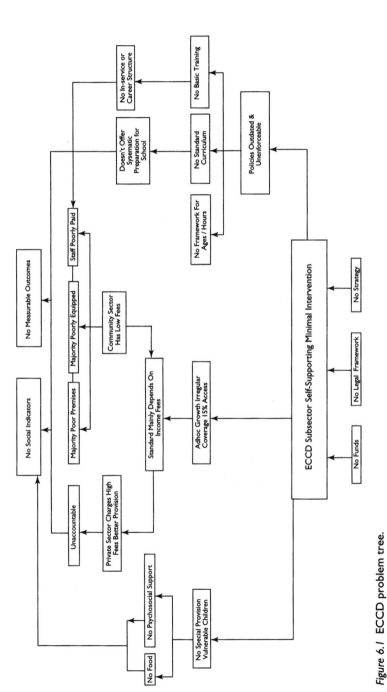

*Figure 6.1* ECCD problem tree.

space granted by the local chief. His blessing is perceived as crucial in mobilizing community support. As a matter of protocol he must be asked, even if he takes his time to reply and has to be won over. He is also regarded as having an important role in identifying those children who are likely to be most in need of help.[14]

The most active donor in supporting the preschool system has been UNICEF. UNICEF offices operate under the aegis of principles laid down by the headquarters in New York. The current prescription requires country offices to take a 'human rights approach' in programme planning. As I have been arguing, this kind of blanket prescription cannot be applied in any straightforward way to Swaziland – or to any other country. UNICEF, like other international donors, is often criticized as an ineffective agency, too much in thrall to Euro-American thinking.[15] However, in Swaziland, the UNICEF office is exceptionally good. The head of the office, in his spare time, has written a series of children's books, illustrated by a local artist, that wittily draw on traditional folktales, to highlight the plight of children and the dangers they face. These stories were piloted with local groups, and have been very successful. More than 17,000 copies of each story have been distributed by churches and used for communal story-telling.

UNICEF has also sponsored the survey reported above. It has facilitated new discussions on policy and regulation of preschools, that it hopes will be taken up by the Ministry of Education. It has also provided practice guidelines. Using a local consultant and working with local people, it has published a manual for caregivers and trainers. This models conventional ideas about development and play, but puts them into a local context. The modules are:

- Health, nutrition and safety
- Language and books
- Pre-reading and pre-writing
- Getting ready for maths
- Discovering our world (pre-science)
- Arts and crafts
- Movement, music and culture
- Good character.

UNICEF is also producing a basic series of leaflets for parents and caregivers modelled on this manual. It will highlight the position of young children affected by HIV/AIDS.

UNICEF is not in a financial position to provide preschools or crèches. But it has been able to support what it calls 'care points', centres for food distribution. In each care point a woman in the community is designated as 'a shoulder to cry on', a woman to whom children can go and talk, who will give them some comfort, as well as ensuring they get access to at least one meal a day. The care points are again designated by chiefs, and the local women involved are chosen by the community. I visited one of these care points. It consisted of a group of women in a stick and wattle enclosure, boiling soya porridge in a cauldron over an open fire. A group of despondent, ragged, listless small children sat on the ground outside the enclosure. One of the women did then come and take the youngest child by the hand and stood with her. Over 150 children came every day for the porridge. The women asked us for money to buy sugar: 'the children like it when it is sweet'. When I asked a UNICEF colleague whether these minimal 'care points', in their dependency on local chiefs, and their very basic provision, could be effective in providing support and protection for young children, he said patiently 'What else is there?'

## Conclusion

I have used the example of Swaziland to illustrate the complexities of the assumptions that are commonly made about early education and care as they are applied to the South. The dilemmas faced by anyone wishing to improve the lives of young children in the South include maintaining critical respect for culture and tradition; anger about the impoverishment and inequalities arising from globalization and its very damaging effects on young children; and urgent recognition of the exceptional crisis in the lives of children produced by HIV/AIDS. It requires enormous intellectual and emotional effort to address such dilemmas. These problems are a long way from the ordinary concerns of early childhood educators in the North, although perhaps not so far as we think. Scheper-Hughes and Sargent (1998), in taking an anthropological overview of children's situation and status, draw convincing parallels between the brutality of the lives of children in the inner cities of the USA and those of the poorest children in the favelas of Latin America.

An average crèche in a rural district in Swaziland might have 20 or 25 hungry children with one or two scarcely literate caretakers in a bare hut with a rough unfenced yard and an adjoining, slippery, pit latrine. In the poorest areas water is fetched laboriously from the bilharzia-infested river. Food, if it is supplied at all, is the soya porridge provided, at least this year, by the World Food Agency. The caretakers, or 'teachers' get paid only if and when the parents can afford the termly fee of E50 – about $6.

Are the children in Swaziland deserving of the same facilities and resources as those who use the best of provision – for example in Reggio Emilia? There, in immaculate, architect designed nurseries, freshly pressed orange juice is offered for a mid-morning snack, and in-service training for staff is weekly and ongoing. It is difficult to see the preschools in Swaziland as part of the same spectrum of childcare provision. The early childhood services that are affordable by poor people in Swaziland are of such a low quality as to be unrecognizable by the standards of the North.

Donors working in the South argue that their interventions must be 'sustainable', that is self-supporting; also that it does not make sense to offer childcare with much better conditions than those of the everyday life that children lead. Woodhead (1997) has argued for 'contextually appropriate' early childhood provision, matched to the level of the best of local circumstances. Childcare in Swaziland illustrates the limitations of such an argument (see also Chapter 8). In Swaziland local conditions vary enormously; the urban well-to-do can access relatively good preschool provision, but poor rural communities have very little. A relative approach leads to the position that the needs and entitlements of poor children are of far less significance than those of well-to-do children. In Swaziland preschools are embedded in their local communities, and the changes that might lead to their reform or development are also those required of their wider society. The complexities and difficulties in achieving more equitable treatment for children – and adults – are almost insuperable, and certainly long-term. Yet from the North we cannot ignore the plight of children whose survival is so precarious and whose lives are so painful, however difficult it might be to act.

# Chapter 7

# India

*Pawan K. Gupta*

**Summary**

This chapter describes the work of the Society for Integrated Development of Himalayas (SIDH) developing education in a Himalayan tribal district. SIDH originally aimed to bring mainstream education to remote communities, but gradually came to realize mainstream education was inappropriate, and that a more locally grounded education, stressing local values and priorities was more important and relevant to the lives people were leading. Mainstream education served to emphasize the inferiority of local people and increase their discomfort. SIDH chose to work with local people to develop a curriculum and a style of teaching that better reflected their own needs and concerns. SIDH continually tries to evaluate and monitor its work through small local research projects and investigations. A key series of research projects has been on the theme of family structure and the way that this influences participation across a range of activities. The chapter concludes with an examination of the damage wrought by modernity and 'development'.

## Introduction

SIDH (Society for Integrated Development of Himalayas) is a voluntary organization, based in Jaunpur, in the Tehri District of the central Himalayas. It is primarily engaged in educational activities. Pawan K. Gupta and Anuradha Joshi founded it in 1989. Today it has a team of 60 people – most of them local young people from Jaunpur. SIDH runs several schools located in remote villages, which cater for different age groups of children and young people. The villages of Jaunpur are small (about 15 families per village) and scattered.

SIDH has a fairly small programme having eight balwadis (ECCE centres for early childhood care and education for children under 6 years of age), three balshalas (balwadis upgraded to class 2), five primary schools (up to class 5), one elementary school (classes 6–8), and a high school (classes 9–10). In all, there are nearly 550 children in these 18 centres. Besides these, SIDH has a research and publication wing and several programmes for youth. It conducts several week-long residential courses in a year, for young people to discuss serious issues concerning their lives. It also runs a year-long residential course for young people in the 17–24 age group. There are no degrees or diplomas given at the end of the course and the emphasis is to make the youngsters think on their own (*how* to think instead of *what* to think) and at the same time learn a few skills that may help them in future to earn a livelihood. Students from this year-long programme have after passing out started their own initiatives in their own villages. These initiatives have taken various forms from setting up a small income-generating unit (e.g. a bakery) to setting up a school for the young children.

SIDH's primary schools are now about 80 per cent self-reliant and are managed by the community. Constant changes are made in teaching methodology, evaluation systems and curriculum. These changes are a result of constant self-reflection, internal critique, research and discussions with the community. Hence SIDH considers its school programmes as 'action research' and the focus is not on increasing their numbers but in taking the learning to others, mainly the government bodies. This is done by organizing seminars where government functionaries, academics and research scholars are invited to interact and discuss core issues. SIDH has also initiated an informal network of teachers – both from government and non-government schools – to take its learning to a larger audience.

SIDH also publishes journals and books (including handbooks for teachers). Recently, a new programme has been initiated with government and private schools in the locality for a closer interaction with both the teachers and students of those schools, on a regular basis. Students and teachers from schools in the Jaunpur area come to the SIDH campus to spend a few days interacting with the SIDH resource team in order to be able to teach using the local environment so that they can make learning more contextual and relevant to the everyday life of students.

SIDH's research wing, called Sanshodhan, is engaged in exploring the assumptions of the mainstream education system, its linkages with other larger systems of governance as well as the contradictions of the system and in the various beliefs of the community. It has conducted various studies; for instance to explore the assumptions and beliefs of the community about various aspects of education and school; a study to understand the impact of family structure on women and children and on the well-being of various people in the family; and a recent comparative study of textbooks prescribed by different pundits in India, in order to understand the hidden values being imparted to the children. These reports are published by SIDH and efforts are made to initiate discussion around the findings of these studies. Learning from these researches also feed into the various programmes conducted by SIDH.

This chapter emanates from 15 years of experience of working in the field of education with a village community in the central Himalayas. Jaunpur is in Tehri Garhwal district in the newly formed hill state of Uttaranchal, still quite rich in its culture and tradition, even though it is constantly under threat of being marginalized, by the instruments of modernization – primarily 'education' and the market. For many of us in India, as for all countries that were colonized, globalization is a new word for colonization.

## Beginning – the trap of 'backwardness'

When we started our work 15 years ago we were under the impression that education was only largely provided in schools and that it could only do 'good'. Although we were dissatisfied with the existing system, we felt privileged for having received the (mainstream) education, which had equipped us to derive benefit from the larger system. At that time we did not realize the basic contradictions in our thinking. How could we be dissatisfied with the larger system and yet feel privileged at having received the kind of education which largely equipped us to exploit it? Much later we realized that either we must accept this system – in which case there would be no need to do the kind of work we were doing, except perhaps to work simply as service providers, supporting and spreading the efforts of the State. But if we were of the view that the problems essentially stemmed from the basic framework of the system then how could we agree with the present mainstream education, which was designed in the first place to serve and support it?

It was a long, painful but interesting journey before this clarity came about. In the initial stages we were quite content doing 'literacy programmes' and increasing access into schools. We had a patronizing attitude – however hard we tried to camouflage it – of the privileged 'us' towards the poor 'them'. We also thought at that time that systems and technology were neutral and they could be used either for the benefit of mankind or to exploit/destroy it – depending on how one used them. We had not realized the power of the system and its instruments in moulding and influencing the individual and societies, in a predetermined manner.

We did not realize then that schools not only teach what is apparent but also impart many underlying values, beliefs and a particular world view in an almost invisible, subtle and unconscious manner.

In this world view there was a universal, standardized and linear definition of not only 'development' and 'progress' but also of 'education' and the 'educated', 'science' and 'scientific', 'modern', 'progressive', 'secular', etc. There was no space for diversity here except in a patronizing manner (e.g. the diversity seen in museums, craft fairs (*melas*) and food festivals) but all efforts were towards making everyone obedient citizens of 'one world'. In this world view the larger majority were 'backward' and a few Westernized individuals or societies were 'modern' and 'developed'. In this world view the rural India (or Indians) were backward and had to become like the urban India (or Indians) and the urban India (or Indians) had to become like Europe or America (or the Europeans and Americans) to become 'modern' and 'developed'. A linear, standardized path to 'development' and modernity was being promoted. But there was one particular flaw here among the many (such as the question of availability of natural resources in case the whole world were to achieve the same levels of consumption as the West), which we only realized much later. By the time – after years of struggle – rural India became (if it were at all possible) almost like urban India, and urban India came to be like Europe or America, the benchmarks of 'development' and 'progress' would have further receded on this linear and endless path to growth. Thus we were condemned to remain backward forever! We started wondering if backwardness was a reality or only a tool to steer societies in a particular direction.

## Learning

This questioning led us to listen to the people with whom we were working. In this process we also learnt what *listening* meant – also examining one's own assumptions. Women from the villages of Jaunpur were the great teachers who taught us to differentiate between education (*shiksha*) and literacy (*saksharta*), between wisdom and knowledge, between *samriddhi* (prosperity) and income, between *sukha* (happiness) and *suvidha* (facilities or conveniences). Basically they taught us to differentiate between *lakshya* or *sadhya* (the objective) and the *madhyam* or *sadhan* (the means). The process of this great learning was difficult and non-linear, sometimes not even falling in the domain of 'rationality'. These great teachers made many insightful observations about our schools, the students and the so-called educated.

'*Gaon ka padha shahar mein aur shahar ka padha videsh mein hi fit hota hai*' (a person educated in the village becomes suited to living in the towns and those educated in towns become suited for living abroad or in other words education is creating misfits in societies). 'So what is in it for us?'

(SIDH 1999)

'*Padh likh kar bache bigar jate hain aur barbad ho jate hain*' (children get spoilt and ruined after getting the education); '*padh likh kar ghar ka, hath ka kaam nahi hota*' (after education they cannot work with their hands and do household chores anymore).

(Ibid.)

'*Padha likha jyada beiman hota hai*' (the educated is more untrustworthy or dishonest); '*padhe likhe ko kam kaam karke jyada paise chahiye*' (the educated wants more money for doing less).

(Ibid.)

'*padhne likhne ke baad aadmi na ghar ka rahta hai na ghat ka*' (after being educated one is neither here nor there, or becomes good for nothing).

(Ibid.)

It was not that they were against education (these schools were started at the insistence of many such women), but these were expressions of their helplessness and pain at what the present education was doing to their young ones. They also expressed grief at the fact that their children stopped respecting their elders after getting 'educated', got alienated from everything their own, and started harbouring a false sense of pride which actually stemmed from a deep sense of inferiority and lack of self-esteem.

In another vein they said: '*bacho ko "hona" sikhao "dikhana" nahi*' (teach them to be, not just to *appear* 'good') (ibid.)

They laid stress on being rather than appearances or pretensions. They were talking of authenticity: '*Únko padhna nahi gunana sikhao*' (teach them how to live by the values not just how to read about them) (ibid.)

The conviction with which these women said: '*dharmi ki jad hari hari*' (one who follows the path of dharma will always be happy) or '*meri baat puri hogi*' (what I say will be done) showed the strength of their character. Here *dharma* as they used the word cannot be translated as religion. Rather it referred to a universal law by which all of us, our entire existence, is bound. According to them the 'educated' tend to loose this conviction in *dharma*.

These distinctions were profound and ones to which all great educationists from Mahatma Gandhi to Rabindranath Thakur to J. Krishnamurthy have frequently referred. But what was remarkable was that it was the simple women of this mountain region who were expressing them so naturally. It was indeed a manifestation of the great wisdom in this community. Slowly we started perceiving this community with a sense of respect. We also became convinced that these were not mere platitudes but that there was great substance and strength of character behind these words.

It was so obvious that the confidence of these women stemmed from somewhere within – call it faith or conviction – and did not depend on something outside or on another person. The confidence of the 'educated' on the other hand, usually depended on the 'other' or outside factors, and very often the confidence had a negative basis, as it depended on the 'other' not having – a particular skill/attitude or material possession – what they possessed. But the confidence of these so-called non-literate (but educated) women was unshakable, absolute. It was independent of any comparisons. The sad part was that education was taking away this intrinsic confidence by eroding the faith and conviction, which essentially came from their cultural roots.

They also explained to us that there was no correlation between income and prosperity. In fact, according to them it was the other way around. They gave examples of how an increase in income from selling milk made them more unhappy and brought misery in their lives. The money earned from the sale of milk went into the hands of men who frittered it away in buying useless things and in alcohol from the market.[1] As a result the women and the children suffered. We learnt a new lesson in economics that day – that income does not necessarily get converted into prosperity and that prosperity was far more important.

The women explained that in the villages, irrespective of the difference in the amount of wealth between different families, their lifestyles are almost similar. The women gave good reason for this: 'the display of wealth (as is the norm in any consumer society), leads to jealousies and false aspirations which give rise to violence, and that is why we do not believe in displaying our wealth'.

These experiences gave us new insights into understanding the two different worlds – the world of the larger majority of our people and our world, the world of the 'educated' few, who were dominating. After that we started observing things in a different manner. We also learnt that diversity was not just in the objects, artefacts, crafts, food, lifestyles, customs, etc., but also in the way we perceive, in our belief systems, knowledge systems, the way we think and the process through which we arrive at our decisions. Essentially it was about the manner in which we deal with our *sansar* (the world around us) and establish relationships with the different entities within it.

## Realization

Slowly we realized that perhaps with all the good intentions, we were doing more harm than good by imparting 'education'. We realized that our education had nothing from or of the *local*, except perhaps the physical environment – outside the classroom. The textbooks and teaching aids had nothing about their locality in them. Often the teachers came from other areas as well. Even if they were from the mountains, it hardly made any difference because they too were now 'educated' and hence were busy trying to prove that they were no longer 'backward'. Now in their world view the village, the mountains and 'these uneducated people' were 'backward' and 'uncivilized' (*'jahil'* and *'ganwar'*). Their lifestyle, their crops, the clothes they wore, the homes they lived in, the language they spoke and their manner of speaking, expressions, the manner in which they took their decisions, their thinking pattern, their 'rationality', their knowledge systems – everything in the eyes of the 'educated' was backward and thus worth getting rid of. And to fill this vacuum the newly 'educated' had to imitate and attempt to acquire a completely alien lifestyle, mannerisms, thinking and world view even if they did not completely believe or comprehend them. With this kind of education no wonder that the sooner one migrated from the village and changed one's identity, the better it was.

We realized that we too were alienating them from their society, culture and families, as well as unknowingly giving them a deep sense of inferiority, which they were camouflaging with a false sense of pride in being 'educated', 'modern' and 'developed'. Perhaps the damage we were doing (unconsciously) could never be undone. This was painful and disturbing. This feeling has still not left us completely.

We realized that the 'educated' started believing unquestioningly in the newly acquired values. They felt ashamed about their beliefs because they were taught that these were not 'scientific', were not 'rational', that these were all backward, regressive, superstitious, etc. The sad thing was that they imbibed, without analysing, anything which appeared to come from the modern world, which was sold to them as 'scientific', that would make them 'developed' and 'modern'.

Education has not helped to enhance their critical or analytical faculties but has only demoralized them by turning them into mindless imitators.

We found that there was a conflict between what the educated had come to believe under the influence of modernity, modern science, modern education, development, market forces, the media, globalization – call it what you like – and what their actual experience or reality was.

In the process we were confronted with our ignorance. We realized we were making huge assumptions and imparting them to these first generation literates. The so-called non-literates also had their assumptions, their beliefs, which we called superstitions but at least they were aware of them and did not justify them. But we the 'educated' were, in most cases, not even aware of our assumptions upon which we based our inferences. And this was having huge implications upon their lives.

## Investigations on the impact of family structures

### Dropping-out

In five of our primary schools, in the last six years, 18 children dropped out before finishing the school. We tried to find out the reason and some factor that was common to all the 18 children. We were looking along predictable lines and failed to arrive at any common element: they were not all girls (12 were girls but there were 6 boys); they were not all from schedule caste families (only 10 were from schedule caste families; 5 boys and 5 girls). Then we stumbled upon a strange commonality – they were all from nuclear families![2] When we explored this further we could understand much more (SIDH 2002).

The requirements of rural livelihood in the mountains are such that a joint family is better suited to the way of life. Rural life, farming or animal husbandry, entails a number of activities. The activities are all inter-connected in a complex web. In a subsistence economy, the number of chores and the time taken in each of these are the same irrespective of the size of the farm or the number of cattle. In any case, in the hills one cannot have a very large farm at one single location. Farms are normally scattered in different locations. In a large family with more working hands, different activities get distributed among many individuals; while in a nuclear family, the same number of activities has to be done by a smaller number of people – often a single couple. This results in an increased burden on the men but more so on the women and children. Joint families are also far better for the women, the disabled and for the old people in many other respects as well. The women have more free time and the old and disabled are cared for in a better manner in joint families.

In nuclear families children are often pulled out of the schools to help at home. Still the work never gets done. If a family member falls sick there is no substitute. Nuclear families are often unable to cope with the demands of an agrarian economy and they fall into a spiral of poverty, which then forces them to migrate to cities in search of a paid job. A salaried job is certainly easier for a nuclear family.

## Work and play

Though all children – both from joint and nuclear families – help with household chores, it is not a huge burden for the children from joint families. The boys help mainly with the work which is done outside the home, like cleaning the cow shed, fetching water, helping to plough the fields, grazing the cattle, etc., while the girls help with cooking, cleaning vessels, washing clothes and taking care of siblings. But there is a difference in the quantum of work between children from joint and nuclear families. Children from nuclear families are overworked. In joint families where there are a number of cousins (often many of the same age), all working together, there is also an element of fun attached to the work. Work and play intermingles in a strange fashion.

The traditional games that children play in this area are different from the modern games like cricket, which are becoming extremely popular, thanks to the money involved and the hype created by the media. Almost all traditional games have no or extremely insignificant elements of competitiveness in them. The rules are flexible and keep changing according to the location, time of day and number of children available or willing to play. These games are inexpensive and can be played anywhere, anytime. The games are played more for fun than to win.

Children from nuclear families complain: 'We get no rest at all' or 'We have to do so much work, we get no time to study.' This was confirmed by several adult responses like: *Unke fajite hote hain* (Children are really exploited in a nuclear family and are quite miserable). Or 'Children are happier in joint families, but in nuclear families they only work and work.'

However, in the nuclear families, the children feel a kind of drudgery while doing the work and are unhappy doing it. This is evident from their responses:

continued

'We have to work because there is no one else to help our family.'

'If we don't work we won't get any food.'

'If we don't work our parents beat us'.

Source: SIDH 2002

These statements from young and old, from nuclear and joint families from different districts in Uttaranchal are revealing:

'Children in joint families grow up and study painlessly' (*Pal bhi jate hain aur padh bhi jate hain*).

'Children can study better in a joint family. In a nuclear family the poor children have to do so much work. They get no free time.'

'Children from joint families can study without being disturbed. I want to send my children to school but I cannot do so. I am alone. Who will then help in cutting grass for the buffalo and how will we survive'? 'Only well off people from nuclear families can afford to send their children to school.'

'Who is there in the nuclear family to look after the studies of children?'

Boys and girls from joint families had this to say:

'We have no problems in going to school, because there are so many children going from the same house and we all know each other.'

'We can study better in joint families because there are many opportunities to study. With so many people around so much information is exchanged, which helps us in the class . . .

There are many people who can help us with our difficulties/problems in a joint family.'

Source: SIDH 2002

Children from joint families say: 'When we fall ill, we are looked after and given medicine at regular intervals.' Children also spoke of a constant monitoring by their grandparents, aunts and uncles about their bathing and eating regularly. There is always someone around to look after, bathe, feed and clothe the children in joint families.

'Children are better looked after in joint families because there is always a special person – like a grandfather or grandmother – to take care of the children. It is only when people at home have enough time or leisure that children can be well cared for.'

'When my grandson fell ill, we had no problem. But if he had been in a nuclear family, then who would have gone to the chhani (cow-shed), who would have worked at home and who would have fetched the doctor?'

'In a joint family different work is allotted to different people and there is no excessive burden on one individual and so every job is done well, whether it is looking after children, or looking after the guests or the buffalo or working in the fields . . .'

Source: SIDH 2002

It is significant that children from joint families do not make any comment on food, whereas all children from nuclear families speak a lot about food and food sufficiency in joint families.

continued

'Children from joint families get food at the right time and are fed.'

'In joint families there are many cows, goats and buffaloes and a lot of milk and butter.'

'In a joint family somebody is always there to give food to children.'

'Children in joint families do not have to wait for food.'

On the other hand their comments about nuclear families were quite damning:

'Children from nuclear families have to often go hungry (*Khali pet rehna hota hai*), because nuclear families are usually poor.'

'In nuclear families we have fewer animals and so less milk and butter at home.'

Source: SIDH 2002

According to the study (*Child and the Family*, SIDH 2002), children from joint families are generally happier, while those from those from nuclear families are lonely and insecure.

Some typical responses of children from joint families:

'Girls in joint families get more love.'

'We get more opportunities to go outside our homes with our parents and take part in marriages in other villages too.'

'We live in a big house and people respect us in the village. Members of joint families get a lot of support when they are in trouble.'

> Even young men are aware of this. A young 20-year-old from a nuclear family from Almora district said, 'Grandparents are more loving than parents who are overworked. Children in joint families are more loving and tolerant than those from nuclear families.'
>
> Source: SIDH 2002

## Self-confidence

Children from joint families appear healthier, happier, more relaxed and at ease in school, while children from nuclear families are more insecure. They display a tendency to say things only for making an impression, without actually meaning it. They speak about the importance of manual labour and how love and affection are more important than money. Yet after some time when the conversation takes a turn in a different direction, they may contradict themselves by saying: 'Farming is the job of the foolish illiterate people, not of people like us' and 'I don't want to work in the fields, I can buy anything, even labour and food with money'. They speak of the importance of being together in a joint family, but later contradict it by saying that it is best to substitute relatives and joint family with neighbours who can give the required support. Thus a certain amount of hypocrisy is noticed among children from nuclear families. In an earlier study (SIDH 1999) it was pointed out by women from rural areas that schools were responsible for putting more emphasis on 'appearance' rather than on 'being'. This study (SIDH 2002) revealed that it was not only the schools but also the nuclear families from where children learnt not to 'be' but to 'look' or 'appear' good. They were ashamed and embarrassed about their customs, when their mothers wore *ghagras* (the traditional dress) or spoke in the local dialect. But became quite alert and talkative when there was discussion of the latest television serials. These are some of the things said by children belonging to nuclear families:

> We feel ashamed to feed our guest with *mandua* (a local grain which is coarse and hence considered inferior though in fact it is far healthier and more nutritious) *roti* (bread).

> The only important thing these days is money.

> I like it when my mother wears *salwar kameez* (which most urbanized Indians wear nowadays), not the *ghagra* (local dress).

## Doing well at school

The teachers' reports show that the children from joint families generally performed better in mathematics, language, general knowledge and were more articulate than children from nuclear families.

There could be many reasons for this. Most children from joint families have grandparents living with them, who speak to them in the local dialect. It is a well-known fact that the local dialects enrich vocabulary and help in creative expression and thinking, which facilitates articulation and language skills. It was also observed that those children who were more confident in speaking in the local dialect were also better in language (Hindi). Children from joint families generally, know more folklore, folk songs, myths and local legends than children in nuclear families. Children from joint families also know a lot more about home remedies.

## Disability

A primary study in 18 villages with 2,096 children (below 15 years), from Jaunpur Block, Tehri District on the incidence of disability, revealed a significant difference in the incidence of disability among children from joint and nuclear families. The joint families had significantly fewer disabled children (1.51 per cent) than nuclear families had (3.55 per cent) (SIDH 2001) (see Table 7.1). Earlier case studies revealed that a lot of mothers in nuclear families had to leave their children unattended and as a consequence the children sometimes had an accident (SIDH 1996). This could be a possible reason for the differences in disability between children from nuclear and joint families. As a 70-year-old woman said:

> In a nuclear family, children are in a bad state. The parents lock them in, and open the door only upon their return. '*Ghuma diya tale men chabi. Vapas ayenge, tabhi khulega*' (They turn the key in the lock, lock the door and open it only when they return – in the evening). Sometimes the children in nuclear families do not even eat properly or have a bath.

Another younger woman aged 40 commented that in nuclear families children are often left in charge of younger siblings: 'In a nuclear families young girls take care of children and how can children know how to look after children?' (SIDH 2001).

In spite of these realities and everyday experience of children, in school they are found parroting '*chhota parivar sukhi parivar*' (a small family is a happy family). The reason can be traced to a lesson in their class 3 Hindi textbook, which teaches them:

> We see in our villages that large families are not happy. The food in their fields is never enough. The children can never get education because the children have to work. Small families are happier because they have to work less hard, their children study well and are healthy.[3]

Table 7.1 Study of disability in children in eighteen villages from Jaunpur Block, Tehri District

|  | Joint family | Nuclear family | Total |
|---|---|---|---|
| Families | 92 | 266 | 358 |
| No. of children | 859 | 1237 | 2096 |
| Disabled children | 13 | 44 | 57 |
| Percentage of disabled children | 1.51 | 3.56 | 2.72 |

Source: SIDH 2001.

## Birth rates and population myths

We conducted a small but detailed survey of 30 villages in Uttaranchal to find out whether the couples in joint families (where a large number of people stay together) have more children. Our finding was a revelation and contrary to the belief held by majority of the policy makers. The survey revealed that the average number of children (3.01) per couple in joint families was in fact less than the average number of children (3.39) per couple in nuclear families. Far more couples (43.78 per cent) from nuclear families had four or more children, as compared to only 38.48 per cent in joint families. While 12 per cent of the couples in joint families had no children at all, in nuclear families there were only 9.28 per cent such couples (see Tables 7.2 and 7.3 below).

Yet the myth perpetuates that those in joint families breed more children. '*Chhota parivar sukhi parivar*' (a family is a happy family) is seen on the back of all public buses, public walls and even textbooks. The small (nuclear) family has almost come to symbolize freedom, modernity, progress and happiness even though the reality, at least in the context of the rural areas of the mountains, is to the contrary. Some people may argue that *chhota* (small) does not mean nuclear but the number of offspring a couple has. But the picture – accompanying this population control

Table 7.2 Population distribution for joint/nuclear families

| Total no. of villages | Total no. of families | Total no. of joint families | Total no. of nuclear families | No. of couples in joint families | No. of couples in nuclear families |
|---|---|---|---|---|---|
| 30 | 902 | 213 (23.61%) | 689 (76.39%) | 725 (3.40 per family) | 948 (1.38 per family) |

Source: Primary survey in 30 Villages of Uttaranchal, 2001.

Note
23.61 per cent families in the 30 villages were joint and 76.39 per cent nuclear. There were on an average 3.4 couples per joint family and only 1.38 couples per nuclear family.

Table 7.3 Number of children born into joint families compared to nuclear families

| Families | Total no. of couples | Those having 4 or more children | Those having 3 children | Those having 1 or 2 children | Those with no children |
|---|---|---|---|---|---|
| Joint | 725 | 279 (38.48%) | 129 (17.79%) | 230 (31.72%) | 87 (12%) |
| Nuclear | 948 | 415 (43.78%) | 183 (19.30%) | 262 (27.64%) | 88 (9.28%) |

programme depicting a couple with two children (now just one girl) with the caption, '*chhota parivar sukhi parivar*' – is misleading. The message conveyed is that the nuclear family is more likely to have fewer children and is happier. The reality is in contradiction to this message.

People in the villages give several reasons for the difference in the number of children between joint and nuclear families. According to the common understanding, the desire to have a son is one of the main reasons for having more children. But the obsession for a son is far stronger among couples in nuclear families. In joint families, if a brother has two daughters (or no children) but another brother has a son then, in most cases the desire for a son (or children) is not felt so strongly, as all children are taken to belong to the entire family rather than to different individuals. So it is quite common to find one brother with two daughters living fairly happily without too much dissatisfaction with a brother who has a son. It was noticed that parents of nuclear families felt more insecure about their old age and thus the need for a son drove them to have more children. Another reason could be that nuclear families in rural areas, engaged in farming activities, require more working hands and hence the need to have more children. Perhaps this is why in rural homes, the total number of children per couple in joint families was found to be significantly fewer than in nuclear families. Another reason could be difference in sexual behaviour of couples in the two families – nuclear and joint.

## The hostile education system

A minute study of the textbooks used in Indian schools is quite revealing. And this bias is prevalent across the board – from the textbooks used in the schools, managed by the right-wing Hindu Nationalist organization, the Rashtriya Swayamsewak Sangha, in the name of Shishu Mandirs (attended mostly by children from the rural areas or from lower middle-class backgrounds); to the textbooks used in government schools; to the ones used in the so-called public schools, mostly managed by various Christian churches (started in the late nineteenth century), or the recently opened expensive but more 'progressive' schools, the last two both attended by children from the elite classes of India. Some books may be superficially more gender sensitive than others but as far as the world view that they represent or advocate goes – there is complete harmony between these different textbooks. Most revealing are the textbooks on languages (Hindi, English, etc.) and social sciences. For instance, in the textbooks:

- When a picture of a kitchen is shown, it is always of one like that found in Westernized Indian homes, where the cooking is done standing up. But even today the reality is that in 80 per cent of Indian homes and in almost 95 per cent of rural homes in India cooking is done sitting down.
- A dirty home (often shown in a rural setting) is where there is filth all around and often there is a cow and cow dung. Side by side there is a picture of a clean home where things have been spruced up but along with the cow dung the cow also disappears. The reality is that in 95 per cent of agrarian families a cow is a necessity. A cow is a rich source of food for children and organic manure for the marginalized farmer who cannot afford the more expensive chemical fertilizer available in the market. Its milk and other products from the milk and urine are used in many home remedies as well as for pesticides and weedkiller. The cow thus plays a very important role in the lives of rural people. And this has nothing to do with the Hindu

religious sentiments, as it is equally true for the Muslims living in rural areas.

- Dirt and filth are mostly associated with the 'rural' while the 'urban' is depicted as clean, sophisticated and knowledgeable. The reality is that most of the rural homes are far cleaner than many urban homes, shanties and slums in urban areas.
- It is always the washer men (*dhobi*) or the simple God-fearing villagers taking their bath in the river that are depicted as the ones dirtying the rivers. But though it is not a well acknowledged fact, the truth is that most Indian rivers are polluted by the filth from the towns and cities and not by the Indian villages.
- In Hindi language textbooks there is a section which invariably praises a child who knows good English and this is perceived to demonstrate the child's intelligence!

Most textbooks perpetuate the view that increasing consumption and usage of resources (cars, televisions, etc.) are synonymous with development and progress. Figures are given comparing these (consumption) levels with Western (developed) countries. These are but a few examples of the underlying values perpetuated by these textbooks, which must be doing great damage to the self-respect and self-esteem of children from the rural areas.

There are no black-and-white nor either/or situations in the real world. But our perceptions seem to be moulded in that direction by our education system. In the language class we teach our children 'opposites' (black/white, morning/evening, yes/no, and then go on to men/women, girl/boy). We train our children to think in terms of (almost non-existent) polarities. In reality there are no opposites – only differences. Even black and white are really different – not opposite. 'Yes' and 'no' are also opposites in a particular context and not in an absolute sense. Men and women – how can they be opposites? But that is what we are doing – creating false assumptions in the name of education.

Modern-day education is making people myopic. They are being 'trained' to make connections between things only in the immediate. There is undue importance on both the immediate and the sensorial inputs. The validation only comes from the outside while what one feels or understands within is ignored. If a child *feels* good when she co-operates (e.g. when she shares a toy with another child) this is not pointed out by the teacher. So the focus turns to the object that made her feel good rather than either the *act* of co-operation or the *feeling*. Values are either being imposed or are being ignored. Children are being asked to speak the truth (because they *should*) or truth is not discussed at all. In SIDH schools, though, an attempt is being made to make the child understand and feel the values. Exercises are done with the children where they are asked to find out the reasons for both lying and speaking the truth. It takes time but the children, with a little help from teachers, can figure out that the benefits of lying are often short term and those of speaking the truth long term. They realize the value of reliability and trust and can relate it to speaking the truth. They also acknowledge that trust is a *feeling* more than anything else. Most schools ignore any mention of feeling, perhaps because it is considered subjective and hence non-scientific.

Uttaranchal is largely a mountainous area. People here seldom die of hunger or cold, while in cities there are people dying every year of the cold, heat and of hunger. There are 1.3 million families living in Uttaranchal while there are 2.2 million homes including those for the cattle, but these facts are glossed over. People are being trained to look at themselves as miserable and poor who need help all the time. So much so, that now the 'educated' feel quite comfortable when they are addressed as 'backward'. On the contrary if their strengths are pointed out they feel cheated or deprived!

An exercise done with nearly 300 young people, mostly first generation literates, has given us an interesting insight into the manner in which new beliefs are being created by the media and the education system. Young people in batches of 30 were shown advertisements from popular English (Indian) magazines. These advertisements depicted a man and a woman in Western dress and postures in luxurious surroundings. The participants were asked to write their impressions about these models (unknown faces for them) in the advertisements. After a few minutes they were asked to share their impressions with other participants. Many participants commented on the looks, the clothes, the surroundings but they all made a remark that these models were *sabhya* (civilized) and *shikshit* (educated).

When asked about the basis for reaching these conclusions, especially as they did not know them, they referred to the style of their dress, the surroundings, the colour of their skin (which is often fair in the case of these models) and the accompanying assumptions that therefore they must be English-language speakers (and hence necessarily must be 'civilized' and 'educated'). We then had a prolonged discussion and asked them several questions to make them aware of their unfounded (and hidden) assumptions: we asked them what might happen if one of these model people got lost on a trek in the mountains and were to come to their village asking for help. It is most natural for the villagers in this community to

extend hospitality to a stranger without ever feeling that they have done
a great favour.

Then we asked them to consider a situation where they lost their own
way in a city where these people may be residing and by sheer coincidence
knocked on the door of one of them. Then they caught on and realized
that these people would be unlikely even open the door fully – let alone
help them. They realized the mistake of their assumption in calling people
civilized based only on looks and attire.

Similarly we informed them that more than 25 per cent (higher than
25 per cent according to some reports) of the high school 'pass' students
in the USA are functionally illiterate (even although they are native
English speakers). This shocks them because they have been made to
believe that education and speaking in English are synonymous. The
exercise is part of an overall module to provoke youngsters into questioning their assumptions.

These are only a few examples of how our education is turning the
educated into mindless imitators and projecting a stereotypical image
of the 'poor', 'deprived', 'undeveloped', people who need to be helped.
Yes, they need help, but more in terms of raising their confidence and
self-esteem.

## The incursions of modernity

The number of cattle has depleted sharply over the years in this area,
resulting in poverty and misery. The reason given by elders is that children
who earlier used to take the cattle for grazing into the forests have now
to go to the schools. Hence the cattle have depleted. There are hardly
any studies to document or verify such phenomena, possibly because
these go against the assumptions and value systems of the dominant
world view. But these are stark realities staring us in the face if we dare to
see them.

As mentioned earlier in this chapter, joint families are better off in most
respects and yet they are breaking up fast. In our study we found that the
number of joint families has declined by 75 per cent over the last 40 years
(SIDH 2002). One reason is the desire for privacy but another strong
reason is the desire for freedom 'to do as one pleases' (*manmarzi*), and to
buy 'good' food, 'good' clothes, etc. Joint families talk about 'enough' food
and 'enough' clothes but this acceptance of 'enough' is now changing to
a growing desire for 'good', which no one knows how to define. The desire
for 'freedom' (devoid of self-discipline) and 'good' is being promoted by
modern education.

Local statistics suggest that the villages have high child mortality rates (higher for girls than boys) and high infant mortality rates (higher for boys than girls) but there are no data to compare them with the situation before modern interventions were made. By looking at the data of the last 40 years or so, sweeping assumptions are made that people must necessarily be better off now than before. But elders tell a different story. According to them the traditional systems of healing, medicines and healers (e.g. midwives) are fast depleting. One cannot find a midwife below the age of 50 in villages now. Young girls do not want to take up this vocation (traditionally the midwives do not charge a fee for their services). They are under the mistaken belief that a child delivered through a caesarean operation is safer and healthier (even under normal conditions) than going in for a natural childbirth. Young men do not like to go to traditional healers or resort to home remedies as they have been 'taught' that these are mumbo-jumbo.

Modern education seems to have cast doubts in the mind of the young about the strengths of their traditions. So traditional support systems are becoming marginalized. Such systems must have been far stronger earlier. The modern system is not a replacement for the old, yet we assume that the villagers are better off than before. It cannot be proved, but it certainly can be argued that in many respects villages may have been better off before. If we are able to shed our prejudices and explore the traditional health-care systems, as they existed in the past, we may discover that people were better looked after in the past than they are now. If the health status is poor now, that does not necessarily mean that it was worse earlier. The old traditional systems have been undermined and the modern systems have not been able to replace them, resulting in the miserable situation of today.

In Uttaranchal there are festivals like *phooldei* and *thesya* which are exclusively for the children. There are festivals and occasions where women play the most vital role and have the freedom to organize things their way and enjoy themselves. In fairs (*melas*) parents give the girls more money to spend (as compared to the boys). These factors are not even mentioned, drawing a dismal, lopsided picture of rural India. These are seldom accounted for while studying the status of children and women in these areas.

A myth perpetuates not only among the international donor agencies but also among the elite of India that most children are under tremendous pressure of work, that girls are grossly discriminated against and that the rural illiterate are largely responsible for this. There are gross generalities in this kind of a perception. Girls in joint families are better off than in nuclear families. By and large, children from joint families are not over-worked. Work and fun often intermingle. Children are mentally healthy and not lonely, which is the case in most modern societies. A number of studies have been conducted to understand the reasons for the large number of dropouts but none has even taken this factor of family structure into consideration, revealing a major flaw in perception.

## Conclusion

In short, our experience of the last 15 years is that on the whole the traditional societies in the mountain areas were not that badly off, in fact they were, and still are, fairly happy and healthy. This is not to say that problems do not exist or that nothing needs to be done. But by and large they have the wisdom and mechanisms to cope with these problems. Instead of making sweeping assumptions that these communities are better off today than they were in the past, we need to acknowledge that gradually these (traditional) societies are disintegrating, are becoming weaker, are losing their spaces of solidarity and are getting marginalized by forces of 'modernity' and 'development'. And as a result they are slowly losing confidence in their own abilities and find it hard to operate the systems with which they are increasingly forced to live. The donor agencies and development workers also need to do some self-reflection on their assumptions and examine whether they are, with the best of intentions, doing something to undermine the confidence of these people.

The alienation of our urban educated from the real concerns of the majority of our country is unfortunately one reason which prevents our political reforms from becoming relevant. The tragedy is that the media and the present education system, as well as other factors, are mesmerizing people into adopting new values (beliefs), which give rise to almost unrealistic expectations and do not match their experiences. The result is that most people in rural areas are worse off than before. The quality of life is far worse even when the educated ones get a job and acquire a few material conveniences.

The irony is that the victims of the system are themselves becoming willing collaborators of the system. The majority may still have modest aspirations, but they have been 'educated' into believing that if they fail to achieve their individual aspirations, then the fault lies with them and not with the system. Sometimes even if there is a dissatisfaction with the system, the protest is about acquiring a larger share (of the shrinking pie) and does not get converted into questioning the very foundations of this system which is essentially discriminatory. The illusion continues.

We need to stop 'helping' people or 'building their capacities' (which basically means adapting themselves to the system that is essentially exploitative and alien) and start working at two levels. We need to (a) explode the myth perpetuated by the modern development paradigm, and (b) we must restore the spaces of the traditional societies and help them build confidence not only in their abilities but also in their knowledge systems so that they can take their own initiatives.

There is no single path to development. The essential thing is to be happy and contented, for which each community must find its own way. It is high time we realized that the path of progress or development that we have taken is flawed. We were backward earlier and we are backward now and this way we will eternally remain backward. We seem to be busy with the symptoms while having no time to diagnose the real cause. Thus it is important to realize that our societies have their unique strengths which need to be supported and we only need to remove the obstacles in their path.

The ruling class must realize that they do not have the answers and that they do not know. Like one wise old man of Jaunpur said, 'science also makes mistakes'. What is propagated today as a wonder drug may be banned the next day. In fact there are *no* universal solutions. The elite and the donors must also realize that by structuring and imposing from the outside they are squeezing out the spaces and taking away the initiatives from the hands of the local communities. This is leaving local communities with no room to operate or utilize their own methods and knowledge systems to cope with their environment. Once this is addressed, soon enough we will find that the communities will find the time, confidence and courage to develop their systems further. But trying to find neat solutions within the existing system is merely misdirecting the effort. What is necessary is to look beyond the immediate difficulty and create spaces so that local initiatives can emerge.

Chapter 8

# Childhood and social inequality in Brazil

*Fúlvia Rosemberg\**

## Summary

Brazil was a Portuguese colony from 1500 to 1822. When the Portuguese began their journeys of conquest to the Brazilian territories, they encountered between three and five million indigenous people organized into approximately one thousand different nations. Portuguese society was rigidly structured, 'centred in hierarchy, founded in religion; service to God and service to the king were the parameters of social activity' (Paiva 2000: 44). The Portuguese Empire had the support of the Catholic religious orders in the colonization process, especially the Jesuits who used formal education of indigenous children as one of their strategies. The Portuguese began to enslave the indigenous people in 1536. The Jesuit priest Manuel de Nóbrega, who founded the Jesuit mission in Brazil, wrote the following to Dom João III, king of Portugal, in 1551:

> When the priests realized that the grown people were so rooted in their sins, so obstinate in their evil ways, gratifying themselves by eating human flesh, and that they called it the true ambrosia and seeing how little can be done with them because they are so full of women, so fiercely engaged in war and given over to their vices, and that is one of the things which most disturbs reason and takes away all meaning, the priests decided to teach the children the ways of salvation so that later, they can teach their parents. Thus going out to the villages, they gathered them together to teach them Christian doctrine.
>
> (Cited in Chambouleyron 2004: 59)

Thus, in the sixteenth century, there began an uninterrupted narrative by the North about the inhabitants of the South, its children and adults, interpreting, as a rule, the specificity of the South as sin, vice, pathology, anomie, underdevelopment, incompetence; a specific which required instruction and counsel from the North so that the natives could acquire civilization. From then until the present day, pirates, colonizers, criminals, travellers, diplomats, queens and princes, governors, academics, scientists, artists, politicians, activists from international and humanitarian organizations, Brazilianists, and advisors to non-governmental and multilateral organizations have interpreted Brazil and its people based on their own parameters, interests, languages and sources. Often, like the Jesuits, they have proposed or imposed solutions. Such solutions, at times, are incorporated by the South itself, which describes itself according to the point of view of the North.

This chapter describes and discusses how social and economic inequality impacts on young Brazilian children (under 6 years of age). It emphasizes how social policies to address inequality have also been defined in the context of North–South relations.

## A brief state of the art

This chapter is based on published and widely available macro data. Brazil has a public agency responsible for national statistics, the Brazilian Institute of Geography and Statistics (*Instituto Brasileiro de Geografia e Estatística*/IBGE) which has been undertaking demographic census since 1872, and annual national household surveys (PNADs) since 1976. Generally, statistical information is reliable and of good quality. Researchers, activists and technical personnel from public agencies who are users of this information, perform critical analyses of its quality and are regularly consulted by the IBGE to in order to improve it.[1] On the whole the literature on early childhood is now wide-ranging, particularly with the publication of *Primeira Infância* (Young Childhood) (IBGE 2001a). There is a literature on early childhood care and education (ECCE), infant and child mortality and malnutrition.[2]

Academic production is dispersed throughout various publications, predominantly in journals of education, psychology, social service, history and public health.[3] Childhood and adolescence have had more attention from educators and social workers, while the fields of sociology and anthropology have shown less interest (Nunes 1999). In Brazil, there has not been the same emphasis towards childhood studies or the sociology of childhood reported in the northern hemisphere (Rosemberg 2003b; Montandon 2001; Sirota 2001; James and Prout 1990).

There has been a long progressive tradition of the human and social sciences in Brazil, heavily influenced by Marxism. In line with this tradition, early childhood activists and researchers have drawn on European psychology – Piaget, Wallon, Vygostsky – rather than on the Anglo-Saxon experimental psychology tradition. (Anglo-Saxon influence has been felt most intensely in the activities of the multilateral organizations such as

UNICEF and the World Bank (Rosemberg 2003a)). This long progressive tradition also explains, in part, the priority focus of Brazilian studies: childhood which is forsaken, poor; adolescents considered to be in 'situations of risk' ('street children', prostitution, adolescent pregnancy, etc.); themes of high media visibility and great international appeal. However, as elsewhere, it is easier to research the poor, who, due to their very condition of subordination, are more welcoming to researchers than the Brazilian middle class, who are more resistant to researchers invading their intimacy.

Writing on childhood by academics, activists and Brazilian governmental agencies shows the same bias as writing from the northern hemisphere about the southern hemisphere: the focus is to treat social inequality from the point of view of the dominated rather than the dominant. Thus, what is problematic are the poor, the blacks, the indigenous, i.e. the 'others'. Rarely is the issue framed from the reverse point of view: what it means to be white, of European origin, to belong to the economic and political elites, to speak a dominant and hegemonic language. We do not examine the effective strategies we use to maintain their (our) dominant position.

At present, the Department for Children and Adolescents within the Ministry of Justice is the national agency responsible for promoting and defending the rights of children and adolescents. Public policies for young children are fragmented (Campos *et al.* 1992) and are interspersed among federal, state and municipal agencies for education, social welfare and health.[4] We have Councils for Children and Adolescents at all three levels of government. The specific legislation, the Statute on Children and Adolescents, is considered to be quite advanced, but suffers from the same tensions observed in the International Convention on the Rights of Children (Boyden 1990; Rosemberg and Freitas 2001). This tension resides between the right to protection and the right to autonomy, the guiding concept being individual, and not collective, rights. The most recent Constitution agreed in 1988 extends the rights of children and adolescents, of women, of the disabled, of the aged, of blacks and of the indigenous. For example, it criminalizes racism and recognizes the collective ownership of the ancestral territories of blacks and indigenous peoples. It also recognizes children's right to education in daycare and preschools, which should fulfill the double role of education and care.

During the 1970s and 1980s, the feminist movement mobilized to struggle for daycare for the young children of working women. At the moment its political agenda is centred on adult women (combating domestic violence, decriminalizing abortion, etc.). Brazilian feminist theory now, like international feminist theory, tends to assume children and childhood are unchanging and not particularly relevant (Rosemberg 1996b). The Brazilian black movement centres more attention on older children, adolescents and adults.

Two Brazilian organizations presently stand out as advocacy organizations for young children: the Interforum Movement for Early Childhood Care and Education of Brazil (MIEIB) and the Pastoral Commission for Children. The MIEIB is a lay organization, created in 1999, with a national presence, whose goal is to monitor ECCE. The Pastoral Commission for Children is an agency connected to the Catholic Church, with national coverage, which acts through voluntary community agents (women) who give maternal–child assistance to the low income population (Pastoral da Criança 2002).

Brazilian public attention is directed more toward older children, adolescents and young people. The multilateral organizations (UNESCO, UNICEF, the World Bank) prioritize elementary education for children over the age of 7 in Brazil, as does the Brazilian government. This priority appears to derive from their greater visibility in the public arena. Adults, both Brazilian and foreign, see the behaviour of older children as potentially disruptive and dangerous. Young children, however, are more likely to be at home or confined within closed spaces, and have less public visibility. Unlike older children they are not yet labelled as victims, nor considered to be a threat – the sentiments which appear to mobilize adult public attention. The relative lack of public attention to young children is not a reflection of parental attitudes in Brazil – but to the very low negotiating power of young children and poor women (Rosemberg 2000a).[5]

If we get some distance from the stereotyping and stigmatizing eye trained to observe the spectacle – 'such as Sebastião Salgado's photographs, or the images used to illustrate the reports of the multinational organizations or fundraising advertisements in the North (such as 'adopt a child from the South for fifty dollars a year') – we encounter clear indications of the appreciation of Brazilian parents for their young children. There are strong signs of change. Recent urbanization, the penetration of the individualistic values of modernity, nearly universal access to television, the drop in infant mortality and fertility rates and the intense expansion of ECCE over the last three decades are social conditions that fuel this changing conceptualization (Rosemberg 1996b).

Early childhood is set off from the other stages of childhood: new spaces in the labour and consumer market are staked out. Parents recognize changes in understandings and patterns of child rearing. The young child is considered to be intelligent, making demands on, but dependent upon, adults. The impact of modernity (television, violence) is feared. The right tone in education is sought, and the role of fathers in caring for their children is being rethought (Moro and Gomide 2003).

Finally, in this section, I would like to make two general points about my analysis. It is worth noting that Portuguese, the hegemonic language of Brazil, unlike English, uses two different terms for children: *filho/a* (*filius* in Latin) and *criança* (*puer*). Thus, the translation of this text, like all production of information and studies of childhood, leaves room for ambiguities deriving from differences in meanings associated with the terms 'child' and '*criança*' (Rosemberg 2003b).

## Social inequality in Brazil

Brazil occupies a territory of 8.5 million km² in the east of Latin America, inhabited by one hundred and seventy million people who generate an annual per capita gross domestic product of US$2,129 (data from 2000). On a worldwide comparison, its per capita income level places it in the upper third of world countries, which means that '77 per cent of the world population lives in countries with a lower per capita income than Brazil' (Barros *et al.* 2000: 17). Given the intense concentration of world income, Brazil is in a good position among the developing countries. Therefore, Brazil is not a poor country, but a country with intense inequality in the distribution of income, which results in having a small number of rich people and a large percentage of poor. The percentage of poor in the country has revolved around 30 per cent to 50 per cent in the 1980s and 1990s, reaching 57.1 million people (34 per cent) in 2002.[6] (See Table 8.1.)

*Table 8.1* The evolution of poverty

| Year | Percentage of poor people | Number of poor (in millions) |
|------|---------------------------|------------------------------|
| 1982 | 43 | 51.9 |
| 1985 | 44 | 56.9 |
| 1992 | 41 | 57.3 |
| 1995 | 34 | 50.2 |
| 2002 | 34 | 57.1 |

Sources: PNAD 1982 and 1995 (cited in Barros *et al.* 2000: 15); PNAD 2002 (cited in *Folha de S. Paulo*).

The Gini index rating of inequality is one of the highest in the world – around 0.60. In Brazil, the wealthiest 20 per cent enjoy an average income thirty times higher than the poorest 20 per cent of the population (Barros *et al.* 2000: 22–3).

The incidence of poverty over time shows an important decline in the 1970s; but beginning in 1980, there is stagnation, and then a higher rate of poverty (Medeiros 2003: 10). This suggests inequality in Brazil is historical and structural. 'The levels of inequality in Brazil have not been significantly modified by urbanization, industrialization, democratization, secularization and growth in the aggregate product of Brazilian society' (Medeiros 2003: 16).

Brazilian social inequalities exhibit two marked tendencies: the social sectors that receive less income are also those that have less access to the benefits of public policy and lesser political participation. These inequalities are persistent. Thus, indicators such as life expectancy at birth, access to schooling (along with the ability to remain in school and be successful) and basic sanitation, show clear improvements in recent years throughout the national territory, yet, at the same time, maintain the pattern of inequality.

Political participation in the political parties, unions or the organizations of civil society, shows a strong correlation with personal income and education (Schwartzman 2004). This situation indicates that the economic elite are also the political elite in Brazil. The professions declared by members of the fifty-second legislative session of the National Congress (2003) are mostly high-earning professions.

> The large majority of the individuals who occupy positions among the political elite, represented by the members of congress, belong to the economic elite. If the economic elite are also the political and social elite, their power is not limited to managing their own wealth in accord with individual and group interests, this power also extends to the management of the wealth of third parties, including public funds.
>
> (Medeiros 2003: 9)

Social inequality in Brazil shows a strong association to colour/race, geographical region of residence and age of the citizen: higher incomes and greater social benefits are appropriated by the white, adult, residents of the south and southeastern regions. The position of women is more ambiguous and will be explored further in this chapter.

## Inequality and race

The enslavement of Africans lasted for more than three centuries and Brazil was the last country to abolish it. Domination of black Africans during the slaveholding regime extended beyond the slaves, also affecting free black people. Colonizers or travellers brought to Brazil the vision reigning in Europe about Africa, the Africans and miscegenation.

> With few exceptions, all the young black girls have no concern beyond that of being mothers. It is an idée fixe that takes hold of their spirits, from the time of puberty, and that they put into practice as soon as they have occasion. This fact, that the ardor of African blood is perhaps sufficient to explain, is above all then a calculated result. In truth, does maternity not lead them with all certainty to well being, to the satisfactions of self love, to the usufruct of sloth, to coquetry and to consume delicacies? A wet nurse is hired for more than a laundress, a cook or a maid . . . At the time of farewell, some even shed tears . . . but what all lament infinitely is [the loss of] the indolent life, the luxury of the clothes, the abundance of all that it is necessary to leave behind.
>
> (Charles Expilly, French traveller to Brazil 1862,
> pp. 202–20, cited in Leite 2001: 31–2)

The abolition of slavery was gradual and regulated by specific legislation. In 1859 transatlantic traffic of African slaves was prohibited; in 1871 freedom was granted to those born of slave mothers and in 1885 to the aged slaves; finally in 1888 the law granting overall liberation of the slaves was promulgated.

Brazilian society at the end of the nineteenth century displayed the following configuration:

> a small white elite, the remainders of a slaveholding economy in decadence, and a multitude of freed slaves, bastard children, descendents of Indians, poor whites and poor immigrants brought from Europe and Japan. They lived mostly in the country, often on large plantations, but for the most part as sharecroppers, producing, at most, enough to survive; but also in the cities as vendors, artisans, clerks, oddjobbers, household servants, the unemployed and occasional beggars. Very similar to Marx's 'dangerous classes', but, far from being residuals from a social and economic order in transition, they were the majority of the population of a country in formation.
>
> (Schwartzman 2004: 20)

After the abolition of slavery, social and political relations between blacks and whites were shaped by three main processes:

1   The country did not adopt legislation to ensure racial segregation (unlike the United States and South Africa), and therefore there was no legal definition of racial identity.
2   The country had no specific policies for integration of the recently freed blacks into the evolving society, which served to strengthen the historical social inequalities between blacks and whites, which have lasted into the present.
3   The country encouraged white European immigration during the transition from the nineteenth to the twentieth century: a state policy of whitening the population in consonance with the eugenic racist policies developed in Europe in the nineteenth century.[7]

To escape the fate of a mixed race country, so despised by Europe, Brazil encouraged European immigration by conceding advantages for Europeans to settle in Brazilian territory, especially in the South and Southeastern regions. This policy caused an increase in the percentage of whites (from 44.0 per cent in 1890 to 63.5 per cent in 1940), and the forcing of the black populations into the Northeast region, which was already showing economic decadence. Today, the Northeast constitutes the poorest region in Brazil and also has the greatest percentage of blacks (blacks and browns). By contrast, the South and Southeast are the wealthiest regions and have the largest percentage of whites (Table 8.2).

This historical process, updated later by structural and symbolic racism, shaped the pattern of race relations in Brazil. Classification now takes the following forms:

(a)   a system of racial classification based on appearance resulting from the simultaneous apprehension of physical traits (skin colour, facial features, hair), socio-economic status and region of residence;
(b)   a large black and mixed-race population (which identifies as brown, not white) – 46 per cent of the population;[8]
(c)   living with patterns of race relations which are simultaneously vertical, producing intense inequality of opportunity and horizontal, where overt hostility and racial hatred are not observed. (This can result in amicable relationships in certain social spaces under certain circumstances.)

Table 8.2 Racial composition and income distribution by geographical region, Brazil, 2001

| Regions | Composition | | Income level (in MW*) | | | | | |
|---|---|---|---|---|---|---|---|---|
| | Whites | Blacks | Under ½ MW | ½ to 1 times MW | 1 to 2 times MW | 2 to 3 times MW | 3 to 5 times MW | 5 times MW |
| North (N) | 27.9 | 71.8 | 28.7 | 29.5 | 21.2 | 7.4 | 5.4 | 5.0 |
| Northeast (NE) | 29.5 | 70.2 | 37.0 | 28.1 | 17.2 | 5.5 | 4.3 | 4.5 |
| Southeast (SE) | 63.5 | 35.0 | 12.1 | 21.8 | 26.6 | 12.6 | 10.5 | 11.6 |
| South (S) | 84.0 | 15.0 | 11.9 | 22.1 | 29.2 | 13.1 | 10.4 | 10.8 |
| Central-West (C-W) | 43.8 | 55.4 | 18.1 | 27.6 | 24.4 | 9.5 | 8.0 | 9.8 |
| Brazil | 53.4 | 46.0 | 18.9 | 24.1 | 24.5 | 10.6 | 8.6 | 9.6 |

Source: PNAD 2001, cited in IBGE 2003.

Note
* MW = minimum wage.

This last particularity of race relations in Brazil, which also appears as intense miscegenation, allied to the process of racial classification based on appearance, resulted in the dissemination, at home and abroad, of the myth of Brazilian racial democracy. This myth presupposes not just amicable, cordial relations, but equality of opportunity as well. Further, the social and economic inequalities between whites and blacks in Brazil were attributed solely to the slaveholding past and class inequality.

The constitutive historical and contemporary racism in Brazil society is evident when the Human Development Index (HDI) is calculated separately for the white and black populations: for whites it is the equivalent of 0.791 (41st place) and for blacks, it is 0.671 (108th place).

The myth of racial democracy has been challenged since the 1950s by both black and white researchers, and especially by black activists at the end of the 1970s. They have pointed out the undeniable racial inequality in access to both symbolic and material goods, and have interpreted this as an expression of structural and ideological racism. They have proposed policies to overcome racism. In 1996, the Brazilian government recognized, for the first time, that the country is structurally racist and acknowledged its historical debt to blacks. Young black children who are residents of the Northeast are the poorest of all children.

## Children under 6 years old

The 2000 Census counted 23 million children under 6 years old, making up almost 13.6 per cent of the population in Brazil. This percentage has been in steady decline as a result of the reduction in fertility and birth rates: from 1990 to 2000, the birth rate per 1,000 inhabitants fell from 23.05 to 20.04 and total fertility from 2.70 to 2.2.

### Income distribution

Despite the reduction in the proportion of children under 6 years old in the population, this group shows the highest percentage of poor and chronically poor people and has the worst ratings on social indicators (Rosemberg and Pinto 1997; Hasenbalg 2001; Sabóia and Sabóia 2001).

The majority of Brazilian children under 6 years old live with the status of children (*filius*) in two-parent families (71.6 per cent). Less frequently children live in extended families (10.3 per cent) or only with the mother (13.5) (PPV, cited in Hasenbalg 2001: 13). As in the overall population, the majority (52 per cent) of children are white, residing in urban areas (76.5 per cent), predominantly in the Northeast (32.4 per cent) and Southeast (38.7 per cent) (IBGE: PNAD 1999).

A comparison among different types of families that have children under 6 show that across social classes they always occupy an unfavourable position when compared to families which do not have young children (Sabóia and Sabóia 2001).[9] The persistence of such indicators about the unfavourable position of families and households with young children 'would justify a national policy of support for these families . . . It indicates that programmes directed to children of school age should be preceded by programmes directed to young children' (Sabóia and Sabóia 2001: 45). This suggestion, however, has not been taken up by the Brazilian government.

Hasenbalg (2001: 10) highlights two aspects regarding the relation between poverty and early childhood: differences in fertility which may explain the disproportionate concentration of young children at the lower levels of income; and oscillations in the level of poverty in the Brazilian population according to the ups and downs of the economy over recent decades. In addition, families that have young children tend to be at the beginning of their working lives; and the present pattern of fertility means that couples are having children closer in age to each other. The school schedule makes working outside the home difficult for mothers with young children, so family income falls. The state accepts a redistributive role and offers some social support, e.g. social security, and some programmes to maintain poor children from the ages of 7 to 14 in school (called *Bolsa-Escola*). Barros and Carvalho argue that 'Although all these programmes lead to a reduction of poverty at all age levels however, the reduction is much more marked among old people than among children'

Table 8.3 Percentage of people with an income of less than half the minimum wage, by age and year, in the Northern region of Brazil, 1992 to 1999

| Age | 1992 | 1993 | 1995 | 1996 | 1997 | 1998 | 1999 |
|---|---|---|---|---|---|---|---|
| under 6 | 58.03 | 54.31 | 41.27 | 41.28 | 41.91 | 44.37 | 45.54 |
| 7 to 14 | 53.58 | 50.03 | 35.47 | 36.93 | 36.63 | 38.42 | 40.08 |
| 15 to 17 | 44.71 | 41.49 | 26.84 | 28.25 | 28.48 | 29,78 | 32.06 |
| 18 to 24 | 39.13 | 36.97 | 23.28 | 24.74 | 25.03 | 25.87 | 27.64 |
| 60 to 66 | 22.98 | 20.40 | 8.45 | 10.28 | 9.87 | 9.26 | 9.32 |
| over 67 | 20.51 | 19.80 | 7.23 | 9.29 | 8.78 | 7.64 | 7.80 |

Source: various PNADs.

(2003: 8) since the amount of resources allocated by the social welfare net is greater for the elderly than for small children.

## Living conditions

The low priority assigned to young children by economic and social policies is shown in their conditions in life and death. Inequality is not just a matter of income distribution, but also of the benefits of public policies.
    An analysis of poverty indicators shows:

(a) Improvement over recent decades for the country overall and for each region.
(b) Marked and persistent differences among them according to region, rural or urban residence, racial segment, family income level, the schooling of the mother and head of the family. Generally, the worst indicators are observed among black and indigenous children,[10] residents of the Northeast region, the rural areas, those coming from families with lower incomes and whose mothers had little educational opportunity. A large number of the indicators also show worse conditions for children residing in households headed by women, but there are exceptions, as for example in access to basic sanitation, where the indicators are better for households headed by women (Rosemberg and Pinto 1997).
(c) A general improvement in the indicators has not contributed to reducing inequalities. The gap that separates children with better indicators (coming from higher income levels and receiving greater benefits from social policies in housing, sanitation, education, etc.) from children who show worse indicators remains.
(d) The literature is contradictory in its use of indicators. UNICEF (2004), for instance, weights mother's education, or lack of it, as a causal factor in mortality and malnutrition whereas Simões (2002) considers it to be just a proxy; family income and sanitation conditions are more likely to cause mortality and malnutrition.

    Information available about some of these indicators is summarized in the following sections on housing, nutrition and mortality.

### Housing

Approximately one third of the population live in conditions of high density (favelas or shanty towns) and lack an adequate supply of water, sanitary sewers and trash collection (IBGE 2001a, Northeast and South-east regions). Such living conditions tend to affect the daily lives of small children more than the other residents of these households, in so far as their circulation in other spaces is more restricted and they depend on older people.

In research on living conditions of young children according to racial background, Rosemberg and Pinto (1997) observed an important racial difference in the access of children from urban areas to adequate sanitation conditions, even when controlling for household income and area of residence. In Brazil, especially in urban Brazil, black populations tend to live in areas alongside poor whites. They do not have access to good services, but they are more likely to be able to deal with racism.

Intense regional inequality and the poverty and lack of opportunity in rural areas have led to continued internal migration and consequent growth of the metropolitan areas. Thus, the rate of urbanization for Brazilians is high (83.9 per cent) and three metropolitan areas house 33.7 million people, i.e. 20 per cent of the Brazilian population: the São Paulo metropolitan area with 18.2 million residents, Rio de Janeiro with 11.0 million and Belo Horizonte with 4.7 million inhabitants (IBGE: PNAD 2001). Mostly migrants congregate in peripheral areas of cities, in favelas or shanty towns, and are in effect environmentally segregated from the city.

The distribution of services and urban infrastructure is deficient in these peripheral areas of the large cities: transport is precarious, adding additional hours to long working days; sanitation is deficient, to which is added non-existent drainage, greater exposure to the occurrence of floods and landslides during the rainy season and cuts in water supply during the dry season. There are fewer opportunities for formal employment, for access to the professions, for access to information; for access to leisure facilities, or to the legal system, or to the administrative apparatus; difficulty in access to health services, school and daycare; greater exposure to violence both from the police and criminals (Maricato 2003: 152). Inadequate basic sanitation and its unequal distribution have been considered one of the factors responsible for the persistently high rates of malnutrition and infant and child mortality.

## Mortality

Two different expressions refer to the death of young children: infant mortality, which refers to the death of children before completing a year of age, and child mortality, which refers to children who die before

*Table 8.4* Rates of infant mortality (under 1 year old) and child mortality (under 5 years old) by year and region (%), Brazil, 2000

| Regions | Infant (under 1 year, per 1,000 population) 2000 | Child mortality (under 5, per 1,000 population) 2000 | Family income, per capita | Child mortality (under 5 years, per 1,000 population) |
|---|---|---|---|---|
| North | 33.01 | 41.3 | 1st quintile | 81.6 |
| Northeast | 52.31 | 66.8 | 2nd quintile | 54.0 |
| Southeast | 24.09 | 29.9 | 3rd quintile | 48.2 |
| South | 20.34 | 23.9 | 4th quintile | 34.1 |
| Central-West | 24.00 | 28.2 | 5th quintile | 29.8 |
| *Brazil* | *33.55* | *41.8* | *Brazil* | *57.4* |

Source: Census and PNADs, cited in Simões 2002: 55 and 62.

completing their fifth year. Both rates refer to deaths within a group of one thousand people (see Table 8.4).

The same trends emerge again and again: young children coming from families with lower incomes, and black children who reside in the Northeast, whose mothers have had few educational opportunities have the least chance of living beyond 5 years (Simões 2002). Their chances of surviving would be better if they lived in households with adequate basic sanitation.

As a reflection of the low investment in services throughout the 1990s, the drops in child mortality related to basic sanitation were not very significant among children residing in poor households, despite the evident progress in child vaccination and the implementation in 1998 of the Programme for the Comprehensive Care of Diseases Prevalent in Childhood (Atenção Integrada às Doenças Prevalentes na Infância (AIDPI)).

Nationally, on average, the drop was 14 per cent during the periods from 1988 to 1992 and 1995 to 1998, a value similar to that observed in the Northeast and Southeast regions of the country. In the South and Centre-west the drop in mortality was more accented (22 per cent and 28 per cent respectively) and was practically double that observed for the other regions of Brazil. From this we can infer that in the Northeast, more than in other regions of the country, the reduction in child mortality still depends essentially on measures directed to distribution of income and access to basic sanitation services.

(Simões 2002: 74)

The most recent macro-economic reforms (of the 1990s and 2000s), valuing the minimal state and seeking to contain the public debt (internal debt and interest on debt incurred to the World Bank) have reduced infrastructure investment, including basic sanitation. Young children living in lower income households have a greater probability of dying because the government withdraws investments in sanitation to pay these debts, in order not to frighten off international investors.

## Malnutrition

The present federal government – led by Luíz Inácio Lula da Silva – gained national and international notoriety in proposing the *Fome Zero* (Zero Hunger) project as its main social project. The project, presently being reformulated, has sparked controversy and criticisms even among progressives (Monteiro 2003: 7). The economic and media manipulation of hunger has been under discussion in Brazil and the northern hemisphere for a long time (Monteiro 2003; Brunel 1990). Sylvie Brunel (1990) calls the international tatics on hunger 'an international hoax'. Like Brunel (1990), Monteiro (2003) emphasizes that the three concepts – poverty, malnutrition and hunger – are not identical. Information available about small children refers to their state of nutrition or malnutrition. Thus, rates of child malnutrition refer to the percentage of children (under 5 years old) with low height – low height is defined at that which diverges from the averages expected for age and sex, according to the international growth standards recommended by the World Health Organization (WHO 1995, cited in Monteiro 2003: 11).

Brazil has a percentage of 10.4 children (under 5 years old) with low height, an indicator of malnutrition. As for other indicators, malnutrition rates show important local variations: higher in rural areas than urban, higher in the North and Northeastern regions than in the Central-West, Southeast and South (Table 8.5); higher for black than white children and those between 2 and 4 years old (Lustosa and Reichenheim 2001: 104–7). The better indicator for children under 1 year old is possibly correlated with breastfeeding which takes place up to 9.9 months (on average) in urban Brazil in 1999.[11]

These figures show improvement over the last three decades, but this improvement is patchy. Based on figures from the period 1989–96, the goal of controlling malnutrition – i.e. reaching an index of 2.3 per cent – will be achieved at very different times according to the region under consideration: in 2003 for the urban southern regions; in 2013 for the urban Northeast; in 2031 for the urban North; for the rural Central-West in 2035 and only in 2065 for the rural Northeast (Monteiro 2003: 13).

*Table 8.5* Prevalence (%) of malnutrition in childhood, Brazil, 1996

| Region | Area | | |
|---|---|---|---|
| | *Urban* | *Rural* | *Total* |
| North | 16.6 | — | — |
| Northeast | 13.0 | 25.2 | 17.9 |
| Centre-south* | 4.6 | 9.9 | 5.6 |
| *Brazil* | 7.7 | *18.9* | *10.4* |

Source: PNDS, cited in Monteiro 2003: 11.

Note
* Includes the Central-West, Southeast and South regions.

Regional differences persist when comparing levels of child malnutrition even when the children come from households with similar purchasing power. This suggests that the malnutrition of children is influenced by other factors, beyond income, such as availability of public health services, education and basic sanitation (Monteiro 2003: 12).

Brazilian educational policy during the 1990s followed the prescription of the World Bank, prioritizing, almost exclusively, elementary education as a strategy to combat poverty and bring the country economic progress. This prioritization was based on the theory of human capital (Torres 1996). Thus, the federal government abandoned its initial commitment to ECCE (early childhood care and education for children under 6 years of age) and concentrated its resources on elementary education (Rosemberg 2003a).

Public schools were required to implement feeding programmes for children from 7 to 14 years of age. But children this age are likely to suffer less from the impact of malnutrition than younger children! Moreover, pressures from the International Labour Organization (ILO) in its campaign to eradicate child labour (and to avoid an international boycott of its exported products), led the the federal government to create, during the 1990s, the *Programa Bolsa Escola* (School Scholarship Programme) for children aged between 7 and 14 from families with low income to enable them to remain in school and not work. In 2001 the federal government finally created a parallel programme, the *Programa Bolsa Alimentação* for children under 6 years of age. But this was done without a linked strategy of expanding vacancies in daycare centres and preschools, so the poorest young children, who were less likely to be attending provision, did not benefit. Further, the amount passed on by the federal government to purchase food for daycare centres and preschools under contract, was worth, up until July of 2004, only half the value of that passed on to feed children aged between 7 and 14. These policies could be read as discrimination against young children.

## Early childhood care and education

ECCE reflects the intense social segregation in the urban areas of Brazil. Despite the poor living conditions in these segregated areas (poor sanitation, crowded households, contaminated outside spaces) UNICEF (in the 1980s) as well as the World Bank (in the 1990s) suggested that caring for young children in the household (family daycare) for Brazil meant low-cost care. It reduced public investment whilst it expanded coverage. This was justified in the name of 'cultural proximity', i.e. daycare homes would reflect the cultural conditions of the children being looked after!

In 2001, 10.6 per cent of children under 3 years of age and 65.6 per cent of those in the 4- to 6-year age range, attended some kind of ECCE. The offer of ECCE in Brazil is mostly public (63.5 per cent in daycare and 75.4 per cent of preschools in 2000) and among the private sector, for-profit education is responsible for 57.0 per cent of enrolments in daycare and 75.3 per cent in preschools (Rosemberg 2003a).

Despite showing high growth between 1970 and 1990 (Rosemberg 2003a), studies of the 1990s (Kappel *et al.* 2001; Rosemberg 2003a) have shown that ECCE was the level of education that grew least during the 1990s.

White children from the higher income levels have better access to ECCE. However, because of the low-cost schemes to provide ECCE in poor areas as a strategy to combat poverty, the distribution of the attendance rates can be misleading (Rosemberg 2003a). This policy of low-cost ECCE expansion for regions considered 'politically dangerous' (the 'poverty pockets' in the Northeast) during the last years of the military dictatorship subsequently influenced the pattern of attendance rates: it is the Northeast region which shows the better rates. Paradoxically higher rates of ECCE attendance in Brazil are associated with lower indicators of quality (Rosemberg 1999). The Northeast shows, at the same time, high coverage and the worst quality indicators: it has the highest rate of 'lay' teachers, who receive the lowest salaries and who work in establishments with the worst physical conditions (i.e. in schools without any basic sanitation) (see Table 8.7).

This model of low cost ECCE expansion seems to suggest that ECCE shows the greatest focus on the poor: it indicates that 'the poorest have greater access than the wealthiest' (Barros and Foguel 2001: 119). This is the result, however, of a perverse and paradoxical process, deriving from

Table 8.6 Rate of ECCE school attendance by age range, colour, income quartiles and geographic regions, Brazil, 1999

| Region | Age range (years) | White | | | | | Not white (black, brown and indigenous) | | | | | Total |
|---|---|---|---|---|---|---|---|---|---|---|---|---|
| | | Income quartiles | | | | | Income quartiles | | | | | |
| | | 1st | 2st | 3st | 4th | Subtotal | 1st | 2st | 3st | 4th | Subtotal | |
| North* | Under 3 | 1.3 | 3.8 | 8.5 | 12.8 | 6.1 | 2.6 | 6.5 | 6.4 | 12.5 | 5.8 | 5.9 |
| | 4–6 | 39.6 | 53.3 | 55.7 | 71.1 | 54.3 | 39.0 | 47.8 | 53.1 | 70.1 | 49.2 | 50.8 |
| | Total (0–6) | 15.5 | 25.7 | 28.9 | 36.9 | 26.1 | 18.2 | 24.5 | 28.5 | 39.6 | 25.2 | 25.5 |
| Northeast | Under 3 | 6.6 | 10.4 | 16.7 | 24.4 | 11.1 | 6.3 | 9.0 | 11.7 | 26.2 | 8.4 | 9.3 |
| | 4–6 | 51.9 | 64.2 | 76.4 | 88.1 | 63.4 | 49.8 | 57.8 | 66.9 | 79.4 | 55.1 | 57.4 |
| | Total (0–6) | 24.5 | 33.3 | 41.6 | 52.2 | 32.6 | 9.5 | 31.6 | 37.0 | 52.1 | 29.9 | 30.7 |
| Southeast | Under 3 | 7.0 | 7.4 | 7.8 | 19.6 | 10.8 | 5.7 | 8.5 | 7.0 | 13.2 | 7.7 | 9.7 |
| | 4–6 | 43.6 | 48.9 | 57.4 | 75.7 | 58.4 | 38.0 | 47.3 | 51.1 | 62.5 | 47.1 | 54.0 |
| | Total (0–6) | 22.9 | 24.3 | 28.8 | 44.9 | 31.2 | 20.4 | 26.4 | 27.5 | 36.3 | 25.9 | 29.2 |
| South | Under 3 | 6.3 | 5.6 | 12.2 | 21.9 | 10.9 | 3.5 | 10.6 | 12.5 | 24.4 | 8.8 | 10.5 |
| | 4–6 | 31.4 | 35.0 | 45.7 | 62.3 | 43.0 | 28.5 | 32.2 | 35.8 | 43.8 | 32.4 | 41.1 |
| | Total (0–6) | 16.9 | 18.5 | 27.0 | 40.3 | 25.0 | 14.7 | 20.9 | 24.7 | 34.4 | 20.1 | 24.2 |
| Central-West | Under 3 | 3.3 | 5.4 | 6.5 | 14.2 | 7.3 | 6.0 | 3.7 | 6.1 | 10.9 | 5.8 | 6.6 |
| | 4–6 | 31.8 | 38.2 | 46.0 | 69.1 | 46.3 | 31.2 | 35.7 | 45.9 | 56.5 | 38.7 | 42.5 |
| | Total (0–6) | 15.4 | 19.6 | 23.5 | 38.4 | 24.2 | 17.0 | 18.6 | 22.7 | 33.6 | 20.6 | 22.4 |
| Brazil | Under 3 | 6.2 | 7.2 | 9.8 | 20.0 | 10.4 | 5.8 | 8.2 | 8.6 | 16.6 | 7.8 | 9.2 |
| | 4–6 | 42.7 | 47.2 | 55.4 | 73.4 | 54.5 | 44.5 | 49.7 | 54.4 | 66.4 | 49.5 | 52.1 |
| | Total (0–6) | 21.4 | 24.1 | 29.4 | 43.9 | 29.3 | 23.3 | 27.3 | 29.8 | 40.4 | 27.0 | 28.2 |

Source: IBGE 1999.

Note
* Exclusively rural population from the North region.

Table 8.7 Number of preschool establishments by physical characteristics of the school and geographic region, Brazil, 1997

| Region | Total establishments | Establishments that do not have | | | | | | | | | |
| | | Water supply | | Electricity | | Playground | | Adequate bathrooms | |
| | | Total | % | Total | % | Total | % | Total | % |
|---|---|---|---|---|---|---|---|---|---|
| North | 6,399 | 902 | 14.1 | 2,348 | 36.7 | 5,719 | 89.4 | 5,448 | 85.1 |
| Northeast | 39,154 | 4,880 | 12.5 | 12 730 | 32.5 | 34,661 | 88.5 | 33,729 | 86.1 |
| Southeast | 19,754 | 314 | 1.6 | 1,086 | 5.5 | 10,350 | 52.4 | 10,980 | 55.6 |
| South | 11,115 | 38 | 0.3 | 36 | 0.3 | 5,898 | 53.1 | 6,735 | 60.8 |
| Central-West | 4,539 | 40 | 0.9 | 251 | 5.5 | 2,738 | 6.03 | 2,959 | 65.2 |
| Brazil | 80,961 | 6,174 | 7.6 | 16,451 | 20.3 | 59,366 | 73.3 | 59,851 | 73.9 |

Source: 1997 School Census (accessed via the internet, 17 September 1998), cited in Rosemberg 1999.

the fact that these daycare centres and preschools were created precisely for the poor, and due to their poor quality, repelled families with higher income levels. The ECCE reinforces the process of social segregation in providing 'poor programmes for poor people'. Oliveira (1994) observed strong racial segregation in the public daycare centres under contract to the city government of São Paulo; but these centres were *meant* to serve children from black families with low income levels.

Children under 3 years of age are those with lowest access to ECCE. Yet it is exactly within the 2- to 4-year age range that children show the highest and most persistent rates of malnutrition. The federal government acknowledges the problem but only supplies the daycare centres with nutritional supplements at *half the value* (which is already low) given to elementary schools.

Children under the age of 3 have the lowest chance of attending daycare; and children under 4 have the highest malnutrition rates. Rather than seeing better daycare as a solution, however, the latest UNICEF report on Brazilian childhood and adolescence stigmatizes daycare as a care and education option for children under the age of 3. In its latest report on *Diversity and Equity in Brazil*[12] one finds the following passage, a masterpiece of diplomacy (or cynicism):

> **Daycare**: UNICEF considers it important for children to have a good beginning in life, and thus takes the position that under 3 years of age they should benefit from family living and parental care.
>
> In this document an analysis of data on early childhood does not include educational indicators for children under 3 years old, given that, despite being recognized by UNICEF as a right, daycare is not the only education possibility for education at this stage of life. It is fundamental that attention offered by parents and adults responsible for caring for the development of children under 3 years of age be valued as well.
>
> (UNICEF 2004: 52)

The statistics about, and analysis of, ECCE in the 2004 UNICEF report do not include children under the age of 3, who, for UNICEF, have ceased to exist except as embedded in their family.

The devaluation of ECCE has resulted in its having the lowest annual average cost (public and private) per student in the Brazilian educational system. According to the OECD (2000), the average Brazilian cost for ECCE was US$820 (28th place), while the cost for higher education was US$10,791 (10th place).

ECCE expansion has been paid for by family and by teachers (thanks to their low salaries). This has had negative consequences for its quality. In fact it is possible to argue that Brazilian ECCE has been paid for by young children themselves – receiving far less than a decent entitlement. The multilateral organizations (UNESCO, UNICEF and the World Bank) continue to disseminate the idea that the costs of Brazilian ECCE can and should be reduced even further.

The issue of quality in ECCE reached the agenda only in the mid 1990s. Until then, the model used by welfare agencies was of emergency programmes to combat poverty. The propagation via UNESCO, UNICEF and the World Bank of low cost models of public investment meant that the expansion was prioritized at any cost. This resulted in a low quality standard of functioning; educators without formal training, insufficient and inadequate toys, books and interior and exterior spaces.

In this political context, the models for evaluating quality produced in the United States (for example, Developmentally Appropriate Practice (DAP) produced by the NAEYC (National Association for the Education of Young Children) have had little circulation in the country because of the absence of context or any discussion of values. The ECCE community in Brazil needed to discuss the concept of ECCE on the political plane, exploring the values and the social actors involved. Since the debate about ECCE quality began, a main conceptual tool in Brazil has been the discussion paper produced by the European Community, *Quality in Services for Young Children: A discussion paper* (Balaguer *et al.* 1992).

In this sense, diversity in Brazil meant inequality. The contemporary effort has been, therefore, to define an acceptable national minimum so that daycare centres and preschools respect children, rather than reinforce inequality in the name of cultural diversity. But this needs to be done in the wider frame of discussion about values.

## Overcoming inequality

How do we overcome such inequality in income distribution and in access to public services when the neoliberal model reigns supreme and the utopia of world revolution has no more followers? The responses of the multilateral organizations and Brazilian economists and administrators (Barros *et al.* 2000; Faria 2000; Medeiros 2003) suggest three areas for reform: an increase in the amassed wealth of the country, population reduction and a change in the distribution of social benefits via public policy.

## Economic growth

Economic growth is considered one of the routes to reducing inequality and combating poverty. 'A growth rate of 3 per cent per year in per capita income, for example, tends to reduce poverty in an amount approximately equal to a percentage point every two years' (Barros *et al.* 2000: 27). That is, it would take 25 years to reduce the level of poverty to below 15 per cent, if other conditions remained constant (which is highly unlikely). However, the Brazilian economy has not been growing at this rate: between 1995 and 2004, the accumulated Brazilian average is 2.2 per cent, the world average is 3.7 per cent and that of the emerging countries is 4.9 per cent. The most recent macro-economic reforms reduced inflation but promoted inequalities. The option to contain the increase in the public debt limited investment in infrastructure. Paying the public debt (domestic and foreign) and the cost of servicing it, imposed an enormous increase in the tax burden, but redirected it. Between 1995 and 2001, collection of social tax contributions increased 33 per cent (as a percentage of GDP) and social spending by the government increased by just 13 per cent.

Considered by some as the 'indispensable morphine', the Brazilian foreign debt, its negotiation with creditors and the agreements with the IMF for loans destined to compensate for deficits, is a producer of inequality: 'From 1994 to 1998 the country remitted R$128 billion on debt service and debt payment and in 1999, more than R$67 billion. In the same years, the federal government destined R$12 billion to education and R$9 billion to health services' (Souza 2002: 1).[13] Presently, Brazilian foreign debt has now reached an amount close to US$120 billion.

Despite the United States being Brazil's major creditor, Brazilian foreign debt began during the Empire period in the nineteenth century, when Brazil inherited Portugal's debt to England as a result of the Aberdeen Treaty. The last payment on this debt was made in 1957. Brazilian foreign debt increased greatly during the military dictatorship (from US$12.5 billion to US$46.9 billion in 1979) which opted for accelerated growth during the 1970s (a 6.8 per cent average rate increase between 1974 and 1979) thanks to the support of loans. The debt got beyond tolerable limits with the world recession of 1981 and the increase in North American interest rates.

Brazil's present Minister of Education, Tarso Genro, has supported the Argentine initiative of negotiating with international institutions to use debt relief for basic education (Dianni 2004: 1). To reach the goals set for

ECCE by the National Plan for Education (which contemplates an expansion and improvement in quality) in 2006, an expenditure totaling 37.4 per cent of the refinancing of the federal debt service would be needed (Gomes 2004: 64). A miracle would be needed in the present economic and political situation for Brazil's creditors to soften their hearts on behalf of young children.[14]

## Birth control

Birth control has been considered by the neo-Malthusians to be one of the most effective strategies to reduce poverty. After carrying out a simulation of the impact of reducing the number of children of the Brazilian poor, Medeiros concluded:

> Brazilian poverty cannot be associated with the high number of children in families. If no Brazilian family had more than four children under 5 years of age, the percentage of poverty would be the same – 33 per cent. If the control were more extreme and in Brazil there was not even one child under 5 years of age, the number of the poor (and the population overall) would diminish, but the percentage would drop by only one percentage point.
>
> (2003: 11)

Despite this fact, the World Bank continues to attribute important weight to the reproductive patterns in producing poverty in Brazil: 'the three factors most associated to the probable causes of poverty are: being located in a poor area, having a low level of schooling and having a large family' (World Bank 2001: 8).

Explaining poverty by causes attributable to poverty itself such as reproductive patterns; linked to 'cultural' explanations of people's poverty, suggests that the moral scorn of the colonizers has not changed very much. The poor and poverty are still stigmatized. The metaphor of the 'vicious circle' of the reproduction of poverty and the 'virtuous circle' for combating it can be interpreted as a form of ideological pressure.

To illustrate the 'vicious circle' of poverty in Brazil, the World Bank gives a 'real-life' of Pedro's mother and her children. This groups together stereotypes about children's poverty, education and work:

- Pedro's mother is illiterate and of rural origin, therefore, poverty is associated with rural–urban migration.

- Pedro's mother comes from a family with thirteen children; she has ten children (a large family is responsible for the cycle of poverty).
- His mother lives with Pedro's step-father who makes two minimum wages (poverty is reproduced through a 'disorganized' family).
- None of Pedro's mother's children go to school because they cannot afford school supplies.
- It is Pedro's mother who decides who should leave school: 'I told them: you have to get some kind of job to be able to buy all those supplies'.
- Pedro's mother's children work, the boys stay on the street.

(World Bank 1995: 66)

This fable is presented as 'a recent study done by a Latin American institute with support from UNICEF' (cited in Rosemberg and Freitas 2001: 101–2).

This process of stigmatization was acutely perceived by Sharon Stephens during the Global Forum of ECO-92 in Rio de Janeiro, when she referred to the images of children in the discourse of environmentalists:

> The first is an image of innocent children in a beautiful environ- ment, this is the image of quality of life that we outline for 'all of us' when we engage in environmental actions. These children are usually white. The second image is of a mass of starving children, who fill the photographic frame and who destroy the environment. As far as I could tell, these children are black, although many of the children of the Third World are Asian, and naturally many of the poor children of the world are white.
>
> There is an undeniable racist component to illustrate 'over- population' – this excess population that needs to be reduced so that 'our children' have the quality of life illustrated by the first set of images'.

(Stephens 1992: 12)

In this paragraph, Sharon Stephens sums up the emphasis that guides discourses, analyses and proposals issued by the international, inter- governmental as well as the national agencies, about poor childhood and adolescence in the developing world generally, and in Brazil in particular. These emphases, which are ideological, revolve around two main axes:

(a) Underdevelopment is homogeneously identical throughout the con- tinents and within the same continent: Latin America is homogenous and its poor are equal.

(b)   In this context of poverty, poor families practice excesses that put their children at 'risk'. In poor families, women are seen, above all, as out-of-control reproducers, who cause and perpetuate poverty and put global ecology and economy at risk.

In these ways the processes of social domination are reinforced.

## Public policies

During the 1940s, the Brazilian State created specific agencies for child protection for the first time, strongly inspired by European experiences. The National Department for Children (DNCR) was created in 1940, linked to the then Ministry of Education and Health. The Brazilian Legion for Assistance was created in 1942. DNCR gradually centralized the assistance policies for mothers and children in Brazil over a 30-year period, making changes of a normative, educational and moralizing nature. It was the DNCR which regulated the few philanthropic daycare centres created in Brazil at the end of the 1960s. Its moralizing nature was underscored by Vieira (1988: 7): 'The predominant cause everywhere, in Europe as here, of high infant mortality is the incompetence of mothers in the matter of childrearing' (Oliveira 1940, cited in Vieira 1988: 7) – a concept not far from that disseminated by UNICEF in 2004.

> Iniquity and poverty form a vicious circle of self reproduction. Poor children are inserted into intergenerational cycles of poverty and exclusion. When this paradigm is not broken, they will be fathers and mothers of children who are also poor. Thus, malnourished children grow up and become malnourished mothers who give birth to low weight babies; parents who lack access to information crucial for becoming capable of feeding and caring for children in a healthful way; and illiterate parents have more difficulties in helping with the learning process of their children. To transform this negative circle into a positive one, a reduction of iniquity and poverty should be given more attention with regard to childhood, without forgetting other phases and situations of life.
>
> (UNICEF 2004: 47)

Barros and Carvalho, evaluating the challenges for Brazilian social policy to 'combat poverty', point out:

> the lack of integration among existing social programmes, the absence of co-ordination among the three levels of government, a precarious

focus on the neediest population, as well as the rare evaluations that have contributed to the transformations which Brazilian social policy has undergone, have not been sufficient to achieve significant reduction in the degree of inequalities of income in the country.

(2003: 15)

Analysing social policies for young Brazilian children, I would argue that they are underwritten by the policy of spectacle – the very poor, the weak and hopelessly vulnerable, the violent. The intervention of international organizations (of the United Nations and the NGOs) build on the policy of spectacle in order to shape Brazilian public policy on childhood.

After the International Year of the Child (1979), multilateral organizations, especially UNICEF, began to develop campaigns in favour of children in situations of 'risk'. There began a process of fragmenting poverty into subgroups or themes such as 'street children', 'child prostitution', 'adolescent pregnancy', 'eradication of child labour'. These campaigns, no doubt humanitarian, focused on these subgroups as representative of underdeveloped poverty in general. Starting with 'guesstimates', they arrived at a catastrophic number which appealed for focused, urgent governmental action. In their oversimplified explicatory models, they stigmatized children and families.

In 1981, the then advisor to UNICEF in New York on issues related to abandoned children and those without a family, Peter Taçon, brought to public light what was perhaps the first estimate of 'street children' in the world:

> Perhaps there exist no more intensely exploited and abused children in our present world than those who are forced to survive on city streets – descendents of economic miracles and human tragedies. Any reasonable estimate can evaluate their number at around one hundred million – and it is possible that half of them live in Latin America.
>
> (Taçon 1981a: 13)

Two components merit highlighting in this text: the exorbitance of the number of street children and the allegory of 'street children' being descendents of the economic miracle and of human misery.

The one hundred million estimated by Taçon fell to seventy million in the 'underdeveloped world' in the book written by Maggie Black (1986) on the history of UNICEF. The category of 'street children' gained sophistication and was attributed to 'an irregular family situation', accentuating the family of origin and its difficulties:

> Concerned individuals, voluntary organizations and governmental departments estimate that approximately seventy million children throughout the developing world fall under the broad definition of being in 'irregular family situation' meaning that they live totally or virtually without parental support . . . Among these children forty million live in Latin America where industrialization has been more intense than in Asia and Africa. This means that one in every five Latin American and Caribbean children live in a very different way than the traditional dependence on a family and relatives.
>
> (Black 1986: 360)[15]

Families that abandon their children, men and women who do not distinguish between good and evil are the dominant – and insulting – discourses:

> Many personalities have related what happens to abandoned minors in Brazil. Thirty million according to some, thirty-two to thirty-six according to others. The boys *naturally* become delinquents (robbery, holdups, attacks on the aged, etc.) and the girls are prostitutes at an early age.
>
> (International Federation of Democratic Jurists 1986: 106, emphasis mine)

Such issues, due to their media appeal, mobilize national governments who channel resources to specific programmes for 'street children', to combat 'child prostitution', to the 'eradication of child labour', etc. This is the same defensive process as in the nineteenth century, when Gobineau cursed our miscegenation. That is, issues of greater media visibility come to receive resources proportional to that visibility, disconnected from an overall policy for childhood.

The examples have been numerous over recent decades. Taking the example of daycare, international agencies, like UNICEF in Brazil, have chosen to emphasize parental discourses, improving parenting as a means of combating poverty (see Chapter 3). Levison (1991) analysing data from Brazil, showed that the most important factor determining whether Brazilian children from the ages of 7 to 14 work rather than study is the existence of a preschool-age sibling. If the mother of a young child has no care alternative for her child, either she stops working and the family allocates the responsibility to earn to another family member or she keeps working and another family member cares for the younger child. Families are not separate individuals living together by chance, but are inextricably interconnected, as the abundant literature from the 1980s on survival strategies has shown.

## Conclusion

So if there are no daycare centres for children under 3 years old, what do the mothers who work do? And what do the women heads of families do who have young children? Should they stop working and beg with a child on the lap? Should they abandon the child? Should they leave the baby with an older child or contract a neighbour to care for the baby? These are the options in Brazil. Who would this person be, capable of caring for a baby for reduced payment while the mother works? The main option is a young female adolescent who is as poor, or poorer. Thus inequality is reproduced: the international advisor from far away creates the problem, which in order to be solved, requires his/her competence, salary, travel, seminars, publications, etc. At the same time, the international advisors mount campaigns to eradicate the domestic work performed by poor and often black, Brazilian girls. Whose is the vice?

I have reversed the usual way of interpreting inequality in early childhood – good agencies teaching us the best way to develop ECCE – by listing the twenty capital *sins* of the multilateral organizations on public policies ECCE issues.

### Twenty cardinal sins

- Disregard the local prior history of ECCE.
- Disregard earlier interventions by international organizations.
- Disregard local trends and current conflicts.
- Disregard local ECCE experiences (propose models, programmes) without having visited local daycare centres and preschools.
- Commission studies to support project/programme models decided upon beforehand to guide the taking of decisions.
- Learn about local ECCE experiences just by references to the literature that circulates among international organizations, without returning to the original sources.
- Transpose experiences and diagnoses of underdeveloped countries in general to Latin America and the Caribbean in particular.

- Transpose experiences and diagnoses of Latin America and the Caribbean in general to a country in particular.
- Transpose conclusions from some experiences in the North to the South.
- Transpose specific local experiences from elsewhere to Brazil, and vice-versa.
- Be guided exclusively by economic analyses (cost/benefit models).
- Disregard the multiplicity of issues, including values about childhood, family, education and work in implementing programmes.
- Establish deadlines to respond to bureaucratic or institutional needs and not reasons intrinsic to the proposal.
- Lose sight of the fact that the first commitment of programmes for children, proposals and projects should be to improve present conditions in the lives of children and their families.
- Disregard the fact that there are often divergences among the interests of the child, the parents, the professionals, the technicians, the governments and the international organizations.
- Disregard the local and international political setting (the correlation of forces) in which the proposals are being discussed or implanted.
- Develop proposals for programmes where administrative costs (including those of headquarters) and the costs of implementation are disregarded or minimized.
- Propose low cost programmes as miraculous, capable or eradicating poverty.
- Use women's labour as voluntary.
- Do not independently evaluate their local interventions.

# Chapter 9

# The ethics of intervention

**Summary**

This chapter explores what can be done on a personal and practical level by early childhood practitioners and others concerned with young children. Most of this book has been concerned with intellectual arguments about inequality, and about the relationship between poverty and the prospects of young children in poor countries. The case studies of early childhood in four very different countries, Kazakhstan, Swaziland, India and Brazil were used to flesh out the arguments and highlight the often traumatic tensions between local understandings and practices and those imported from the North. The one thing the case studies have in common is that they illustrate that these tensions are not new but part of a historical process of domination and change.

In this chapter I switch genres. I abandon the cautions and caveats of academia (although not entirely) and try to make some practical suggestions. As someone from the North (although with close links to the South) I am aware of my presumption in attempting to give advice. The discussion is directed at others who, like myself, live in the North. I do not wish to presume to speak for those who live in the South, nor offer advice to them; but I hope a statement about what I think we can do in the North is a negotiating position; and negotiate we must.

I suggest that we can act on several fronts: on an intellectual front, questioning the 'facts' about development in the South; as consumers making choices about the goods and services we use; as givers, giving our money generously and judiciously; and as colleagues and collaborators in the field of early childhood. In this last role, we need to think about what we do with young children and if and how this compares with what most of the world's children experience. I put forward some suggestions about what kind of projects might be supported from the North.

## Introduction

People living in rich countries, are continually tempted, one might even say, taunted, to indulge in conspicuous consumption: a house with a swimming pool, champagne, a fast sports car with a retractable hard hood, a meal at a Michelin-starred restaurant, designer clothes, works of art by trendy avant-garde artists, expensive holidays in the sun in winter, hothouse orchids to decorate our homes. A flick through the colour supplement of a Sunday paper reveals all these temptations and more. There is certainly a stratum of society that enjoys this level of self-gratification. And even if we cannot aspire to such worldly goods, few of us have not experienced some covetousness and envy towards those that possess them.

Most people in rich countries live modestly and shop sparingly by the standards of the elite. Bringing up a family is often a time of cheese-paring, of making sure that income covers outgoings. In the North, however, even cheese-paring is relative. The majority of people in the North are, by the standards of poor countries, wealthy beyond the dreams of avarice. The annual expenditure on petfood in the UK, for example, would provide more than enough palliative drugs for HIV/AIDS sufferers in Swaziland for a year. Consumerism and individualism almost inevitably lead to blinkered perspectives.

Glover (2003), a medical ethicist, points to the complex, multi-layered ethical decision-making that now underwrites any medical intervention with children in the UK. Making a decision to operate on one vulnerable child with a life-threatening illness requires many protocols involving the family and medical teams. Yet the death of millions of children occurs casually and almost unrecorded in wars or through poverty or epidemics. As Glover comments: 'war kills many people, but each person has a life no more lightly to be destroyed than that of a child in hospital' (2003: 7). Gottlieb shows how infant death from tetanus, a frequent killer, is almost unrecorded in Côte d'Ivoire, for a variety of reasons (Gottlieb 2004). In the North we justifiably value life and the right to life and are shocked by child deaths or abuse in our own country, but overlook the prevalence of those same phenomena in the South.

How do you arrive at a sense of scale in order to understand these issues of relative wealth and poverty in any proportionate way? Where do one's responsibilities begin and end? How do you arrive at any kind of boundary line for what it is reasonable to spend on oneself and what should be set aside for others? These questions were continually raised and answered by major religions in their discussions of morality and what constitutes a good and devout life. Christians, Moslems, Jews, Hindus, Sikhs and Buddhists all had a view on giving and taking that underwrote religious observance. Today, in secular societies, these precepts are largely ignored.

Yet, as the sociologist Zygmunt Bauman argues, globalization (in all its complexity) means that our knowledge of everyday events is no longer parochial. We can no longer plead ignorance of gross and distorting inequalities:

> We live in a globalizing world. That means all of us, consciously or not, depend on each other. Whatever we do or refrain from doing affects the lives of people who live in places we'll never visit. And whatever those distant people do or desist from doing has its impact on the conditions in which we, each one of us separately and together, conduct our lives. Living in a globalizing world means being aware of the pain, misery and suffering of countless people whom we will never meet in person . . . our world, whatever else it might be is also a 'producer of horror and atrocity' . . . [there is] an abysmal gap between the suffering we see and our ability to help the sufferers.
>
> (1995: 287)

This book is directly and indirectly about the lives of poor children, children whose experiences of life are bitter – if indeed they survive. Poverty, as I have been at pains to explain, is relative and can be a blessing rather than a curse. But not having enough to eat over a long period, not being able to afford medicine that will prevent simple illnesses becoming fatal or debilitating, not being able to afford schooling, leading hard, arduous lives in degraded environments, experiencing exile and conflict: these conditions are very far from ideal. Our toleration of the extent of child poverty on an international scale undermines any claims we might make as civilized people to care about young children.

If as professionals, practitioners, academics or parents, we care about children's health and well-being, we cannot localize our caring and concern to a small group of children in the neighbourhoods where we live or work. The very large numbers of young children who are at risk in the world – through HIV/AIDS, through conflict, and through chronic poverty – are surely our concern too. As Bauman explains, the fact that they may not live on our doorstep is not an excuse for not knowing or not caring or not understanding what happens to them.

General knowledge of and concern about inequality is not, however, the same as specific knowledge of individual people or communities. From the North the question is how to translate good intentions into acts that do not trespass on local self-determination or ignore local realities. As the book has illustrated, in an unequal world, giving and taking are fraught with moral and political difficulties.

## Understanding the arguments

Engaging in economic and geopolitical discussion is a world away from early childhood. Yet the case being advanced in this book is that economics and geopolitics frame children's lives. Understanding about economic inequalities and about the operation of political power may indirectly better the lives of children. Some (perhaps many or most) of the causes of the poverty children experience can be traced back to the rich countries of North America and Europe. It is wrong to blame or write off poor countries as malfunctioning states or 'basket cases'. The problems with which African, Asian or South American governments struggle on a daily basis would probably defeat any European or North American politician.

Global politics and economics act as colonialism once did, to impose a particular kind of rule over others in the name of progress. As the book has also shown, globalism is a contested issue. At the most extreme, global institutions such as the World Bank have been accused of operating a kind of 'global apartheid', favouring and protecting the interests of the rich and ghettoizing the poor, just as white South Africans once oppressed black South Africans (Alexander 1996).

Even from a less extreme position, the international organizations that have been set up to regulate the world economy arguably reinforce inequality. The IMF, the World Bank, the World Trade Organization and a host of other international regulatory bodies are necessary but not benign. The world economy is too complex to do without their brokerage and regulation; but as these bodies are currently constituted, they serve essentially to articulate and fulfil the needs of the rich.

The Royal Society, the UK's most prestigious and august scientific body, commissioned a report on sustainability. It soberly points out that those of us who live in the North live beyond our means. We are depleting the planet of its natural resources. The report concludes that the *only* way forward is to engage in major changes in the lifestyles of the most developed countries (Heap and Kent 2000). Presently we exploit the poor in the South in order to obtain those resources. From oil and gas imported from the Middle East and West Africa to broccoli grown in Peru; from prawn fishing in Thailand to cheap shirts sewn in Bangladesh; from lilies cultivated in Kenya to coffee picked in Colombia; we are supporting our lifestyles on the backs of others.

The *Guardian* newspaper in the UK in 2002 ran a series tracking the production of every day goods such as tennis balls, shoes and teabags. The workers picking the tea or producing the raw goods are paid very little – 90p per day is a good rate for a tea picker. The goods are then transformed several times, sorted, cut, dyed and packaged, and then shipped across the world to the people who will eventually use them. Chussodovsky (1997; and see Chapter 2) has detailed this process for garment production in Bangladesh. The labour cost – what a woman gets paid – for making a shirt retailing at $292 in the USA is $5. Other costs include transport across continents, shipping the material for the shirts to the Bangladesh factory and flying the finished garments across the world. Even so, the profit for the entrepreneur or designer label is approximately $200 (Chussodovsky 1997: 90).

One way to describe the South is as a collection of exploitative industrial and factory farm zones, set up in order to provide the North with cheap out-of-season food, cut-price minerals and chemicals, and inexpensive goods and services. Above all lifestyles in the North are dependent on oil (not for nothing called liquid gold). We overlook the inconvenient fact that at the other end of this process of 'economic development' fostered by the IMF and World Bank are the impoverished families who are paid a pittance and are unable to prevent their children from living such hard lives or worse still, watching their children die young.

The United Nations and the multifarious agencies it has spawned, UNICEF, UNESCO, UNDP, WHO, UNAIDS and many others, draw our attention to inequality and injustice in exquisitely detailed reports. Like the economic regulatory bodies, they may be necessary organizations in a tricky and fast-moving world. They give overviews and comparisons. They provide useful benchmarks and targets. They offer models of governance and civil liberties. They articulate a range of human rights including the rights of the child. But unfortunately they are weak when set against the power of corporations and the governments – especially the USA – who protect the corporations. The UN agencies are required to be 'politically neutral'. In their efforts to be neutral, they may even perpetuate inequality in so far as they fail to challenge some of the basic tenets of economic development and the marketplace. And like any very large institution they have their own internal momentum and bureaucratic habits that are inevitably self-perpetuating.

Keeping abreast of all these arguments is difficult, especially taking on board a range of contradictory views. I have given less credence to the arguments of those like Krugman (2003; and see Chapter 1) who are unapologetic about the benefits of world trade and globalization. In the overall scheme of things, early childhood services are a minor backwater. But if there is a connection between a particular economic stance and the life situation of children we should know what it is, if only to support the case for or against it.

## The power of consumers

There are some very modest means of action in this unequal world. Consumer power works, as the story of the limitation of genetically modified crops illustrates. Judicious purchasing and careful consumption if practised on a large enough scale can bring about change. Eating mainly seasonal, unprocessed foods, from local providers, avoiding ingredients shipped across the world; buying tea and coffee through fair trade co-operatives; checking where clothes and shoes are made, and by whom; and above all cutting back on fuel: these strategies have already changed consumption patterns. No individual by herself can make a change, but many individuals together can reshape the demand for particular kinds of goods.

Consumer power can also exert some (small) influence in financial markets. I discussed in Chapter 1 how financial markets are based on speculative bets, in which enormous amounts of money change hands, distorting the prices of commodities and undermining currencies. For those that have money to invest, there are an increasing number of 'ethical investments' which can be placed through brokers who will not engage in speculative buying of stocks and shares and who will only invest in 'green' companies whose policies have been ethically scrutinized. Some pension funds offer ethical investments. The money market, above all, needs scrupulous investors.

Again, the connection between these kinds of actions and concerns about childhood, is laboured, and not immediately obvious. But as Bauman points out, in a globalizing world we depend on each other, and in deliberately not supporting agricultural and industrial practices that are essentially harmful, we are also supporting the children who are the unwitting victims of such practices.

## Giving

In Chapter 4 I discussed how governments give aid. The UN recommendation is that countries spend 0.7 per cent of GDP per year on aid.

On a personal level, however, the religious obligation of giving has been mostly forgotten – or perhaps people consider such obligations are already met through their taxation! This brings us back to the question, when is wealth obscene? Is it possible to agree or at the very least discuss standards for personal conduct in an individualistic society? If we adopted the same standard ourselves as we have adopted for nation states, we would individually pay a very low amount. The equivalent would be less than £500 for an income of £50,000 per year. I would argue that the circumstances of young children are so dire that we should do both: press governments to meet, or even exceed, their international obligations to contribute towards aid, but also debate whether it is reasonable to aim (voluntarily) for a fixed amount of individual income – say 5 per cent – to be donated to an international fund.

Given the difficulties – discussed in Chapter 4 – of distributing aid, to whom should money be given? Many aid agencies provide a trenchant critique of the global economy. In the UK, Oxfam, Christian Aid, Action Aid and Save the Children are examples of aid organizations who, through their campaigning and advocacy, are trying to highlight injustice and to show what being poor really means. Supporting the challenges they mount is a small step towards a fairer world. A new generation of charities and aid organizations are trying to work on a North/South basis in formulating policies and objectives. INTRAC, as an example, works with non-governmental organizations (NGOs) and civil society organizations around the world exploring policy issues and strengthening management and organizational effectiveness, using perspectives from the South (www.intrac.org). There are many non-governmental organizations in the south who can be supported directly.

## Early childhood colleagues and collaborators

In particular, as early years practitioners, policy makers and researchers, should we be supporting specific early years models or particular projects? Or should we be supporting particular people, sponsoring volunteer workers through organizations such as the UK INGOs, Skills Share or Voluntary Services Overseas (VSO)?

As the case studies have demonstrated, there is no prototype model which can be exported; no typical training which can transported from one situation into another. In Mongolia, a desert and steppes country peopled by pastoralists, I met a very dedicated volunteer nursery teacher, trained in the UK, and sponsored through a volunteer organization in the UK. Her mission was to introduce 'play' into the kindergartens; and she told me how she hoped to encourage sand and water play into what she saw as barren classrooms. For most people in Mongolia, sand is something to keep at bay and water is scarce and hoarded. Children are dressed in their best clothes in order to go to school and school is for learning. All toys and books are very expensive and not often used at home or in school; teachers have developed other methods of relating to – and inspiring – children (Demberel and Penn 2005). In the capital of Ulan Bator, the kindergartens are more cosmopolitan and sand and water play may have been a novelty. But the volunteer teacher's actions symbolized the missionary point of view; that we in the North have the tried and tested methods and we need to show backward and uninformed people in poor countries how to do better.

In the North we have generally accepted (with the exception of the USA) that the state should play a major role in supporting and regulating early years provision. In Chapter 2 I explored the position set out by the OECD (2001) in its summary of early years services, *Starting Strong*. In brief this is that equitable access to early years services brings positive benefits; it enables women to participate in the workforce on equal terms with men; and it enhances the learning capacities of young children and prepares them for the demands of schooling.

It would be good if this OECD position could be taken as one of Rawl's minimum conditions for a decent life. But this position presumes a certain structure and organization to communities and societies that does not exist in many places. The participation-in-the-workforce argument envisages a documented and regulated workforce. In the South, the 'workforce' is a much more nebulous concept. In some countries relatively few people belong to the formal, regulated sector. People may be peasants eking a livelihood from the land, or small traders, or engaged in many small tasks on the periphery of the economy. They contribute little if at all to the tax revenue base, and receive very little from it in the way of benefits or services. Only those directly employed by government or by firms and organizations who observe minimum conditions of employment, are likely to have a regular income. On the other hand, poor women are likely to be working very long hours. In the shanty towns that surround most cities, housing recent (and not so recent) migrants, women eke out a livelihood as domestic servants, as hawkers and petty traders, or brewing beer or making snacks to sell. Munyakho (1992) describes daily life for women and children in one such township on the edge of Nairobi where mothers of young children work 14 hours a day or more.

The education argument is also open to question. Having an education and being literate is for sure better than not having one and being illiterate.

But as Chapter 7 in this book vividly illustrates, many education systems are unpleasant experiences for children, serving to reinforce their sense of failure and incompetence, dangling before them a world they can imagine but to which they can never aspire and at the same time devaluing the world from which they actually come.[1] Some critics such as Serpell (1999a) writing about Zambia, describes education as an extractive process. At each stage the better off and clever pupils progress, leaving those behind with a double feeling of failure, a sense of being doubly peripheral. Teacher absenteeism (or illness and death in the case of HIV/AIDS); corporal punishment; a strange language and an alien curriculum; and anxiety about the incidental costs of schooling – providing pencils, exercise books, shoes and clothes; all these act as deterrents to schooling. There is not much point in getting a head start in an unfair system in which there are very heavy odds of failure.

So the rationales for providing early education and care are weaker, or rather, very much more complicated than in the OECD countries. Any universal provision, for example lowering the school starting age from 6 or 7 years to 5 or 6 years, is contingent on wider educational reforms which may be slow in coming. But if the OECD arguments do not reflect the realities of life in the South and if the rather different arguments about poverty reduction used by the World Bank and others (discussed in Chapter 2) are suspect, what remains? If the theoretical underpinning of child development does not underpin anything except the implicit practices of highly individualistic and consumerist societies, what then?

## What kind of early childhood projects?

Young children are very vulnerable, and their deaths in such large numbers are unacceptable in the North as well as in the South. Here I argue that, for those from the North considering intervention, 'immediacy of need' is a more acceptable justification than putative long-term benefits modelled on Western conceptions of childhood.[2] Some kinds of practical interventions are useful and necessary to relieve immediate need, whatever their wider implications.

Pragmatism implies that one is dealing with the obvious: that needs are self-evident. They are not, of course, and in resource-poor environments there are many competing needs. But abstract and universalistic justifications for intervention may be even more problematic. Local solutions arrived at in discussion with local people is the mantra put forward as an alternative. But as many studies have shown, notions of 'community' and 'participation' and 'local' blur all kinds of wider oppressions, as well as tensions between individuals. Campbell in her book *Letting them Die* examines efforts to involve local people in peer education preventative campaigns against HIV/AIDs in a very poor mining community in South Africa. Despite the efforts to encourage participation in the project it was not successful. Poverty (women so poor that they sold their bodies to survive) and gender inequality (male expectations of women's passivity) undermined prevention efforts, leading Campbell to conclude that 'grass-roots participation is by no means a "magic bullet"' (2003: 196). Campbell argues for more careful analysis of the processes involved, as well as of the power structures that shape what change is possible.

'Immediate need' and 'pragmatism' then beg many questions. Hedged around with 'careful, accountable, transparent and critical', 'telling the truth', they may offer some basis for aid intervention in early childhood. With these cautions in mind, I have drawn on my experience, mostly with SCF-UK, to suggest some examples of situations where early childhood programmes might make a contribution to the well-being of young children in the here and now. But realistically none of these programmes will be sustainable, in the sense that they will carry on without external funding or support in very poor communities. Like the UNICEF immunization programme described above, they depend in the long run on wider societal change, and a society wealthy enough to pay for them.

## Support for time-poor working women with young children

I have described in detail elsewhere (Penn 2001) a programme run by SCF-UK for farm-workers' children in Zimbabwe. The commercial farms were staffed mainly by untenured labour, migrants from Malawi and Mozambique, as well as very poor Zimbabweans. Many of these farms were (and still are) run directly by multinational corporations or by those contracted to supply to them (for instance supplying asparagus to an upmarket UK supermarket chain, or sweetcorn or green beans for canning by well-known brand names).[3] The workers were isolated – it was often a considerable distance to the nearest town. Working conditions on the farms were usually very poor, with meagre accommodation, limited access to water,[4] little or no sanitation and regular use of poisonous chemical sprays to protect crops. Young children would usually accompany their mothers working in the fields and be subjected to the sprays and the harsh working conditions.

SCF negotiated with farm owners to provide a safe fenced piece of land to serve as a playground; some very basic play equipment such as a log climbing frame or tyre swing, a shaded area or hut, basic sanitation and a water supply. Children stayed in these playgrounds whilst their mothers were working in the fields. Two women with basic health training were assigned to look after the children (often 70 or 80 of them) and provide them with one nutritious meal at lunch time, which was provided by the farmer or overseer. SCF provided a very small support team that negotiated with farmers over difficulties that arose, and offered limited training to farm workers in making out-door equipment for the children. The children played together, as they might in a village, multi-aged groups, older ones caring for younger, making up their own games and activities. There were very few signs of friction or fighting as far as it was possible to tell as an outside observer visiting briefly. This was no frills care. It offered no false dawns, but provided a utilitarian service under circumstances it recognized as difficult and sought elsewhere to try to change.

There are many examples of such practical arrangements for working women. SEWA (the Self-employed Women's Association) in India has a long history of providing crèches to support working women, initially for low-caste women in the textile industry (www.sewa.org).

The question is whether these attempts to provide basic care for children should become something more, an attempt to provide a learning environment for children, a place where they do more than pass the time in safety – although this begs another set of questions about what constitutes a good environment for young children or good training for their caretakers. This is a local as much as a national or an international debate.

### Support for orphans and vulnerable children

An estimated 15 per cent of households in some Southern African countries are child headed. Mothers and fathers have died, often painfully and messily, nursed by their children. The oldest child is then left 'in charge' of the family. As well as the grief children suffer, and the loss of financial support and parental guidance, often there are complications about official records (of birth, death, etc.) and inheritances. Relatives and neighbours may step in, but children may be left to fend for themselves. This situation is described in more detail in the chapter on Swaziland. It constitutes an unimaginable horror story.

There is a consensus that orphanages are not the answer; they are too expensive and too institutionalized. Instead there is a focus on community support. Grandparents or neighbours may be able to offer some support, if they in turn are practically supported; so might schools if they are offered support and training and school fees are waived for the most vulnerable.

The youngest and most dependent children are the most vulnerable of all. They require more looking after and they take up more time. Crèche support relieves the burden on carers (older children, relatives, neighbours) and can offer food and nutrition. Although some moves have been made to describe what crèches might offer and to develop such support systems (UNESCO 2002) very little has been done. This is an important area where a systematic consideration of early childhood programmes and support might contribute to the alleviation of suffering, without any accompanying rhetoric about future benefits.

## Support for existing care workers

In almost all cities in the South there is a substantial informal care market. There are hundreds and thousands of backyard crèches, in huts, converted garages and more rarely in purpose built accommodation (which is likely to cost parents much more). There is unlikely to be fenced outside space and there may not be water or sanitation or electricity. The women (almost always) who work in these crèches may be illiterate or barely educated. The crèche is a small and not very remunerative business that women take on when there is little else they are qualified or competent to do. Many churches and other small organizations also run crèches, along very similar lines. With the best will in the world it would be hard to describe the children who attend as having a positive experience, or being prepared for school (unless learning to sit still without complaint is preparation for school). Some crèches may be better than others, but the absence of outside space (unlike the farm crèches) means children are cooped up for much of the time.

This sector is informal and unregulated. To introduce regulation without resources would be self-defeating. Most owners or church groups do not have the resources to make the improvements to meet higher standards. In order to do so they would have to raise fees; but parents are unlikely to be able to pay for higher fees. The question then is what kinds of improvements might work? Many small NGOs offer training courses. I have reviewed some of these in South Africa (Penn 1997). They are of variable quality, as might be expected. Some are extremely good in the way they tap into local traditions and ideas; others draw on curricula and pedagogic ideas almost unaltered from the North. But in addition to any conceptual or pedagogical challenges, attending training presents severe obstacles for the very poor: maintaining contacts without even a telephone; travelling to a course; paying for it; being supported subsequently in carrying out the ideas that are presented. Course organizers have to provide food – people are often hungry and one of the attractions of a training course is the food that goes with it.

There is also the question of the extent to which such training reinforces gender stereotyping. Biersteker (1996) interviewed early childhood trainers in Cape Town and demonstrated how working in early childhood was the only option possible for highly marginalized women; but because of low pay (parents cannot afford to pay more for care) training has to be its own intrinsic reward. There are rarely financial incentives.[5]

Offering training and support to childcare workers is a strategy for meeting 'immediate need', in this case the barrenness of the daily experiences of so many young children. But its efficacy to an extent depends on being embedded within wider sectoral changes. This means more investment in the system as a whole – grants for capital improvements, equipment, literacy aids, some regulatory activities – as well as support for individual training programmes. The quality and relevance of the training matters, but given the gendered position of the carers, marginalized women who live in poverty (as do the users of the services they provide), it is fanciful to talk about empowerment or long-term benefits from, say, a week's training course which, alongside an introduction to childcare, has to catch up on a lifetime's near-illiteracy. On the other hand, providing one is modest about such interventions, training can offer up practical benefits such as some few new ideas about activities to undertake with children and the establishment of supportive links between trainers and participants.

### Making existing systems work for the poor

Most transitional countries had good kindergarten systems offering a more comprehensive range of services, more comprehensive than in the West. Since transition, services for children in these countries have become very run down. Many countries have adopted a policy of introducing charges for these services, so that only those who can afford to pay for them can continue to use them. (This process of exclusion is described further in the chapter on Kazakhstan.)

In Mongolia, for example, an extremely remote and inaccessible country, kindergartens had nevertheless been established for distant settlements and village centres. Working with the Ministry of Education, it was possible to introduce a system which set aside a proportion of places for the poorest children, and to suggest ways in which kindergartens could generate the income to support such children (Penn 1999). If state services do exist, and public money is being spent on them, then it is important that children from poor families are able to attend them.

These are only some examples of 'needy' circumstances. I have not discussed the position of children in refugee camps or displaced children who have experienced conflict, although these certainly merit urgent consideration (Lloyd *et al.* 2004). The point is to be clear why services are provided at a local level, and what they might reasonably seek to achieve.

## What kind of standards?

I have argued that, in some circumstances, providing some kind of centre-based care, or supporting those who work in centre-based care, is a useful strategy to support poor children and those looking after them. But what kind of facility should be provided, bearing in mind that many of the assumptions that underpin early education and care in the North do not travel well to the South? Organizations like the Bernard van Leer Foundation which focus on young children have been concerned about what constitutes quality in resource-poor communities. The organization commissioned Woodhead to carry out a review of quality in early childhood programmes in the South (briefly discussed in Chapter 2). He compared programmes in four countries, Kenya, Venezuela, France and India. He produced a model for 'contextually appropriate practice' and argued that quality should be judged by the best of what is available locally, using criteria of staffing ratios, curriculum, premises, etc.

This relativist approach has been criticised on the grounds that it legitimizes a poor service for poor communities. Any approach needs to be contextually sensitive; but on the other hand the relativity of this approach raises all kinds of questions of inequality – why should poor communities have the poorest services?

In 1998 I visited early childhood services in Dar es Salaam in Tanzania carrying out a needs analysis for SCF. Like most cities in the South, there was a plethora of provision. There were a handful of government nursery classes, maintained to the basic standard of the school. Mostly children sat on the ground, and the teaching I saw relied on chalk and a black-board, although the teachers were trained, and the numbers of children were controlled. There were the usual back street huts with children crammed in rows on mud floors in hot tin-roofed rooms with little to do except recite what the care-worker or teacher told them, if indeed she gave them instructions to follow. I did not visit the Madrassahs, the preschools that are based on Koranic religious teaching in Arabic. And then there was a Montessori nursery school – funded at that time by an Austrian donor – in a light airy ventilated room, floored with lino, where the children had chairs and tables and the full range of Montessori equipment. The children were taught by Montessori-trained staff, one Austrian, one Tanzanian. Outside there was a lovely, shady flower garden for the children to use.

Even in one city like Dar es Salaam – or as discussed in Chapter 6, Mbabane, the capital of Swaziland – what constitutes local and what constitutes community? Should the Montessori school be taken as a beacon school, a centre of excellence, by which the rest are judged? In many middle-income or even poor countries, the elite have services that match those of the best in Europe; should much lower standards be acceptable for the children of the townships or *favelas* (Rosemberg 2003a)?

In South Africa, despite very great inequalities, the government has accepted the responsibility for providing equitably for all children. It has done this by lowering the school starting age, and introducing a curricular framework, national qualifications and a modular training scheme for those working with children. But as in the UK, the level of qualification is pitched at a lower level than for those who trained as nursery teachers. The British style free-standing nursery schools, usually with extensive grounds and good outdoor equipment which were developed under the apartheid regime, have become privatized and are open only to those who can afford the fees. The township crèches are very slowly improving. The post-apartheid ANC government in South Africa is still young – less than 10 years old – and turning a country around from a brutal, divisive and highly unequal regime is a long, imperfect and fraught process. But ultimately the case they have advanced (whether or not it has been attained or is even attainable) for equality of provision for all children is unanswerable.

## Evaluation

In the South there are many examples of projects in which minimally trained paraprofessionals visit homes where there is a child under the age of 2, once a week over a one year period or so, in order to teach 'child development' to parents or carers. Such programmes are usually justified on an a priori basis using 'evidence' from the literature. If indeed they are evaluated, it is standard procedure to use anecdotal evidence collected from participants or staff and/or external consultants' reports for their evaluations. The evaluations tend to focus on process rather than on outcomes. They often have another purpose besides rational enquiry about effectiveness: to sell the project to donors and ensure future funding, so they are selectively enthusiastic about the comments they quote as evidence.

Evaluation of projects is often not taken seriously, for very good reasons. It is expensive, it can be threatening and it may require a level of expertise that is unobtainable. In order to find out whether a project really does what it says it is doing, however, there needs to be a wider theoretical perspective – why are people doing what they are doing, and what is the justification for it? Baseline measures and outcome measures based on the justification then offer some rigorous data in addition to people's opinions and feelings – which whilst important may also be heavily influenced by those who have set up the project. Research ethics are now sophisticated enough to deal with complicated questions of procedure; and academic evaluations at least, are usually subject to some kind of ethical scrutiny.

## Conclusion

I began this book with two quotations from philosophers, Richard Rorty and John Rawls. They are both concerned with injustice and have put forward models of conduct for dealing with it. They agree that we should try to describe and address injustice, and that doing so is a complex and multi-layered undertaking, whether one takes an approach that is relativist (progress can only come through understanding and negotiating with local realities) or universalist (there are minimum standards of justice for everyone). I have tried to describe some of these complexities with regard to young children, although I am acutely aware that my account is a partial one. If nothing else this book is an argument against simplistic formulations and parochial perspectives in dealing with an outrage: the unnecessarily impoverished lives and early deaths of millions of young children.

# Notes

## Preface

1 Even grouping countries according to their wealth or poverty presents difficulties since the categories are never clear-cut. Poor countries used to be called 'The Third World'. This was regarded as perjorative and has been more or less dropped by some progressive scholars but not by journalists or ordinary people. The preferred term, still in widespread use became 'developing countries'. This begs the question of what 'development' is, and many radical commentators steer clear of it. Some colleagues use the expression 'Majority and Minority World' to indicate that the poor are the majority of people in the world, and the rich the minority. This has proved too confusing, and in any case was objected to by colleagues in very polarized countries like Brazil, where great wealth and great poverty sit uneasily together.

Other words in use are the more geographically orientated terms 'the South' to indicate poor countries and 'the North' to indicate rich countries. These are also imprecise terms, since countries like Australia and South Korea could be described as 'South' but are certainly not poor countries. In addition 'Transitional countries' refer to ex-communist countries which are in transition from a centralized planned economy to a liberal free market economy. Transitional countries tend to use the 'West' to describe Euro-American countries.

I am adopting the words 'the South', 'the North' and 'Transitional' for the purposes of this book, on the basis that they are the most commonly used in the field by international agencies. Some of the articles and books I draw upon or quote from may use other terminology. I hope the text will make the meanings clear.

## I Global inequalities

1 See Chapter 4 for details of the different kinds of aid agencies.
2 A recent edition of the *British Medical Journal* was dedicated to exploring health inequities for those affected by or living with AIDS (*BMJ* 2002).
3 Channel 4 News, 16 November 2003.
4 In fact, history in a sense is the history of empire. Throughout history, in every

era for which we have records, various powerful groups have sought to control and dominate others.

## 2 Interpreting poverty

1 Although her book is widely quoted, she has also been criticized heavily within Brazil, as an outsider pronouncing – in English – about the condition of the poor without any engagement with the social movements in Brazil trying to bring about change. See Chapter 8 for more details.
2 A similar argument is also presented in Chapter 7.

## 3 Understanding early childhood

1 Author's translation.
2 The most frequently cited brain studies are that by Chugani *et al.* (1987) carried out on a group of epileptic children aged 5–15, some of whom were under severe medication; and studies carried out by Hubel and Weisel (1977) in the 1970s of the visual cortex of kittens who were blinded at birth!
3 On its current ECD website the World Bank's only mention of the UK is a casual reference to something called the 'Playground Movement', presumably a misreading of playgroups.
4 The recent film 'The Weeping Camel' (2004) is a reasonably accurate portrayal of life in a nomadic Mongolian family. In the film the children are determined about what they want, but always within the context of the wider group and their obligations within it.
5 Personal communication, Paivi Lundberg, Ministry of Social Welfare, Finland.
6 See the chapters by Gupta and Rosemberg.
7 Although still prepared to inflict it on others, for example in Afghanistan and Iraq – see Glover 2003.

## 4 Lending a helping hand

1 Colonialism is only a more recent episode in the history of human conflict and empire building, but has been a particularly savage one.
2 The most extreme example of this were the Bantustans, the native homelands, created by the apartheid government of South Africa. The ANC government continued to pay tribal leaders when apartheid was dismantled, hoping to minimize disruption and fighting, particularly in KwaZulu Natal.
3 See Chapter 8 for an account of the Portuguese colonization of Brazil.
4 In South Africa it has proved the most tremendous challenge to adapt and change Afrikaaner government structures. In 1996–7 I was seconded to help set up a new early years section in the education department of the new Regional Government in Gauteng (Johannesburg and the mid-rand). The regional government brought together the previously separate Black, Indian and Afrikaaner administrations. Every rule, regulation and code of practice had to be renegotiated (down to how you ordered replacements for the missing drawers of a filing cabinet!).
5 See also chapters 7 and 8.

6 The World Bank has a number of sister organizations. For example the Inter-American Bank specializes in Latin America; the Asian Development Bank (ADB) finances developments in Central and South-East Asia. They also rely on macro-economic analyses for determining aid (although the ADB has a reputation for being more concerned with social issues and local context). They, too, operate on a loan basis, and much of their work is tendered out to consultancy organizations.

7 See Chapter 8 on Brazil for more details.

8 The most accusatory accounts of USA/World Bank funding are provided by Chomsky (2003).

9 *Fifty Years is Enough*. Factsheet produced by the Inter-Church coalition on Africa, on the fiftieth anniversary of the founding of the World Bank

10 see Chapter 8 for a critique of Scheper-Hughes.

11 It was previously directed by an academic, but partly because of USA pressure, it is now lead by Carol Bellamy, an ex-businesswoman and ex-US senator.

12 A UNESCO colleague in South-East Asia told me that he had witnessed such corruption in his work that when he retired he wanted to work on a voluntary basis for Transparency International.

13 I write this having been one such consultant, working in four continents in six months on short-term contracts. Knowing the difficulties I still do it. I justify this to myself somewhat ambivalently on the grounds that first of all I earn money for my employer, a university; and second that the material I obtain I can, as in this book, also use for research purposes, an opportunity to document circumstances that might otherwise remain untold. But most international organizations require intellectual property rights undertakings. So even 'telling it like it is' is a circumspect process.

14 Although he now considers governments should curb and regulate the excesses of capitalism: Soros 2000.

15 See Chapter 5.

16 The UK government have set themselves a target of reaching 0.7 per cent by 2010.

17 DfID does have a small research budget to fund research centres in the UK to work on and evaluate development projects and it issues research publications.

18 On a visit to South Africa, February 1998.

## 5 Kazakhstan

1 The President of Kazakhstan and his wife were guests at the wedding of the son of the King of Spain in June 2004.

2 The President's wife has taken an interest in kindergartens and has supported the rebuilding of the kindergarten which her grandchildren attend as a model kindergarten.

3 Like many ex-Soviet bloc currencies the Kazakh currency fluctuates considerably against the dollar. The exchange rate when I was there was approximately 138 tenge to the dollar. Although the dollar is still the best-known currency, local entrepreneurs such as taxi drivers are now asking to be paid in euros rather than dollars!

4 There were considerable problems in devolving finances to local districts – these were the subject of a separate financial review.

5 For example 'conductive education' is a special form of intense physiotheraphy designed for children with cerebral palsy, which was developed in Hungary and has had some influence in the UK. Speech therapy is extremely well developed in Bulgaria where speech is regarded not only as pronounciation, but as a complex system of communication and expressiveness.

6 This was the main recommendation of the report I wrote for ADB.

7 Except environmental ones, concerned about the pollution of the Aral Sea and Semiplatansk.

8 I visited the world photo journalism exhibition held in August 2002 in Perpignan. One set of exhibits was from a Russian prison in Siberia. I was struck by the similarity of the prison regime to a kindergarten in the design of facilities (what the photographer called the 'industrial aesthetic') in the activities portrayed and in the collective demeanour of the prisoners. One of my translators in Kazakhstan described her own experiences of kindergarten as being like a boot camp – on the other hand she still elected to send her own children to the local kindergarten.

## 6 Swaziland

1 Chieftains still receive generous allowances from the new South African state (for example £3 million a year for the Zulu King Buthelezi) and co-exist uneasily besides democratic government; a price that Mandela deliberately chose to pay in order to effect a peaceful transition.

2 Although anti-apartheid activists were angry that he gave them no support.

3 The EU mission in Southern Africa has been pressurizing Mswati to adopt the constitution, as has the British High Commissioner. Mswati has sent this constitution to Robert Mugabe, in Zimbabwe, for advice.

4 His book is banned in Swaziland.

5 In the short time I was in Swaziland there were two major scandals concerning the king's expenditure. One concerned the proposal by the king to use government funds to buy himself an expensive jet plane for his personal use. The other was a conference for heads of state called 'Smart Partnership'. This jamboree, which was poorly attended, but which consumed the time of senior government officials for months, had no obvious content other than as a showpiece for the King to entertain visiting dignitaries, and cost the country millions of dollars.

6 Geographically Swaziland is an enclave within South Africa. Many South Africans joke about Swaziland's backward politics, and call it 'Micky Mouseland'. It is compared to a Bantustan under apartheid, where chiefs, bought off by the apartheid regime, exercised similar kinds of absolute powers and indulged themselves with the money used to buy them off.

7 DfID – Department of International Development, UK. As an ex-colony, the UK maintains a High Commissioner in Swaziland. Until recently DfID was an active donor in Swaziland. It still funds small projects, mainly to try to strengthen civil governance.

8 There was a continuing argument about the EU education review, about whether the grant should be spent on prestigious secondary school buildings

or used to support poor children in school. The King and his advisers strongly favoured the former.

9 Neprovirene is by no means a perfect cure and may increase drug-resistant strains of HIV; it has an estimated 60–70 per cent success rate in preventing mother–child transmission. Any alternative is even more costly.

10 She lent me the Kuper books. She also was working with a group of teachers in Swaziland to write an alternative history book, one which did not take the royal family as its focus.

11 This is likely to be an underestimate of the number of centres. In discussion with stakeholders and in the course of field trips, we came across a number of centres that had not been included in the survey.

12 Eight emalgeni (E8) = approximately one dollar ($1).

13 For example, an Italian environmental organization, supports two crèches and a number of informal schools alongside an environmental regeneration project.

14 The Government has set up an independent National Emergency Response Committee for HIV/AIDS, known as NERCHA. It has attracted funds from a variety of sources including the global aids fund. Some of this money is designated to support orphans and vulnerable children, in particular child headed households. NERCHA, after much debate, decided that the most reliable way of identifying children in need was to use the chieftaincy system. Chiefs are asked to provide lists of vulnerable children in their area.

15 For instance see Scheper-Hughes and Sargent, 'Small Wars' (1998) in which the widespread use of oral rehydration schemes is criticized.

## 7  India

1 In Jaunpur, traditionally, wine is brewed in almost every home and is of extremely high quality containing herbs, roots and local grains and made in a highly sophisticated and elaborate manner. This is consumed by both men and women and one never heard of domestic or any other kind of violence, which often accompanies alcohol consumption in other areas, specially the urban areas. But now under the urban influence alcohol is increasingly being bought from the market by the men and consumed only by them. The educated women neither know how nor like to make alcohol at home and are being discouraged from drinking it.

2 In this context a nuclear family is one where the only adults present in it are the mother and father.

3 Gyan Bharti Part 3, Lesson 15, page 53, Basic Shiksha Nideshalaya 1999

## 8  Childhood and social inequality in Brazil

* Fúlvia Rosemberg is Brazilian, a senior researcher with the Carlos Chagas Foundation, and a full professor of social psychology at the PUC-SP, where she coordinates the Nucleus for Studies on gender, race and age relations (NEGRI). Her academic and political activities have dealt with issues related to the creation and overcoming of social inequalities. To access her publications in Portuguese or another language go to www.cnpq.br/ plat formalatts/index novo.htm. The translation from Portuguese to English was done by Ann Puntch.

1 I have not used statistics and indicators systematized and published by UNICEF and the World Bank, references which are almost obligatory in analysing the poverty of the South. This was (and has been) a political option, since I and other researchers and activists consider that international agencies propose policies for Brazilian childhood that, as a rule, reinforce stigma and social inequalities, and the statistics they use reinforce these perceptions.

2 Two publications from the 1980s deserve to be highlighted: *Infância e Desenvolvimento* (Childhood and Development) (Magalhães and Garcia 1993) and *Criança pequena e raça* (Young children and Race) (Rosemberg and Pinto 1997).

3 The academic journal that comes closest (to gathering these materials) is entitled *Revista Brasileira de Crescimento e Desenvolvimento* (The Brazilian Journal of Growth and Development), created in 1992.

4 Since, 1889, Brazil has been a federal republic comprised of 26 federal units and a federal district. The federated units (the states) are subdivided into municipalities (5,560 in the overall federation).

5 Infant mortality in a rural region of the state of Pernambuco, was the subject of an award winning interpretation by a North American academic. Through this one can perceive that the anathema launched over Brazilian poverty can also have its origin in academic writing, even when motivated by 'good intentions'. I am referring to *Death without Weeping*, a book by Nancy Scheper-Hughes, who began travelling to Brazil at the start of the dictatorship as a member of the Peace Corps (USAID–North American). Her book deals with the negligence of poor rural mothers in the region of Pernambuco known as the Zona da Mata, as one of the intermediaries of premature death of infants.

It is a Brazil observed by Americans and includes visions of primitivism and primevalism as well as the hardened emotiveness and distorted characterizations of the poor people who are shaken by misery and violence in a country that has still not experienced full development. 'American national anthropology reinforces its dominant pose, and Brazil, poor and primitive, aids in the construction of this anthropology' (Scott 2004: 3–4). The author has not published a single text in Portuguese, which makes a debate with the national academic community difficult. The impact of this book extends beyond anthropology, escaping the walls of academia. The maternal negligence related by Scheper-Hughes in this circumscribed region came to be reported in the media as poor Brazilian mothers who kill their children. e.g. *Publishers Weekly*. 'In Brazil's shantytowns, poverty has transformed the meaning of mother love. The routine-ness with which young children die, argues University of California anthropologist Scheper-Hughes, causes many women to affect indifference to their offspring, even to neglect those infants presumed to be doomed or "wanting to die". Maternal love is delayed and attenuated, with dire consequences for infant survival, according to the author's two decades of fieldwork.'

6 Brazil does not have a legal definition of a poverty line. Here we use the criterion that the poor are people who do not have the minimum income level necessary to satisfy basic needs. There is a national debate about the validity of measuring inequality in Brazil, in so far as the rich tend to omit reporting part of their income (Hoffmann 2000).

7 A European of the nineteenth century, who was outstanding in the propagation of racist theories in Brazil, was Count Gobineau (1816–82), author of the *Essai sur l'inégalité des races humaines*, who served here as the head of the French diplomatic delegation. A monogeneticist, Gobineau introduced the notion of 'degeneration of the race', 'understood to be the final result of mixing different human species'. Following are two excerpts from his writing:

> The two varieties of our species, the black race and the yellow race are the gross background, the cotton and the wool, that the secondary families of the white race soften, mixing their silk into them, while the Aryan group, putting its finer fabric into circulation through the ennobled generations, apply their arabesques of silver and gold to the surface, in an amazing masterpiece.
>
> (Gobineau 1940, vol. II: 539)

8 Brazil can be considered the second largest country, after Nigeria, with a majority black population in the world (composed of blacks and browns).

9 This conclusion is based on a study by Sabóia and Sabóia (2001) based on data from the PPV 96/97 which analysed eight types of families using ten variables by the grouping method of analysis. The sole exception found was for families headed by men residing in the Southeast region.

10 The indicators for indigenous children are not always available since in addition to having received little attention from indigenists and anthropology (Nunes 1999), their low presence in the population generates difficulties in interpretation of the data collected in research by sampling.

11 In recent decades, Brazilian mothers have been nursing their babies longer. Between 1989 and 1999 the average age for weaning babies increased by 4.4 months (Ministry of Health, cited in Brazil 2003: note 39).

12 The report was developed under contract with the IBGE, the official Brazilian agency which has been collecting data on daycare since 1995, under pressure from the social movements.

13 One US dollar is approximately equal to R$3 (July 2003).

14 See Chapter 3 and comments by the Inter-American Development Bank.

15 During the 1990s several studies were done that estimated the number of children and adolescents in a street situation in Brazil. All arrived at much lower numbers than the international media estimates. I co-ordinated a study that did the counting in the city of São Paulo (1993). We found fewer than 5,000 children and adolescents during the day (the large majority working) and fewer than 900 during the night (Rosemberg 2000b).

## 9 The ethics of intervention

1 In one school we visited in Swaziland, two grade 5 classes (children of 11–17 years old, a variation of age because of repetition of grades and late age of entry to school) were combined into a class of 70 because of the absence of one of the teachers. All the children were outside in the yard because they couldn't fit into the classroom. The home economics lesson, a hangover from the days when blacks were being trained to act as servants to whites, consisted of teaching the children how to polish black leather shoes (something very few

of them actually owned). There was only one pair of shoes and one tin of black polish for the demonstration.

2 As I stressed at the beginning of the chapter, this is no more than a negotiating position with 'stakeholders' in the communities/countries concerned.

3 A salutary lesson to avoid out of season vegetables imported from the South – I have never eaten any of them since then.

4 One tap for 1000 workers, at a very well-known brand-name farm-factory where the lawns in front of the main building were watered daily.

5 There is now a ladder of qualifications in South Africa, and a transferable credit system means that trainees can build up a qualifications profile. But the end result is the same, except for a few fortunate women. Training does not result in more pay or opportunities.

# Bibliography

Abley, M. (2003) *Spoken Here: Travels amongst Threatened Languages*, New York, Random House.

Alderson, P. (2000) *Young Children's Rights*, London, Save the Children/Jessica Kingsley.

Alexander, T. (1996) *Unravelling Global Apartheid*, Cambridge, Polity Press.

Amin, S. (1990) *Maldevelopment: Anatomy of Global Failure*, London, Zed Books.

Balachander, J. (1999) 'World Bank Support for Early Childhood Development: Case studies from Kenya, India and the Philippines', *Food and Nutrition Bulletin*, 20(1) also at www.unu.edu.unupress/food/v201e

Balaguer, J., Mestres, J. and Penn, H. (1992) *Quality in Services for Young Children: A Discussion Paper*, European Commission on Childcare Network.

Barbarin, O. and Richter, L. (2001) *Mandela's Children*, London, Routledge.

Barnett, T. and Whiteside, A. (2002) *AIDS in the Twenty-First Century*, Basingstoke, Palgrave/Macmillan.

Barnett, W., (1995) 'Long Term Effects of Early Childhood Programs on Cognitive and School Outcomes', *The Future of Children*, 5(3), 25–50.

Barros, R.P. and Carvalho, M. (2003) *Desafios para a política social brasileira*, Discussion Paper 815, Rio de Janeiro, IPEA.

Barros, R.P. and Foguel, M.N.(2001) 'Focalização dos gastos públicos sociais em educação e erradicação da pobreza no Brasil', *Financiamento da educação no Brasil, Em Aberto*, 74 (18 July):106–20.

Barros, R.P., Henriques, R. and Mendonça, R. (2000) 'Evolução recente da pobreza e da desigualdade: marcos preliminares para a política social', *Cadernos Adenauer*, 1: 11–22.

Bauman, Z. (1995) *Life in Fragments: Essays on Postmodern Morality*, Oxford, Blackwell.

Bergesen, H. and Lunde, L. (1999) *Dinosaurs or Dynamos? The United Nations and the World Bank at the Turn of the Century*, London, Earthscan.

Berman, P. (ed.) (1995) *Health Sector Reform in Developing Countries*, Cambridge, MA, Harvard University Press.

Bernard, D., Cantwell, N., Cherp, A., Falkingham, J. and Letarte, C. (2000) *Societies in Transition: A Situational Analysis of the Status of Children and Women in the Central Asian Republics and Kazakhstan*, Almaty, UNICEF.

Bickel, R. and Spatig, L. (1999) 'Early Achievement Gains and Poverty-Linked

Social Distress: The Case of Post Head-Start Transition', *Journal of Social Distress and the Homeless*, 8(4): 241–54.

Biersteker, L. (1996) *Non-formal Education in the Early Childhood Development Sector and Women's Empowerment: Experiences of Some Women Trainers in the Western Cape*, Evaluation study submitted to the Centre of Adult and Continuing Education, Cape Town, University of the Western Cape.

Black, M. (1986) *Children First: The Story of UNICEF*, Oxford, Oxford University Press.

Boli, J. and Thomas, G. (eds) (1999) *Constructing World Culture*, Stanford, CA, Stanford University Press.

Bourgois, P. (1998) *Families and Children in Pain in the U.S. Inner City*, in N. Scheper-Hughes and C. Sargent (eds) *Small Wars: The Cultural Politics of Childhood*, Berkeley, CA, University of California Press, pp. 331–51.

Boyden, J. (1990) 'Childhood and the Policy Makers: A Comparative Perspective on the Globalization of Childhood', in A. James and A. Prout (eds) *Constructing and Reconstructing Childhood*, London, Falmer Press.

Brazil, Ministério da Saúde (2003) *Relatório sobre saúde infantil*, Brasília, Ministério da Saúde.

Bradbury, B. and Jantii, M. (1999) *Child Poverty Across Industrialized Nations*, Florence, UNICEF Innocenti Centre, EPS 71.

Bredekamp, S. and Copple, C. (eds) (1997) *Developmentally Appropriate Practice in Early Childhood Programs*, Washington, National Association for the Education of Young Children.

Briggs, J. (1970) *Never in Anger: Portrait of an Eskimo Family*, Cambridge, MA, Harvard University Press.

British Medical Journal (2002) 'Global Voices on the AIDS Catastrophe', *British Medical Journal*, 7331, 26 January.

Bronfenbrenner, U. (1974) *Two Worlds of Childhood: US and USSR*, London, Penguin.

Bruer, J. (1999) *The Myth of the First Three Years*, New York, The Free Press.

Brunel, S. (1990) *La faim dans le monde*, Paris, Hachette.

Burman, E. (1995) *Deconstructing Developmental Psychology*, London, Routledge.

Campbell, C. (2003) *Letting them Die: Why HIVAIDS Prevention Programmes Fail*, Oxford, James Currey.

Campbell, F., Pungello, E., Miller-Johnson, S., Burchinal, M. and Ramey, C. (2001) 'The Abecedarian Project: The Development of Cognitive and Academic Abilities: Growth curves from an early childhood educational experiment', *Developmental Psychology*, 37: 231–42.

Campbell, F., Ramey, C., Pungello, E., Sparling, J. and Miller-Johnson, S. (2002) 'Early Childhood Education: Young Outcomes from the Abecedarian Project', *Applied Developmental Science*, 6(1): 42–7.

Campos, M.M., Rosemburg, F. and Ferreira, I.M. (1992) *Creches e Pré-escolas no Brasil*, São Paulo, Cortez.

Chambers, R. (1997) *Whose Reality Counts? Putting the First Last*, London, Intermediate Technology.

Chambers, R. (2002) *Power, Knowledge and Policy Influence: Reflections on an Experience*, in K. Brock and R. McGee (eds) *Knowing Poverty: Critical Reflections on Participatory Research and Policy*, London, Earthscan, pp. 135–65.

Chambouleyron, R. (2004) 'Jesuítas e as crianças no Brasil Quinhentista', in Mary Dez Priore (ed.) *Hist Prioree as crianças no Bra*, São Paulo, Editora Contexto, pp. 55–83.

Childcare Information Exchange Home Page: www.ccie.com

Chomsky, N. (2003) *Power and Terror*, New York, Seven Stories Press.

Chua, A. (2003) *World on Fire*, London, Heinemann.

Chugani, H.T., Phelps, M.E. and Mazziota, J.C. (1987) 'Positron Emission Tomography Study of Human Brain Function Development', *Annals of Neurology*, 22: 487–97.

Church of England/Christian Aid (2000) *New Start Worship*, London, Church of England.

Chussodovsky, M. (1997) *The Globalization of Poverty: The Impacts of IMF and World Bank Reforms*, London, Zed Books.

Cole, M. (1990) *Cultural Psychology: A Once and Future Discipline*, Cambridge, MA, Bellknap Press/Harvard University Press.

Cornia, G. and Sipos, S. (1991) *Children and the Transition to the Market Economy*, Aldershot, Avebury.

De Vylder, S. (1996) *Development Strategies, Macro-economic Policies and the Rights of the Child*, Stockholm Discussion Paper for Radda Barnen.

De Waal, A. (2002) *Famine Crimes: Politics and the Disaster Relief Industry in Africa*, Oxford, James Currey.

De Waal, A. (2003) 'Review of Aids in the 21st Century', *London Review of Books*, July.

DeLoache, J. and Gottlieb, A. (eds) (2001) *The World of Babies: Imagined Childcare in Seven Societies*, Cambridge, Cambridge University Press.

Demberel and Penn, H. (2005) *Education in Nomadic Society: An Autobiography*, Oxford, Bergahn Books.

Dianni, C. (2004) *Tarso Genro discutiu com ministro argentino acordo*, Folha de São Paulo online, www.bookfinder.us/review2/0520075374.html.

Diderichsen, F. (1995) 'Market Reforms in Health Care and Sustainability of the Welfare State', in P. Berman (ed.) *Health Sector Reform in Developing Countries*, Boston, Harvard University Press, pp. 183–98.

Epstein, A. and Weikart, D. (1979) *The Ypsilanti–Carnegie Infant Education Project: Longitudinal Follow-Up, Monographs of the High/Scope Educational Research Foundation*, No. 6, Ypsilanti, Michigan, High/Scope Press.

Evans, J. with Myers, R. and Ilfeld, E. (2000) *Early Childhood Counts: A Programming Guide on Early Childhood Care for Development*, Washington, World Bank Institute.

Falkingham, J. (2000) *From Security to Uncertainty: The Impact of Economic Change on Child Welfare in Central Asia*, Innocenti Working Paper 76, Florence, UNICEF.

Faria, V.E. (2000) 'Estabilização e o resgate da dívida social', *Cadernos Adenauer*, 1: 23–33.

*Folha de São Paulo*, 27 June 2004.

The Future of Children (1995) 'Long-term Outcomes of Early Childhood Programs: Analysis and Recommendations', Washington, *The Future of Children*, 5(3, Winter).

Gasperini, L. (1999) *The Cuban Education System: Lessons and Dilemmas*, Human Development Department LCSHD Paper, Series no. 48, Washington, World Bank.

Geldof, B. (2004) 'Brand New Aid', *Guardian*, 27 February, p. 27.

George, S. and Sabelli, F. (1994) *Faith and Credit: The World Bank's Secular Empire*, London, Penguin.

Ghosh, A. (1998 edition) *In an Antique Land*, London, Granta, p. 200.

Giddens, A. and Hutton, W. (2001) 'Fighting Back', in W. Hutton and A. Giddens (eds) *On the Edge: Living with Global Capitalism*, London, Vintage, pp. 213–24.

Gilliam, W. and Zigler, E. (2001) 'A Critical Meta-Analysis of all Evaluations of State-Funded Pre-school from 1977–1998: Implications for Policy, Service Delivery and Programme Evaluation', *Early Childhood Research Quarterly*, 15: 441–73.

Glover, J. (2003) 'Can we Justify the Killing of Children in Iraq?', *Guardian*, G2, 5 February: p. 6.

Gobineau, Joseph Arthur, comte de (1940) *Essai sur l'inégalité des races humaines* (1st edition pub. 1854), Paris, Firmin-Didot & Cie.

Gomes, C.A. (2004) 'Financiamento e custos da educação infantile', in Coelho, R. de C. and Barreto, Â.R. (eds) *Fundamento da Educação infantil*, Brasília, UNESCO, pp. 31–72.

Goodnow, J. and Collins, A. (1990) *Development According to Parents*, New Jersey, Lawrence Erlbaum.

Goody, J. (1990) *The Interface between the Written and the Oral*, Cambridge, Cambridge University Press.

Gottlieb, A. (2004) *The After-life is Where We Come From: The Culture of Infancy in West Africa*, Chicago, Chicago University Press.

Gupta, A. (2001) 'Governing Population: The Integrated Child Development Services Program in India', in T. Hanson and F. Stepputat (eds) *States of Imagination: Ethnographic Explorations of the Post-Colonial State*, Durham, Duke University Press.

*Guardian* (2002) 'The Life of a Tennis Ball', G2, 5 February, 24.

Hancock, G. (1991) *Lords of Poverty*, London, Mandarin (revised edn published 1996).

Harkness, S. and Super, C. (1996) *Parent's Cultural Belief Systems: Their Origin, Expressions and Consequences*, New York, Guilford Press.

Harper, C., Marcus, R. and Moore, K. (2003) 'Enduring Poverty and the Conditions of Childhood: Lifecourse and Intergenerational Poverty Transmissions', *World Development*, 31(3): 535–54.

Hasenbalg, C. (2001) 'Condições de socialização na primeira infância', in IBGE (ed.) *Primeira infância*, Rio de Janeiro, IBGE, pp. 9–24.

Head, B. (1993) *The Cardinals*, Cape Town, David Philip.

Heap, B. and Kent, J. (2000) *Towards Sustainable Consumption: A European Perspective*, London, The Royal Society.

Hensher, M. and Passingham, S. (1996) 'The Impact of Economic Transition on Kindergartens in Kazakhstan: Problems and Policy Issues, *Compare*, 26(3): 305–13.

Hertz, N. (2001) *The Silent Takeover: Global Capitalism and the Death of Democracy*, London, Arrow.

Hinton, W. (1970) *Fanshen: A Documentary of Revolution in a Chinese Village*, London, Penguin (reprinted 1997, University of California Press).

Hochschild, A. (2001) 'Global Care Chains and Emotional Surplus Value', in W. Hutton and A. Giddens (eds) *On the Edge*, London, Vintage.

Hoffman, R. (2000) 'Mensuração da desigualdade e da pobreza no Brasil', in R. Henriques (ed.) *Desigualdade e pobreza no Brasil*, Rio de Janeiro, IPEA, pp. 81–107.

Hrdy, S. (1999) *Mother Nature: A History of Mothers, Infants and Natural Selection*, New York, Random House.

Hubel, D.H. and Weisel, T.N. (1977) *Functional Architecture of the Macaque Monkey Visual Cortex*, Proceedings of the Royal Society of London, B, 198: 1–59.

Hulme, D. and Edwards, M. (eds) (1997) *NGOs, States and Donors: Too Close for Comfort?*, Basingstoke, Macmillan.

Hulme, D., Moore, K. and Sheperd, A. (2001) *Chronic Poverty: Meanings and Frameworks*, Working Paper 2, Manchester, Chronic Poverty Research Group.

Hutton, W. and Giddens, A. (eds) (2001) *On the Edge: Living with Global Capitalism*, London, Vintage.

IBGE, *Pesquisa Nacional por Amostra de Domicílios* (PNAD) 1982, 1985, 1995, 1996, 1997, 1998, 1999, 2001 and 2002.

IBGE (1999) *Microdados da PNAD 1999*, Rio de Janeiro, IBGE.

IBGE (2001b) *Censo Demográfico 2001*, Resultados Preliminares, www.IBGE. gov.br

IBGE (2001a) 'Pesquisa sobre padrões de vida, 1996, 1997' (PPV) in *Primeira infância*, Rio de Janeiro, IBGE.

IBGE (2003) *Síntese de indicadores sociais 2002*, Rio de Janeiro, IBGE.

Inter-American Development Bank (1999) *Breaking the Poverty Cycle: Investing in Early Childhood*, Washington, Inter-American Development Bank.

The Inter-American Development Bank (1999) *Breaking the Poverty Cycle: Investing in Early Childhood*, New York, Inter-American Bank.

International Federation of Democratic Jurists (AIJD: Association Internacionale des Jurisites Democrates) (1986) *Bulletin d'Informacion sur les Activités de l'AIJD en 1986*, Brussels, AIJD, pp. 29–30.

Jahoda, G. and Lewis, I. (1987) *Acquiring Culture: Cross-cultural Studies in Child Development*, London, Academic Press.

James, A. and Prout, A. (eds) (1990) *Constructing and Reconstructing Childhood: Contemporary Issues in the Sociological Study of Childhood*, London, Falmer Press.

Jaramillo, A. and Mingat, A. (2003) *Early Childhood Care and Education in Sub-Saharan*

*Africa: What Would it Take to Meet the Millenium Development Goals?*, Mimeo, Washington, The World Bank: Africa Region.

Justice, J. (2000) 'The Politics of Child Survival', in L. Whiteford and L. Manderson (eds) *Global Health Policy, Local Realities: The Fallacy of the Level Playing Field*, London, Lynne Reinner Publishers.

Kagan, J. (1998) *Three Seductive Ideas*, Cambridge, MA, Harvard University Press.

Kaldor M. (1999) *New and Old Wars*, Cambridge, Polity.

Kappel, M., Dolores B., Kramer, S. and Carvalho, M. Cristina (2001) 'Perfil das crianças de 0 a 6 anos que frequentam creches, pré-escolas e escolas: uma análise dos resultados da pesquisa sobre padrões de vida', *Revista Brasileira de Educação*, 16 (January–April): 35–47.

Kessen, W. (1981) 'The Child and Other Cultural Inventions', in E. Kessel and S. Siegel (eds) *The Child and other Cultural Inventions*, New York, Praeger.

Khor, M. (2001) *Rethinking Globalization: Critical Issues and Policy Choices*, London, Zed Books.

Kirschenbaum, L. (2001) *Small Comrades: Revolutionizing Childhood in Soviet Russia 1917–1932*, London, Routledge.

Krugman, P. (2003) 'The Good News', article from *New York Times* reprinted in *This Day*, 2 December, p. 22, Johannesburg.

Kumar, A. (2003) *World Bank Literature*, Minnesota, University of Minnesota Press.

Kunbur, R. (2001) *Economic Policy, Distribution of Poverty and the Nature of Disagreement*, paper presented to the Swedish Parliamentary Commission on Global Development, 2000, Revised January 2001, www.people.cornell.edu

Kuper, H. (1978) *Sobhuza II: Ngwenyana and King of Swaziland*, London, Duckworth.

Kuper, H. (1980) *An African Aristocracy*, New York, Africana Publishing Co.

Lamb, M. (1999) *Parenting and Child Development in 'Non-Traditional' Families*, New Jersey, Lawrence Erlbaum.

Lamb, M. and Sternberg, K. (1992) 'Socio-cultural Perspectives on Non-Parental Care', in M. Lamb, K. Sternberg, P. Hwang and A. Goteborg (eds) *Childcare in Context: Cross-cultural Perspectives*, New Jersey, Lawrence Erlbaum, pp. 1–26.

Leite, M.M. (2001) 'A infância no século XIX', in M.C. de Freitas (ed) *História social da infância no Brasil*, São Paulo, pp. 25–38.

Levin, R. (1997) *When the Sleeping Grass Awakens*, Johannesburg, Witwatersrand University Press.

LeVine, R. (2003) *Childhood Socialization: Comparative Studies of Parenting, Learning and Educational Change*, Hong Kong, Comparative Education Research Centre.

LeVine, R., Dixon, S., LeVine, S., Richman, A., Leiderman, P., Keefer, C., and Brazleton, T. (1994) *Childcare and Culture: Lessons from Africa*, Cambridge, Cambridge University Press.

Levison, D. (1991) *Children's Labour Force Activity and Schooling in Brazil* (tese de doutorado), Ann Arbor, Michigan.

Lloyd, E. *et al.* (2004) *How Effective are Measures Taken to Mitigate the Impact of Armed*

*Conflict on the Psychosocial and Cognitive Development of Children aged 0–8?*, www.eppi.ioe.ac.uk, accessed March 2004.

Lustosa, T.Q.O. and Reichenheim, M.E. (2001) 'Perfil nutricional da primeira infância', in IBGE (ed.) *Pesquisa sobre padrão de vida, 1996–1997*, Rio de Janeiro, IBGE, pp. 89–127.

Magalhães, A.R. and Garcia, W. (1993) *Infância e desenvolvimento*, Brasília, IPEA.

Magagula, C.M. (1987) *An Inventory of Preschools in the Kingdom of Swaziland*, Mbabane Swaziland Institute of Educational Research, UNISWA with support of Bernard van Leer Foundation.

Mamdani, M. (1996) *Citizen and Subject: Contemporary Africa and the Legacy of Late Colonialism*, New Jersey, Princeton University Press.

Maricato, E. (2003) *Alternativas para a crise urbana*, Petrópolis, Vozes.

Masse, L. and Barnett, S. (2003) *A Benefit/Cost Analysis of the Abecedarian Early Childhood Intervention*, www.nieer.org at March 2004.

Mayall, B. (2002) *Towards a Sociology of Childhood: Thinking from Children's Lives*, Bucks, Open University Press.

Medeiros, M. (2003) *Os ricos e a formulação de políticas de combate à desigualdade e à pobreza no Brasil*, Discussion Paper 984, Brasília, IPEA.

Montandon, C. (2001) 'Sociologia da infância: balanço dos trabalhos em língua inglesa', *Cadernos de Pesquisa*, 112 (March): 33–61.

Monteiro, C.A. (2003) 'A dimensão da pobreza, da desnutrição e da fome no Brasil', *Revista de Estudos Avançados*, 48 (May–August): 7–20.

Moore, K. (2001) *Frameworks for Understanding the Inter-generational Transmission of Poverty and Well-being in Developing Countries*, Working Paper 8, Manchester, Chronic Poverty Research Centre.

Moro, C. de S. and Gomide, P.I.C. (2003) 'O conceito de infância na perspectiva de mães usuárias e não usuárias de crèche', *Paidéia*, 13(26, July–December): 171–80.

Munyakho, D. (1992) *Child Newcomers in the Urban Jungle*, The Urban Child in Difficult Circumstances series, Kenya/Florence, UNICEF.

Myers, R. (2000) *Thematic Studies: Early Childhood Care and Development*, Paris, UNESCO.

Narayan, D. with Patel, R., Schafft, K., Rademacher, A. and Koch-Schulte, S. (1999) *Can Anybody Hear Us?*, Washington, World Bank/Oxford, Oxford University Press.

Narayan, D., Chambers, R., Shah, M.K. and Petesch, P. (2000) *Crying Out for Change*, Washington, World Bank/Oxford, Oxford University Press.

National Association for the Education of Young Children (NAEYC) (1995) *Developmentally Appropriate Practice*, USA, NAEYC.

New Internationalist (2003) *The World Guide: An Alternative Reference to the Countries of Our Planet*, London, ITGD Publishing.

Nichter, M. and Lock, M. (2002) *New Horizons in Medical Anthropology*, London, Routledge.

Norberg-Hodge, H. (1992) *Ancient Futures: Learning from Ladakh*, London, Rider/Random Century.

Nunes, Â. (1999) *A sociedade das crianças a'uwê-xavante*, Lisboa, Instituto de Inovação Educacional.

Ochs, E. and Schieffelin, B. (1984) 'Language Acquisition and Socialization: Three Developmental Stories and their Implications', in R. Shweder and R. LeVine (eds) (1984) *Culture Theory: Essays on Mind, Self and Emotion*, Cambridge, Cambridge University Press, pp. 276–320.

OECD (2000) *United States: Early Childhood Education and Care Country Note*, 1 July, Paris, OECD. Also on web at www.oecd.org

OECD (2001) *Starting Strong: Thematic Review of Early Education and Care*, Paris, OECD.

Oliveira, E. de (1994) *Relações raciais nas creches paulistanas*, São Paulo, PUC-SP.

Paiva, J. M. (2000) 'Educação jesuítica no Brasil colonial', in E.M. Tehal Lopes (ed.) *500 anos de Educação no Brasil*, Belo Horizonte, Autêntica, pp. 43–60.

Pastoral Da Crianca (2002) 'Portal Pastoral da criança', www.pastoral dacrianca.org.br. Accessed 2 July 2004.

Penn, H. (1994) 'Working in Conflict: A Dynamic Model of Quality', in P. Moss and A. Pence (eds) *Valuing Quality*, London, Paul Chapman/Teachers College Press, pp. 10–28.

Penn, H. (1997) 'Diversity and Inclusivity in Early Childhood Studies in South Africa', *International Journal of Inclusive Education*, 1(1): 1204–114.

Penn, H. (1999) 'Researching Childhood in the Majority World', in B. Mayall and S. Oliver (eds) (1999) *Social Policy Research: Issues of Power and Prejudice*, Buckingham: Open University Press, pp. 25–39.

Penn, H. (2001) 'Research in the Majority World', in T. David (ed.) *Promoting Evidence Based Practice in Early Childhood Education: Research and its Implications*, London, JAI, pp. 289–308.

Penn, H. (2004a) *Childcare and Early Childhood Development Programmes and Policies: Their Relationship to Eradicating Child Poverty*, Child Poverty Research Centre, London, Save the Children Fund.

Penn, H. (2004b) *Understanding Early Childhood: Issues and Controversies*, Maidenhead, Open University Press/McGraw Hill.

Penn, H. (2005) 'Parenting and Substitute Parenting', in G. Bentley and R. Mace (eds) *Alloparenting in Human Societies*, Cambridge, Cambridge University Press, forthcoming

Penn, H. and Gough, D. (2002) 'The Price of a Loaf of Bread: Some Conceptions of Family Support', *Children and Society*, 16.

Phipps, S. (2001) 'Values, Policies and the Well-being of Young Children in Canada, Norway and the United States', in K. Vleminckx and T. Smeeding (eds) *Child Well-being, Child Poverty and Child Policy in Modern Nations: What Do we Know?*, Bristol, The Policy Press, pp. 79–98.

Pieterse, J.N. and Parekh, B. (eds) (1995) *The Decolonization of the Imagination: Culture, Knowledge and Power*, London, Zed Books.

Pollitt, E. and Triana, N. (1999) 'Stability, Predictive Validity, and Sensitivity of Mental and Motor Development Scales and Pre-school Cognitive Tests among

Low-income Children in Developing Countries', *Food and Nutrition Bulletin*, 20(1, March).

Prout, A. and James, A. (1990) *Constructing and Reconstructing Childhood*, London, Falmer Press.

Quarles van Ufford, P. and Giri, A. (2003) *A Moral Critique of Development: In Search of Global Responsibilities*, London, EIDOS/Routledge.

Rabain, J. (1979) *L'enfant du Lignage*, Paris, Payot.

Raffer, K. (1992) *What's Good for the United States Must be Good for the World*, Kreisky Forum Symposium, Vienna, reprinted by Jubilee (2000).

Rahnema, M. with Bawtree, V. (eds) (1997) *The Post Development Reader*, London, Zed Books.

Rampal, S. (1999) *Debt Has a Child's Face*, Unicef Website, unicef.org/pon99/debtcom

Rawls, J. (2000) *A Theory of Social Justice*, Oxford, Oxford University Press.

Republic of Kazakhstan (2001) *Preschool Education and Training: Main Regulations*, Astana, Ministry of Education and Science.

Reynolds, P. (1989) *Children in Crossroads: Cognition and Society in South Africa*, Capetown, David Philips.

Reynolds, P. (1991) *Dance, Civet Cat: Child Labour in the Zambezi Valley*, London, Zed Books.

Reynolds, P. (1996) *Traditional Healers and Childhood in* Zimbabwe, Ohio, Ohio University Press.

Rorty, R. (1989) *Irony, Contingency and Solidarity*, Cambridge, Cambridge University Press.

Rosaldo, R. (1993) *Culture and Truth: The Remaking of Social Analysis*, London, Routledge.

Rose, S. (ed.) (1998) *From Brains to Consciousness? Essays on the New Science of the Mind*, London, Penguin.

Rosemberg, F. (1990) *Panorama da educação infantil brasileira nos anos 1990*, São Paulo, Fundação Carlos Chagas, mimeo (2003).

Rosemberg, F. (1996a) 'Contemporary Trends and Ambuiguties in the Upbringing of Small Children', in E. Barretto and D. Zibas (eds) *Brazilian Issues on Education Gender and Race*, São Paulo, FCC, pp. 87–110.

Rosemberg, F. (1996b) 'Teorias feministas e subordinação de idade', *Pro-posições*, 7(3): 17–23.

Rosemberg, F. (1999) 'Expansão da educação infantil e processos de exclusão', *Cadernos de Pesquisa*, 107 (June): 7–40.

Rosemberg, F. (2000a) 'Ambiguites in Compensatory Policies: A Case Study from Brazil', in R. Cortina and N. Stromquist (eds) *Distant Alliances: Promoting Education for Girls and Women in Latin America*, New York and London, RoutledgeFalmer, pp. 261–94.

Rosemberg, F. (2000b) 'From Discourse to Reality: A Profile of the Lives and an Estimate of the Number of Street Children and Adolescents in Brazil', in A.M. Rosely (ed.) *Children on the Streets of Americas*, London and New York, Routledge, pp. 118–35.

Rosemberg, F. (2003A) 'Multilateral Organizations and Early Child Care and Education Policies for Developing Countries', *Gender and Society*, 17(2): 250–66.

Rosemberg, F. (2003b) 'Quelques points d'un plan de recherche sur la sociologie de l'enfance', *Journées francophones de sociologie de l'enfance*, Lisbonne, Octobre.

Rosemberg, F. and Andrade, L.F. (1999) 'Ruthless Rhetoric: Child and Youth Prostitution in Brazil', *Childhood*, 6(1, February): 113–32.

Rosemberg, F. and Freitas, R. (2001) 'Will Greater Participation of Brazilian Children in Education Reduce their Participation in the Labor Force?', *International journal of Education Policy Research and Practice*, 2(3): 249–66.

Rosemberg, F. and Pinto, R.P. (1995) 'Saneamento básico e raça', *Revista Brasileira de Crescimento e desenvolvimento humano*, 112 (January–December): 23–38.

Rosemberg, F. and Pinto, R.P. (1997) *Criança pequena e raça*, São Paulo, Textos FCC, 13.

Roy, A. (1999) *The Greater Common Good*, Bombay, India Book Distributors.

Ruel, M., Levin, C., Armar-Klemesu, M., Maxwell, D. and Morris, S. (1999) *Good Childcare Practices can Mitigate the Negative Effects of Poverty and Low Maternal Schooling on Children's Nutritional Status: Evidence from Accra*, FCND Discussion Paper 62, Washington, International Food Policy Research Institute.

Sabóia, J. and Sabóia, A.L. (2001) 'Condições de vida das famílias com crianças até 6 anos', in IBGE (ed.) *Primeira infância*, Rio de Janeiro, IBGE, pp. 25–48.

Sange Agency (2001) *Listening to the Poor*, Almaty, UNDP.

Scheper-Hughes, N. (ed.) (1983) *Child Survival*, Dordrecht, Holland, D. Reidel Publishing Co., pp. 293–324.

Scheper-Hughes, N. (1993) *Death Without Weeping*, Berkeley, CA, University of California Press.

Scheper-Hughes, N. and Sargent, C. (eds) (1998) *Small Wars: The Cultural Politics of Childhood*, Berkeley, CA, University of California Press.

Schwarcz, L.M. (2004) *O espetáculo das raças*, São Paulo, Companhia das Letras.

Schwartzman, S. (2004) *As causas da pobreza*, Rio de Janeiro, FGV.

Schweinhart, L. (2003) *Benefits, Costs and Explanation of the High/Scope Perry Preschool Program*, Paper presented at the Meeting of the Society for Research in Child Development, Tampa, Florida.

Schweinhart, L. and Weikart, D. (1997) 'The High/Scope Preschool Curriculum Comparison Study Through Age 23', *Early Childhood Research Quarterly*, 12: 117–43.

Schweinhart, L., Barnes, H. and Weikart, D. (1993) *Significant Benefits: The High/Scope Perry Preschool Study Through age 27*, Monographs of the High/Scope Educational Research Foundation, 10.

Scott, J.C. (1989) *Weapons of the Weak: Everyday Forms of Peasant Resistance*, New Haven, Yale University Press.

Scott, J.C. (1998) *Seeing Like a State: How Certain Schemes to Improve the Human Condition Have Failed*, New Haven, Yale University Press.

Scott, K., Avchen, R. and Hollomon, H. (1999) 'Epidemiology of Child Development Problems: The Extent of the Problems of Poor Development in

Children from Deprived Backgrounds' *Food and Nutrition Bulletin*, 20(1): 2, also on www.unu.edu/unupress/food

Scott, P. (2004) *Antropologias nacionais e articulações internacionais, Brasil e Estados Unidos*, Recife, UFPE.

Sen, A. (1999) *Development as Freedom*, Oxford, Oxford University Press.

Serpell, R. (1993) *The Significance of Schooling: Life Journeys in an African Society*, Cambridge, Cambridge University Press.

Serpell, R. (1999a) 'Local Accountability in Rural Communities: A Challenge for Educational Planning in Africa', F. in Leach and A. Little (eds) *Education, Cultures and Economics: Dilemmas for Development*, London, Falmer Press, pp. 111–39.

Serpell, R. (1999b) 'Theoretical Conceptions of Human Development', in L. Eldering and P. Leseman (eds) *Effective Early Education: Cross-cultural Perspectives*, London, Falmer, pp. 41–66.

Shweder, R. and LeVine, R. (1984) *Culture Theory: Essays on Mind, Self and Emotion*, Cambridge, Cambridge University Press.

SIDH (1996) *Culture and Gender Beliefs*, Mussoorie, Society for Integrated Development of Himalayas.

SIDH (1999) *A Matter of Quality: A Study of People's Perceptions and Expectations from Schooling in Rural and Urban Areas of Uttarakhand*, Mussoorie, Society for Integrated Development of Himalayas.

SIDH (2001) *Primary Study on Incidence of Disablity in Jaunpur*, Sansodhan–Block Tehri District, Mussoorie, Society for Integrated Development of Himalayas.

SIDH (2002) *Child and the Family: A Study of the Impact of Family Structures upon Children in Rural Uttarakhand*, Mussoorie, Society for Integrated Development of Himalayas.

Simões, C.C. (2002) *Perfis de saúde e de mortalidade no Brasil*, Brasília, OPAS.

Sirota, R. (2001) 'Emergência de uma sociologia da infância: evolução do objeto e do olhar', *Cadernos de Pesquisa*, 112 (March): 7–32.

Soros, G. (2000) *Open Society: Reforming Global Capitalism*, New York, Public Affairs.

Souza, Silvio Araujo (2002) 'A impagável dévida externa', CMI Brazil, www. midiaindependente.org, Accessed 27 October 2003.

Spiro, M. (1990) 'On the Strange and the Familiar in Recent Anthropological Thought', in J. Stigler, R Shweder and G. Herdt (eds) *Essays on Comparative Human Development*, Chicago, Chicago University Press, pp. 47–61.

Stephens, S. (1992) *And a Little Child Shall Lead Them: Children and Images of Children at the Conference on Enviroment and Development*, Trondheim, Mimeo.

Stephens, S. (1995) *Children and the Politics of Culture*, New Jersey, Princeton University Press

Stigler, J., Shweder, R. and Herdt, G. (1990) *Cultural Psychology: Essays on Comparative Human Development*, Cambridge, Cambridge University Press.

Stiglitz, J. (2002) *Globalization and its Discontents*, London, Penguin.

Stirrat, R. (1999) 'Economics and Culture: Towards an Anthropology of Economics', in F.E. Leach and A. Little (eds) *Education, Cultures and Economics*, London, Falmer, pp. 33–47.

Super, C. and Harkness, S. (1986) 'The Developmental Niche: A Conceptualization at the Interface of Society and the Individual', *Journal of Behavioural Development*, 9: 545–70.

Sure Start (2003/4) www.ness.bbk.ac.uk

Sutton-Smith, B. (1986) *Toys as Culture*, New York, Gardner Press.

Sutton-Smith, B. (1999) 'The Rhetorics of Adult and Child Play Theories', in S. Reifel (ed.) *Advances in Early Education and Day Care*, 10, London, JAI pp. 149–62.

Taçon, P. (1981a) *El seminario sobre el menor en situación de abandono y/o atención al niño*, New York, UNICEF.

Taçon, P. (1981b) *My Child Minus One*, New York, UNICEF.

Theroux, P. (2003) *Dark Star Safari: Overland from Cairo to Cape Town*, New York, Houghton Mifflin.

Tobin, J. (1995) 'Post-structural Research in Early Childhood Education', in J. Hatch (ed.) *Qualitative Research in Early Childhood Settings*, Connecticut, Praeger, pp. 223–43.

Tobin, J. (1996) *Making a Place for Pleasure in Early Childhood Education*, New Haven, Yale University Press.

Toroyan, T., Roberts, I., Oakley, A., Laing, G., Mugford, M. and Frost, C. (2003) 'Effectiveness of out-of-home day care for disadvantaged families: randomized controlled trial', *British Medical Journal*, 327: 906–9.

Torres, R.M. (1996) 'Melhorar a qualidade da educação básica? As estratégias do Banco Mundial', in De Tommasi, L., Warde, M. and Haddad, S. (eds) *O Banco Mundial e as políticas educacionais*, São Paulo, Cortez, pp. 125–93.

UNCTAD (1999) *Trade and Development Report*, New York, United Nations.

UNDP (2003a) *Perceptions of Corruption in Kazakhstan: By Parliamentarians, Public Officials, Private Business and Civil Society*, Sange Research Centre, Almaty, UNDP.

UNDP (2003b) *Human Development Report 2003: A Compact Amongst Nations to End Human Poverty*, New York, United Nations.

UNESCO (2000a) *World Education Forum 2000: The Dakar Framework for Action*, Paris, UNESCO.

UNESCO (2000b) *World Education Forum 2000: Thematic Studies: Early Childhood Development and Care*, Paris, UNESCO.

UNESCO (2002) *Workshop on Young Children Affected by HIV/AIDS*, Paris, UNESCO.

UNESCO/MoE (2000) *Case Study: Kazakhstan Preschool Education System at the Doorstep of the 21st Century*, Astana, MoE.

UNICEF (2000) *Societies in Transition: A Situational Analysis of the Status of Children and Women in the Central Asian Republics and Kazakhstan*, Almaty, UNICEF.

UNICEF (2001) *Annual Report for Swaziland*, Mbabane, UNICEF.

UNICEF (2002a) *The Right to Quality Education: Creating Child-friendly Schools in Central Asia*, Florence, MONEE/Innocenti Centre.

UNICEF (2002b) *Early Childhood Development in the Central Asian Republics and Kazakhstan*, prepared by Konstantin Osipov and Cherie Etherington-Smith, Almaty, UNICEF.

UNICEF (2004) *Relatório sobre infância e adolescência no Brasil: equidade e diversidade*, Brasília, UNICEF.

van der Gaag, J. and Tan, J. (1998) *The Benefits of Early Child Development Programs: An Economic Analysis*, Washington, World Bank Education Section, 18992, V. 1.

Vieira, L.M. (1988) 'Mal necessário: creches no Departamento Nacional da criança', *(1940–1970) Cadernos de Pesquisa*, 67 (November): 3–16.

Viruru, R. (2001) *Early Childhood Education: Postcolonial Perspectives from India*, London, Sage.

Vleminckx, K. and Smeeding, T. (eds) (2001) *Child Well-being, Child Poverty and Child Policy in Modern Nations: What Do we Know?*, Bristol, The Policy Press.

Wade, R. (2001) 'Showdown at the World Bank', *New Left Review*, Second Series, 7: 124–37.

Walt, G. (1994) *Health Policy: An Introduction to Process and Power*, London, Zed Books.

Whiteford, L. and Manderson, L. (eds) (2000) *Global Health Policy, Local Realities: The Fallacy of the Level Playing Field*, London, Lynne Reinner Publishers.

Whitfield, S. (1999) *Life Along the Silk Road*, London, John Murray.

Whiteside, A., Hickey, A., Ngcobo, N. and Tomlinson, J. (2003) *What is Driving the HIV/AIDS Epidemic in Swaziland and What More Can we do About It?*, Mbabane, National Emergency Response Committee on HIV/AIDS (NERCHA) and United Nations Programme on HIV/AIDS (UNAIDS).

WHO (1999) *A Critical Link: Interventions for Physical Growth and Psychological Development: A Review*, Geneva, WHO, Department of Child and Adolescent Health and Development.

WHO (2004) *The Importance of Caregiver-child Interactions for the Survival and Healthy Development of Young Children: A Review*, Department of Child and Adolescent Health and Development, Geneva, WHO.

Woodhead, M. (1997) *In Search of the Rainbow: Pathways to Quality in Large Scale Programmes for Young Disadvantaged Children*, The Hague, Bernard van Leer Foundation.

Woodward, D. (1992) *Debt, Adjustment and Poverty in Developing Countries: The Impact of Debt and Adjustment at the Household Level in Developing Countries*, London, Pinter Publications/SCF.

World Bank (1998) Project information BRPA 6525, Washington, World Bank.

World Bank (2001) *O combate è pobreza no Brasil, Vol. 1, resumo do relatório*, Departamento do Brasil, Setor de Redução da Pobreza e Manejo Econômico, Região da América Latina e do Caribe, Brasília.

www.worldbank.org (15 March 2000, 12 April 2001, 18 July 2001)

World Bank (1995) *Children: School or Work? Brazil Country Assistance Strategy*, Washington, World Bank.

World Bank (2000) *The World Bank and Children*, Washington, World Bank Social Protection Human Development Network.

Young, M.E. (1998) 'Policy Implications of Early Childhood Development Programmes', *Nutrition, Health and Child Development*, Washington, Pan American Health Organization/World Bank.

Zeitlin, M. (1990) 'My Child is my Crown: Yoruba Parental Theories and Practices in Early Childhood', in S. Harkness and C. Super (eds) (1996) *Parents Cultural Belief Systems: Their Origin, Expressions and Consequences*, New York, Guilford Press, pp. 496–531.

# Index

_214_ **Index**